PRAISE FOR *DATELINE JERUSALEM*

"How could such a tiny speck of land on the global map be of such strategic importance on today's geopolitical landscape? Chris Mitchell answers that question in his book *Dateline Jerusalem*. Chris knows the land of Israel because he lives there and has walked the ground and studied the history, but most of all, he knows Bible prophecy. This is a fascinating book that captures the essence of diplomacy, economics, military strategy, and events yet to come. A great read! Well done, Chris."

—GENERAL JERRY BOYKIN, FORMER COMMANDER DELTA FORCE

"Chris Mitchell is not only a gifted newsman, he is an equally talented writer. His book is a spellbinding narrative of his own eyewitness accounts, covering more than a decade of Middle East reporting. These historically significant stories are interwoven with measured analysis, background geopolitical history, and a rich biblical perspective. But above all, from beginning to end, shines the bright thread of faith, offering readers not only hope but inspiration to watch today's unfolding events with discernment, and to pray without ceasing."

—LELA GILBERT, COAUTHOR OF *PERSECUTED: THE GLOBAL ASSAULT ON CHRISTIANITY* AND AUTHOR OF *SATURDAY PEOPLE, SUNDAY PEOPLE*

"Chris Mitchell is a man who knows the Middle East. In his years leading the Christian Broadcasting Network news bureau in Jerusalem, he has been an eyewitness to the marvelous evidence of God's hand on Israel and the surrounding nations. When Chris speaks about Israel and the Middle East, those who know, listen. Filled with fascinating stories and insights, this book is a must-read for all genuine 'watchmen on the wall' and all who love Israel."

—JOEL RICHARDSON, SPEAKER AND *NEW YORK TIMES* BEST-SELLING AUTHOR

"Chris Mitchell understands Israel and the Middle East like few people in this world today . . . Chris doesn't merely report the news, he lives through it . . . clarifying it with history while anchoring it to the pages of the Bible. You can't get this perspective anywhere else . . . I could not put this book down! It is a thrilling read. If you are tired of getting your worldview from cable news, you have got to read this book! Let Chris help you navigate through the complicated and politicized world of Israel, the Middle East, and radical Islam. You will understand it like never before . . . Buy a copy for yourself and your pastor as well!"

—TOM DOYLE, VICE PRESIDENT OF E3 PARTNERS AND AUTHOR OF
DREAMS AND VISIONS: IS JESUS AWAKENING THE MUSLIM WORLD?

"There's no more informed journalist in Jerusalem than Chris Mitchell! My decades of knowing and observing him mark him as a brilliant analyst, a sensitive observer, and a distinguished, discerning reporter amid the mixed milieu of the Middle East's conflicts, confusion, and present convergence of political, religious, military, and social disruption. He has the pulse and knows the stakes at risk in these parts, and he brings Dateline Jerusalem to us with a rare professional and prophetic awareness."

—DR. JACK W. HAYFORD, CHANCELLOR, THE KING'S
UNIVERSITY, LOS ANGELES AND DALLAS

"Chris Mitchel is one of those rare journalists in the Middle East who understands that the history of the region did not begin with yesterday's headlines. In his wonderful book *Dateline Jerusalem*, his vision is always stereoscopic; with one eye on the news he is reporting from the front line, many times at great risk to himself, and the other eye on the biblical narrative, miraculously unfolding before us. A must read!"

—DAN GORDON, CAPTAIN IN THE IDF RESERVE AND SCREENWRITER

"*Dateline Jerusalem* is a gripping and compelling firsthand account of what is happening in the Middle East today. From his front-row seat of history, Chris Mitchell has told a story that every believer needs to read."

—CINDY JACOBS, AUTHOR AND FOUNDER OF GENERALS OF INTERCESSION

"While many of us believe the pace of prophetic events is rapidly increasing and approaching its climax, few observers can offer the front line perspective and significant insight presented by Chris Mitchell in *Dateline Jerusalem*. *Dateline Jerusalem* explores and explains the explosive nature of the struggles in the Middle East. With clarity and precision it details the back story and the current players, peels back layers of confusion and propaganda, and should be required reading before anyone attempts to understand . . . let alone discuss . . . the desperate situation confronting Israel and the Western world. A must read, *Dateline Jerusalem* is one of the most important books of our time."

—BODIE AND BROCK THOENE, BEST-SELLING AUTHORS

"I can think of no person who would be better equipped to write a book about Israel's current challenges than my friend Chris Mitchell. Not only is Chris a highly professional journalist with a brilliant analytical mind, he also has high spiritual antennas and a deep biblical knowledge about the issues shaping the Middle East today . . . I consider Chris an integral part of the journey which has led to the rediscovery and global dissemination of the San Remo resolution of 1920 as Israel's true legal foundation. The news industry needs journalists with integrity and courage like Chris Mitchell to help us make sense of all the complex and often conflicting processes facing Israel today. This book is a must read for anyone who wants to understand the various challenges facing Israel today."

—TOMAS SANDELL, FOUNDING DIRECTOR OF
EUROPEAN COALITION FOR ISRAEL

"Chris Mitchell has had a heart for Israel and the Middle East ever since I've known him. That passion adds an understanding and defining quality to every report he brings us from this most strategic location. He doesn't just report on details, he realizes the significance and impact of all that happens in this region. His book is compelling; his perspective invaluable. He has been called to this role 'for such a time as this.'"

—TERRY MEEUWSEN, COHOST, THE 700 CLUB;
DIRECTOR, ORPHAN'S PROMISE

"Chris Mitchell has served as our CBN Middle East Bureau Chief for more than a decade. During that time we've been together on the front lines of war and met face-to-face with the people shaping Israel's modern history. Dateline Jerusalem offers a firsthand, one-of-a-kind eyewitness account of the prophetic trends unfolding before our eyes and during our time. With so much misinformation these days, it's an invaluable perspective to help you to be like the sons of Issachar who the Bible says 'understood the times.' I highly recommend it."

—Pat Robertson, CBN founder

"In a word, sobering. Here are the words of a man well-versed in both Scripture and current events—a man who sees the news from a global perspective—and what he has to say should wake us up and cause us to pay attention to what is really happening in the march of time from eternity to eternity. If you want to feel the pulse of humanity, look to Jerusalem . . . Dateline Jerusalem presents a viewpoint that is historical, biblical, universal, as well as current. It is as important for us to read as the daily newspaper."

—Pastor Robert Rieth, founder and CEO of Media Fellowship International and an ordained Lutheran minister

DATELINE JERUSALEM

AN EYEWITNESS ACCOUNT OF PROPHECIES
UNFOLDING IN THE MIDDLE EAST

CHRIS MITCHELL

NELSON
BOOKS

An Imprint of Thomas Nelson

Dateline Jerusalem's goal is to be up-to-date with the major Middle East developments. With the Middle East more volatile than in a generation, it's particularly difficult. Someone once said keeping up with current events in the region is like trying to "nail Jello to the wall." From its final revision to first publication, significant events could erupt throughout the region. An Israeli attack on Iran's nuclear facilities, the fall of the Syrian regime, or a number of potential events might unfold.

Despite these potential developments, the theme of *Dateline Jerusalem* remains the same: the focus of the world is turning toward the "naval of the earth" and history's final chapter will be written in Jerusalem.

Published in Nashville, Tennessee, by Nelson Books. Nelson Books and Thomas Nelson are registered trademarks of Thomas Nelson, Inc.

Thomas Nelson, Inc., titles may be purchased in bulk for educational, business, fund-raising, or sales promotional use. For information, please e-mail SpecialMarkets@ThomasNelson.com.

Unless otherwise noted, Scripture quotations are taken from THE NEW KING JAMES VERSION. © 1982 by Thomas Nelson, Inc. Used by permission. All rights reserved.

Scripture quotations marked NIV are from HOLY BIBLE: NEW INTERNATIONAL VERSION®. © 1973, 1978, 1984 by International Bible Society. Used by permission of Zondervan Publishing House. All rights reserved.

Scripture quotations marked KJV are from the King James Version of the Bible.

Library of Congress Cataloging-in-Publication Data

Mitchell, Chris, 1952-

Dateline Jerusalem : an eyewitness account of prophecies unfolding in the Middle East / Chris Mitchell.

pages cm

Includes bibliographical references and index.

ISBN 978-1-4002-0528-8

1. Arab-Israeli conflict--Influence. 2. Arabs--Middle East--Politics and government--21st century. 3. Palestinian Arabs--Middle East--Politics and government--21st century. 4. Middle East--Politics and government--21st century. 5. Foreign correspondents--Travel--Israel--Personal narratives. 6. Mitchell, Chris, 1952---Anecdotes. 7. Bible--Prophecies--Israel. I. Title.

DS119.7.M58 2013

956.05'4--dc23

2013008971

Printed in the United States of America

13 14 15 16 17 18 RRD 6 5 4 3 2 1

Dedicated to my loving wife, Elizabeth, and our children, Philip, Kathleen, and Grace, who came on the journey and stayed for the adventure. Remember, the best is yet to come.

CONTENTS

INTRODUCTION

All roads lead to Rome.

—ANCIENT SAYING

DATELINE: THE ROMAN FORUM, 20 BC

MORE THAN TWO THOUSAND YEARS AGO, ROMAN EMPEROR Caesar Augustus set a golden column in the center of the Roman Forum. He called it the "Golden Milestone." In Latin it's called the *Milliarium Aureum*.[1] This gilded column marked the beginning of all Roman roads. So when Roman engineers built their highways, they measured distances from the Golden Milestone. That's where the saying "All roads lead to Rome" comes from. They really did. If a traveler anywhere in Rome's far-flung empire walked toward the capital of the ancient world, they'd eventually end up in Rome itself. The city sat at the hub of a road system radiating throughout the sprawling Roman Empire. More than fifty thousand miles of paved roads connected conquered Roman land from Great Britain to the Middle East. Two thousand years later, Rome's highway system stands as one of history's engineering marvels.

Many roads still exist today.

For example, just outside Jerusalem, Roman mile markers dot the

"Road of the Patriarchs." Long before Rome ruled the world, many believe Abraham walked that road to sacrifice his son Isaac on Mount Moriah. When Rome later ruled Judea, those markers showed Abraham's descendants how far they had to trek on that same road to the Second Temple. There they celebrated the three great biblical feasts of Passover (*Pessach*), Pentecost (*Shavouot*), and the Feast of Tabernacles (*Succot*).

Now two millennia after the Romans built their highway masterpiece with Rome at its center, another city sits at the crossroads of history, Jerusalem.

Dateline Jerusalem examines this modern-day phenomenon.

If you're like many observers of the Middle East, you may wonder what's happening in this part of the world our history books called the Fertile Crescent. Iran threatens Israel with annihilation while its mullahs are building a nuclear bomb. The Arab Spring turns into an Islamic Winter. Egypt's Muslim Brotherhood threatens to break its thirty-year peace treaty with Israel. Turkey's prime minister vows to send warships against Israel's naval blockade of the Gaza Strip, home to the terror group Hamas. While Israel braces for war, the United States prepares for a regional conflagration.

The images of brutal street fighting in Syria, cries of "Allah Akbar" in Iraq, or American soldiers fighting and then withdrawing from both Iraq and Afghanistan all might seem confusing, chaotic, and unrelated. Current events often look like a blur. When we're bombarded with information in an age dominated by the Internet, TV, Twitter, Facebook, and Instagram, sometimes it's hard to make sense of it all. A two-minute nightly news story simply can't explain the "rest of the story" when you need to know the difference between the Sunnis and Shiites; understand why, not just how, Ahmadinejad wants to destroy Israel; or if the Arab Spring will have a worldwide impact on your life.

You might remember a game where a series of unconnected dots is spread on a page. As you connect the dots, you begin to see a picture emerge. It's like all of a sudden seeing a celestial constellation like the Big Dipper or Orion's Belt among so many other stars in the night sky.

Today, hidden within the headlines, images, press conferences, political shakings, and rhetoric throughout the Middle East are dots making sense of an often complicated region and time.

When an Iranian president thunders a murderous threat or an obscure Turkish drunkard gets a dream in Mecca or a Jewish couple from Brooklyn lands at Tel Aviv's Ben Gurion airport, these dots might seem disconnected. But they aren't. Those biblical, geopolitical, religious, spiritual, natural, and even supernatural dots are connecting in a profound and historic fashion. That's the purpose behind *Dateline Jerusalem*, to connect the dots and provide a grid of understanding for our times. We live in a world now where we cannot afford to be ill informed. What happens in the strategic Middle East, Israel, and Jerusalem is critical and matters to you.

Many of these dots point back to Jerusalem. In a very real sense, the world is shifting its attention to this ancient city like it once turned to Rome. Whether it's a Jew from the former Soviet Union on his way back to "Eretz Israel" (the land of Israel), a Scandinavian diplomat involved in negotiations for peace, a Christian "tentmaker" on the Silk Road evangelizing their way "back to Jerusalem," or a Brazilian pastor taking his congregation on a pilgrimage to the Holy Land, Jerusalem sits like a homing beacon attracting the affairs and peoples of the world.

Today, the Middle East surrounding Jerusalem is undergoing historic changes. These explosive convulsions rival other historical epochs like World Wars I and II or the fall of the Soviet Union. These convulsions can be seen rippling around the world. *Dateline Jerusalem* chronicles many of these changes. Some of them I'm sure you have heard of or read about in the news. Others are under the world's radar but no less significant.

One change, though, that's been quite noticeable to the world is the ascendance of classical Islam throughout the Middle East. The so-called Arab Spring with its tantalizing scent of democracy instead is turning into an Islamic Winter with the smell of Sharia law. Many Muslims throughout the region from Istanbul to Cairo now hunger and thirst for the restoration of what they call the caliphate. The *caliphate* means a government ruled by a *caliph* or "successor" to Muhammad using Sharia (or Islamic) law as their guide. They dream of a world under the dominion of Muhammad's seventh-century religion.

However, another restoration—Israel's—fulfills the dreams of Jews since the fall of Jerusalem in AD 70. Many see Israel's founding in 1948 as a modern-day miracle and the answer to the prayers of both Jews and Christians for centuries. When Israeli paratroopers captured Jerusalem's Old City and the Temple Mount during the 1967 Six Day War, it satisfied the cry "Next year in Jerusalem" that Jews had faithfully prayed for centuries.

Another phenomenon: Jews are returning to their ancient homeland from the four corners of the earth. This divine migration—foretold by Hebrew prophets thousands of years ago—includes "lost tribes" from faraway places like India and China. Yet along with its biblical restoration, Israel finds itself under more threat than ever in its modern history. The nations surrounding the Jewish state pose an existential threat and regularly thunder threats of a Middle East without Israel. This, too, seems to have been foretold and to be a harbinger of things to come when the nations will one day surround Jerusalem.

Other developments transcend politics. Instead, they seem to herald a dramatic move of God in human history.

For example, the Muslim world resisted Christian evangelism for centuries. Yet spiritual cracks have appeared in this seemingly impenetrable bastion. Now veteran Mideast observers report more Muslims coming to faith in Jesus Christ than at any other time in the fourteen-hundred-year history of Islam. While some convert through the influence of satellite television or the Internet, other conversions can only be explained as supernatural. Many Muslims report they behold "a man in white" in their dreams who identifies Himself as Jesus. This phenomenon is piercing the world of Islam from Morocco to Indonesia and beyond. It's shaking the foundations of this religious colossus.

Along with dreams and visions, some Middle East Christians testify the same kinds of miracles once seen in the Bible are happening again today, whether it be people raised from the dead in Iraq or multiplication of food in Egypt. There's a crescendo of concentrated prayer that some believe hasn't ever been heard before. Events like the 2012 World Prayer Assembly in Jakarta, 24/7 Houses of Prayer springing up throughout the Middle East, and the Day of Prayer for the Peace of Jerusalem link millions of Christians around the world with the same prayers. Because of this unprecedented move, some wonder if prayer itself will act like a rudder steering our world through the history of our time.

Furthermore, veteran Christian workers announce we're witnessing an unprecedented marriage of prayer and evangelism with astounding results. Groups like The Call, International House of Prayer (IHOP), Global Media Outreach (GMO), and Every Home for Christ are folding their hands together and witnessing never-before-seen results. They report a harvest so profound and new technology so advanced, they believe it holds promise that the Great Commission—the charge by Jesus Christ to take the gospel to the whole world—could be completed in our generation. One of the spearheads of this new evangelistic thrust called "Back to Jerusalem" carries with it a potential of penetrating the Buddhist, Hindu, and Muslim areas of the earth.

While the headlines of the day trumpet the news on earth, others wonder if heaven had a newspaper, wouldn't these reports of miracles, evangelism, and prayer be making front-page news? Here on earth, it's hard to deny these are truly amazing days to be alive.

As an exclamation point to all these developments, a global focus on Jerusalem—for good or ill—is intensifying. On the one hand millions of Christians worldwide are praying for the peace of Jerusalem with a fervor and intensity never seen before. While at the same time millions of Muslims are participating in events like the Global March on Jerusalem with the cry raising throughout the Muslim world that Jerusalem will be the capital of an Islamic caliphate.

What then—in light of all these events—does that mean for us, for our daily lives? As the Christian thinker Francis Schaeffer asked many years ago, "How should we then live?"

Dateline Jerusalem traces these accelerating trends of history and unravels what it means to you. As a correspondent for CBN News here in Jerusalem since 2000, I've had the opportunity—and privilege—to see the world turn more and more of its attention toward the ancient capital of David. I believe this trend will increase and eventually shape the history of the world and the destinies of its people. The news today might focus on Washington, New York, London, or Moscow, but history's final chapter will be written in Jerusalem.

Dateline Jerusalem begins in Cairo and threads its way through places like Istanbul, Jakarta, Mozambique, the Italian Riviera, Hong Kong, and the West Bank with one unifying theme: history is on its way "back to Jerusalem." It is one man's journey and perspective through the often chaotic, challenging, interesting, and fascinating days we call "our time."

The journey starts in Cairo, in the eye of the storm.

1 IN THE EYE OF THE STORM

Currently the mobs targeting journalists are right
outside the Hilton but have not breached the premises.[1]
—ALERT FROM CAIRO'S HILTON RAMSES HOTEL

DATELINE: CAIRO'S TAHRIR SQUARE

CBN NEWS REPORT: TUESDAY, FEBRUARY 1, 2011

We're standing in Tahrir Square, the epicenter for events here in Cairo, now beginning their second week. They expect one million in Tahrir Square, one million in Alexandria, and another million in Suez. People have been congregating here all day, some walking hours since the government shut down the public trains.

The evidence of the week's violence are all around: burned-out vehicles, Egyptian tanks, armored personnel carriers, and soldiers surrounding the square and Mubarak's burnt-out headquarters nearby.

The one thing unifying the people here is that they want to see Mubarak go. We saw signs saying "World without Mubarak"; we heard people chanting, "Mubarak, go to the U.S."; "Go to Tel Aviv"; shouting, "This is the last day for Mubarak."

Egypt is very much a nation on the brink.

Many say here Egypt will never be the same again, that it can never go back to where it was. But the questions many are asking are: Where will it go from here? Will it sink more into anarchy and chaos? Will it go morph into an oppressive theocracy like Iran? Or will it find its way to greater freedom and stability?

Will Mubarak go? Can he withstand the pressure of the streets or the political pressure of the United States? What role will the Muslim Brotherhood have?

These are questions no one has the answers for. That's why church leaders feel Egypt—this pivotal nation in the Middle East—is at a tipping point and they're calling for prayer and fasting for Egypt—that this land rich in the Bible will fulfill its biblical destiny.

That was our report when the heat of Egypt's revolution burned white hot. But things would burn hotter.

Here's our CBN News report we filed the next day:

Egyptian president Hosni Mubarak pledged not to seek reelection in September, but it may not be enough to satisfy millions of demonstrators who want him to leave office.

The day after Mubarak's announcement, demonstrators gathered in Central Cairo for yet another day of protests. Many demonstrators here in Tahrir Square vow they will stay on the streets until Mubarak leaves. They feel Mubarak's promise not to seek reelection came too little, too late. The demonstrators here are exuding a sense of power; a feeling that all together they can force their president of thirty years to go; that at least for now that for the first time in a long time, they have the upper hand.

A young Egyptian told us, "Yes, we can make him go. And we will. We have had enough of him."

A middle-age Egyptian added, "Today we are making our own history."

The next major confrontation will likely come on Friday, the day of Muslim prayers. Some are threatening to march on the presidential palace itself. For the first time today there were minor clashes between pro-Mubarak supporters and the demonstrators.

Different factions and personalities are jockeying to control this revolution. But everyone is united on one goal: to make Mubarak go. After that, it's unclear what happens next.

Everyone agrees this revolution represents a sea change for Egypt. Some see it as the first scene in the first act in a long drama over the future of Egypt. Its present is precarious and its future uncertain, and many wonder what will be the outcome for the most influential Arab nation in the Middle East and a bell weather for the region. It's why Christians here continue to call for prayer and fasting for Egypt in its hour of crisis.

Before we left the square, around 11:30 a.m., we heard two ominous and prophetic warnings. One man told us Mubarak would use his thugs to disrupt things. Another lady—in a full burqa with only a slit for her eyes—warned us that people were now being allowed in the square without being checked. She said her large bag was not opened. Mubarak supporters would bring in weapons, she cried. She sensed the violence to come. Both felt the quiet wouldn't last.

We went back to the bureau and sent our report by satellite at 1:20 p.m. local time.

After our satellite feed—from the production house six stories up—we watched hundreds and then thousands of Mubarak supporters heading to Tahrir Square. I thought, *That's odd. Why allow them to go there? Isn't that a prescription for disaster? A combustible mix?*

Curious, I walked out of the bureau and followed them down to the square. Mubarak supporters carried one policeman on their shoulders and smothered him with kisses. Certainly not the feelings of the anti-Mubarak crowd just a short walk down the street.

I walked deeper into the crowd. The two opposing groups squared off. I stood just a couple of hundred feet from the epicenter. Something seemed different from the day before: ominous, wrong. I felt the whisper of the Holy Spirit: *Something's going to happen.*

Then, as if someone pulled a trigger, something did happen. A spark ignited the masses. The crowd surged back toward me. Like a field of wheat blown in the wind, the mass swept back in my direction. The crowd as one began to run, including everyone around me. The sounds of feet, panting, people jostling, shouting, and running crackled in the air. Fear and panic—you could feel them.

Then I saw shoes being thrown between the two groups, a profound insult in the Arab world.

I got out my camera and began filming while simultaneously being swept along with the herd. Thankfully, I found myself near the sidewalk, saw a fence, and like many others climbed over it. Still the throng swarmed. Like riding a human wave, it carried me with it and I remember clearly thinking, *Don't fall down, that's how people get trampled.*

But this small eddy of humanity on the sidewalk found an opening in a metal corrugated wall. We poured in. The wall separated a construction site from the street. Sand and rubber tubing filled the area getting ready for a soon-to-be-laid concrete foundation. I saw a young kid pick up a rock, a big one. Then I turned and saw that now the shoes had become rocks, showers of rocks. Back and forth the rocks flew between the pro- and anti-Mubarak forces. *Where did all those rocks come from?* I wondered. I didn't see any rocks when I walked down the street just a few moments before, but now hundreds of rocks filled the air. Somebody brought them.

Some of the rioting spread down side streets. The crowds surged back and forth. Roars swelled when one side or another made advances. I had never seen anything like this. Smoke rose. Soldiers, tanks, and military personnel dotted the scene but took a neutral "you can both fight it out" stance. I saw one photographer in the middle of the melee who climbed up on a statue to get a better vantage point. I feared for his safety as rocks whizzed by his head. I'm sure he wished he had a helmet. Of the hundreds of wounded that day, many, if not most, sustained head injuries.

I continued to videotape with our small JVC handheld camera while hanging on to the fence. An Egyptian clung on to the fence beside me and shared these front-row seats to pandemonium. The relative quiet of thirty minutes before had been replaced by a full-blown riot.

I called back to CBN News. They needed to know. Fast. This changed everything. Our report filed less than an hour ago was already outdated. I tried to text with my fingers shaking. Adrenaline surged. I prayed, "Lord, help me dial right. Help someone answer." One text message: no reply. Another voice mail: no call back. What's that other number? I knew I wrote it somewhere. I found it. I called and reached Steve Little, CBN News's 8:00 a.m. show producer, and told him about the riot.

Then I saw the most surreal scene. Horses raced down the boulevard right in front of us! Then a camel came past me, surging through the crowd. "There's a camel going down the street!" I shouted to Steve.

He passed the phone to Drew Parkhill, our *700 Club* news producer. I told Drew about the riot. Suddenly a man came up beside me. He shouted in Arabic. I didn't know what he said, but I knew what he meant: "Stop videotaping!" I put the small JVC camera in my pocket. But the man and then a second stayed right beside me. I told Drew to pray since I thought the men were from the secret police. I heard stories about their involvement in the demonstrations and knew they wanted to stop incriminating video from reaching the outside world.

I turned and walked away. I had to put some distance between them and me.

I walked about seventy-five feet while still talking with Drew and then turned around. Suddenly, one man grabbed my BlackBerry out of my hand, the other the camera out of my coat pocket. In less than five seconds it was over. They ran away, climbed up on some construction material, jumped a fence, and vanished.

My first instinct was to get my camera back. My second instinct was, well, there were two of them and one of me and I didn't know if they were armed. They had run away so quickly the scene was a blur.

But now I stood there dazed with no phone. I lost my contacts and the video of the riot, two days of personal recollections, pictures, and video of Cairo's historic turning point.

I left the construction site the same way as the thieves, half hoping I'd find them, half not knowing what I'd do if I did. The street I landed in ran perpendicular to the main boulevard where the riot was still raging. Strangely, this street remained relatively quiet. Within a couple of minutes I strode along the Nile still flowing by, a silent witness to this latest chapter in one of the world's most ancient civilizations. But what was taking place just one block away was anything but civilized.

Still trying to process what had just happened, I felt upset at myself. How could I let them steal the phone and the camera? I thought I had better street smarts than that. I pondered, *What do I do next?*

When I got back to the production house, I ran into a producer and reporter I had met earlier in the day. My story gushed out. They expressed shock and offered me a phone to use. I called back to CBN, reported what had happened, and then recorded a phone feed for a new and updated story for the *700 Club*.

About an hour later, I talked on the phone live with Pat Robertson on the *700 Club*. We talked about what happened to me, the riot, the growing concern of the Muslim Brotherhood, how many Christians were asking for prayer and even fasting for the situation in Egypt, and how Egypt's turmoil might affect Israel.

After our call, people in the production house buzzed about other journalists who had been attacked. One example: a crowd had surrounded and accosted CNN's Anderson Cooper and his cameraman. By this time, the mood in the production house had changed. You could see the growing concern on the faces. All of a sudden the streets had turned dangerous, uncertain, and unwelcome.

About thirty minutes later, I joined CBN News's daily editorial meeting by phone. We discussed my situation. Should I leave? Stay? Some implied it might be time to leave, especially since I had no backup and no reinforcements on the way. At the time, I leaned the other way. I thought I could stay in the hotel and the production house in relative safety for the next two days and then head home. The decision ultimately was mine.

At the production house, many huddled around a monitor feeding a live shot of the riot that still raged just a few blocks away. Now the bureau seemed much more vulnerable. There was little or no security. What security I did see was a willowy young teenage girl who opened and closed the front door. Not the kind of physique you want between you and an angry mob. I talked with the head of the production house. What did he recommend? He said he'd never been in this kind of situation and was feeling his way through. A very kind Egyptian, he provided crucial help for me as I sent stories to the *700 Club*. I was deeply grateful for him and felt his aid was an answer for those praying for my trip.

At 5:30 p.m., I walked to my hotel, eager to look inconspicuous. The mood on the streets had turned. You could taste it. Angry crowds spoiling for a fight, eager for a brawl. Dozens of Mubarak supporters passed me headed for the square armed with clubs. I shuddered quietly inside.

Shortly thereafter I reached the hotel and found the hotel staff—bellmen, security, and others—forming a human barrier at the front door. I showed my room key and then one of the bellmen recognized me and allowed me to pass through this impromptu human shield.

The hotel itself housed mostly journalists from all over the world. In fact, the restaurant sounded like the United Nations; French, German,

English, Arabic, and several other languages could be heard. Going into the lobby or sharing a ride in the elevator provided valuable snippets of information. Whose equipment got confiscated, what was safe, where you could go. The hotel morphed into an instant club, a company of reporters sharing the same dangers and glazed together in the same furnace.

I walked into the lobby and ran into old friend, Andrew Wilson of Sky News. Despite the riot going on outside, it was a delightful reunion. Ironically, the last time we had seen each other was on the Israel/Lebanon border when Israel fought Hezbollah during the 2006 Second Lebanon War. Our children went to the same school when he was assigned to Jerusalem. We caught up on family news; then he left to see for himself what was happening outside.

I went up to my room and witnessed something I don't think I'll ever forget: the battle for Cairo.

The conflict—now three hours old—that I had just watched on a monitor at the bureau raged just two to three blocks from my hotel. It had begun with shoes, then rocks, and now had sunk into a brutal battle. Pro- and anti-Mubarak forces fought like medieval warriors with crude weapons like rocks and firebombs hearkening back to the Middle Ages. A revolution that began with twenty-first-century technology—Twitter, Facebook, and the Internet—took a turn back centuries.

After I got to my room, I talked once more with my boss, Rob Allman, and discussed our plans. At this time in the early evening and before the sun had set, I still leaned toward staying, feeling I could manage our news coverage—and still remain relatively safe—by walking between the hotel and the news bureau around the corner.

Meanwhile, the battle continued raging with no signs of abating.

It was a barbaric, bloody siege.

Demonstrators threw petrol bombs from rooftops to the streets below or from one rooftop to the next. Darkness shrouded Cairo by then, and the explosions lit up the night for a moment, then the streets dimmed down into a smoky haze.

I went downstairs for dinner. Riding on the elevator provided more information from other journalists. One divulged two of his remote satellite dishes were taken. The journalists—who by now were all targets—shared an instant camaraderie. "Be safe" became a comforting salutation. My sumptuous dinner in a five-star hotel felt surreal with a revolution taking place outside. I wondered if this was how wealthy Russians felt during the Bolshevik revolution.

Back upstairs in my room after dinner, I had the unusual experience of watching the news live on TV and live from my balcony. I turned to either CNN or BBC and watched their live feed of the battle and then walked a few feet to my balcony and saw the very same image. They might have been broadcasting to the world, but just two blocks away their coverage provided me with valuable information.

Around 7:00 p.m., several thousand miles away, my CBN News colleague George Thomas led the noon chapel at CBN in Virginia Beach. He arranged a Skype connection with my hotel phone, which thankfully was still working. For the first time in days, I heard a worship service, a spiritual tonic for a weary soul. George explained to those in the chapel where I was and what I was doing and then had me share my experiences since I'd been in Cairo. I told them what was happening and my feelings about the situation. Then George led us in prayer both for Egypt's predicament and for my safety.

I could imagine the faces of the CBN family. I sensed their love and support and expressed my love. So far away, alone and in the midst of precarious circumstances, their love and support pushed back the emotional and spiritual darkness. This welcome, sweet respite from the events of the day and the battle near the hotel filled my temporary haven.

I thought, too, of my own family, Liz and our three children. For the first time I questioned: *Would I see them again?* The thought flooded my soul with a profound melancholy. But Liz and I knew the path we had chosen. Our covenant was to be faithful to Jesus and, if necessary, we'd see each other "on the other side." Our mutual heart cry: never to deny the Lord. I reread the e-mail she sent just before I left for Cairo:

Since you are going into a dangerous area . . . remember what we talked about years ago. Whatever happens remember stand for the Lord. Listen carefully. Always follow that little nudge. I trust God to keep you in the palm of His Hand. You are the love of my life.

Love you always, Liz

Courage flooded my soul.

I knew intercessors—many who have prayed faithfully for me for years—were interceding. Their prayers brought the Scriptures to life.

"He who dwells in the secret place of the Most High shall abide under the shadow of the Almighty" (Psalm 91:1).

As the night wore on, the battle grew more intense. The combatants lit on fire cars unfortunate enough to be parked near the battle. Then around 11:00 p.m., gunfire—lots of it—punctuated Cairo's night air. It sounded like heavy-caliber machine-gun fire. Then small-arms fire erupted. I couldn't tell where most of the gunfire was coming from but I did see red tracer bullets flying next to the hotel and arcing out over the Nile River.

Eventually, because of the gunfire, I turned off the lights in my room. Standing up was no longer an option, so I crawled to my balcony.

I thought I should sleep but kept watching the battle both on TV and from my balcony. I reminisced about my dad and what his experience must have been like in World War II. He won the Bronze Star and served as head of a medical hospital unit near the front lines in the Italian campaign. One time through tears he told my sister and me how he prayed to live through a particularly terrifying artillery barrage. It's a long way from the Italian campaign during WWII to Cairo in 2011, but the shared danger on those respective front lines knit together this father and son bond across the decades.

I started thinking I should pack and be ready to leave just in case I needed to evacuate. With those thoughts running through my head, I fell asleep and had a dream. In my dream, the battle reached the hotel and raged just below my window. I saw rocks strewn on the street as one demonstrator hurled a large rock at other protestors. The dream felt so real, so vivid, I woke up and went to the balcony to see the scene for myself. I felt relieved to see the street just below my balcony was quiet, but by now the violence swirled a lot closer to the hotel, just two streets away. The dream's meaning to me was clear: *Pack! It's getting closer!*

About a block away, I watched a skirmish between about thirty on one side and twenty on the other. I couldn't tell who was who, the pro-Mubarak and anti-Mubarak forces. They threw rocks and petrol bombs at each other. One scored a direct hit and a demonstrator lit up like a torch, but within seconds he and an accomplice smothered the flames. The mobs jeered each other, threatened each other, and nearly killed each other.

What struck and sobered me throughout the night was the complete and pervasive lack of law and order. Anarchy in full bloom. The mobs ruled. You could feel it.

"You will not fear the terror of night" (Psalm 91:5 NIV).

Throughout the night and into the morning, a rhythmic beating on the metal barricades reverberated in the darkness. It reminded me of a scene out of the movie *Braveheart* with warriors beating their shields to terrify their enemy: a raw battle to the death. Close quarters combat. From my front-row seat I watched this remarkable and violent drama. Thousands contending over the fate and future of Mubarak and Cairo while Egypt hung in the balance. Neither side willing to give in or give up.

Egypt launched out in uncharted territory. So did I.

"Yea, though I walk through the valley of the shadow of death, I will fear no evil" (Psalm 23:4).

There came a time during the night when my situation seemed to get serious. Very serious. A time when the refuge of the hotel itself seemed vulnerable. Would the mob storm the hotel? Did they know the hotel harbored journalists from around the world? Would the protestors who unleashed such animosity toward journalists earlier in the day turn on the hotel? Was it strong enough? I thought of barricading my room. I looked across the street to the burnt-out hulk of Mubarak's political headquarters, lit on fire just days before. I wondered if they could or would set this building on fire like that. It looked about the same size as the Ramses Hilton where I was staying. If so, what would be my escape route? All of a sudden, I didn't appreciate my seventh-story perch.

Later I found out I wasn't the only journalist concerned about the safety of the hotel. During the heat of the battle, another news agency sent an urgent message to the Hilton Hotel management that said in part:

> Currently the mobs targeting journalists are right outside the Hilton but have not breached the premises.
>
> Word is that staff are getting edgy, the journalists' equipment has been confiscated, and there is danger both that the staff will hand the journalists over or the mobs will breach the hotel.
>
> This is just an email to request that Hilton does all they can to protect those journalists currently inside the Hilton.
>
> Yours in hope.[2]

Yet the sounds of battle kept pounding, kept piercing the atmosphere. "Your rod and Your staff, they comfort me" (Psalm 23:4).

During the night I turned my attention away from my own plight and prayed that the Lord would intervene and redeem this deadly drama I was witnessing. My prayer felt feeble when compared to the intensity of the battle, but at the very least I thought I could as an eyewitness "pray onsite with insight."

In those proverbial darkest hours just before the dawn, I wondered when the sun would come up. I longed for it. When would light shine on this "long day's journey into night"? This desperate, defiant, and deadly day.

Early in the morning, about 5:00 a.m., CNN reported the latest US State Department advisory: all Americans were advised to go immediately to the airport when the curfew lifted. "Further delay is not advisable," it added.

Shortly after that, Rob called. He had seen the same State Department advisory and recommended I follow its advice. I agreed. It was a welcome call offering timely, godly counsel. One factor we considered: my compatriot had never made it into the country. He was supposed to be my guide and translator. He knew Cairo well and had excellent local contacts. He flew in from another Middle Eastern country and despite his best efforts failed to reach me. Egyptian authorities stopped him at the airport. His work with the local church had earned him a black mark. He could not pass "go."

The words from Ecclesiastes 4:9–10 rang true once more: "Two are better than one, because they have a good reward for their labor. For if they fall, one will lift up his companion. But woe to him who is alone when he falls, for he has no one to help him up."

George Thomas called, too, with some needed encouragement, prayer, and savvy advice. One suggestion: don't tell the hotel staff I was leaving until I showed up at the front desk.

Then I called a local Christian. I spoke with her earlier in the week about the biblical and spiritual significance of what was taking place in Egypt. This time we talked about logistics and timing. She urged me to leave for the airport—soon. She didn't want me to wait. Her words resonated: One more confirmation. It's time to leave!

Now I knew I was going, but the question was how. I felt the squeeze of circumstances, but I wasn't quite sure how to get out. One thing I do know is that I was focused in a way I have seldom been before. I may not have known how I'd escape, but I did know the small, incremental steps I needed to take along the way. Shower, dress, empty the safe of valuables. Looking back, I know the alertness was a direct result of the people who were faithfully and fervently praying for me.

"He leads me in the paths of righteousness for His name's sake" (Psalm 23:3).

I called the head of the production company I had talked with before. He graciously invited me to his home but because his English was poor and my Arabic nonexistent, I chose not to accept his offer or ask him for a ride to the airport. The communication hurdle seemed too high.

With no immediate or visible means of escape, I decided to do what many people do when they check out of a hotel: I went outside and got a cab. Simple! And it worked. The bellman went outside with me, and we found a taxi driver who said he was available.

I asked him to give me fifteen minutes and I'd be back down. Not knowing when or where my next meal would come from, I scarfed down a quick breakfast, went upstairs, and grabbed my bags. As the first rays of light revealed the carnage and chaos of the night, I took some last pictures from my still camera from my balcony. I wanted something to remember that night.

I checked out. Ramy, the desk clerk, assured me everything would be okay. The look in his eyes told me otherwise.

Hassan (not his real name) would be my driver. Just as we pulled away, another cab driver stopped Hassan and told him letting journalists videotape out of his cab could get him in serious trouble. Hassan warned me, no cameras! I assured him no pictures, even with the still camera. He drove me through the narrow streets next to the hotel that happened to be his neighborhood. Friends called him out by name, which reassured me. The contrast between the five-star hotel and his neighborhood just blocks away was striking: dirty streets and hovels for homes. The streets built so narrow we had to stop and wait for other cars to squeeze past.

Finally, we emerged from his neighborhood and pulled out to the main street. He looked right. We saw a tank and several cars waiting in line at a checkpoint. Too many, he felt. So he turned left into the oncoming flow of traffic! He flashed his lights as cars whizzed by. Somehow it seemed normal in Cairo. After a block, he bore right and entered into the flow of traffic back on the right side of the road. We saved some time and a checkpoint. We drove on and again he warned me about pictures.

We came up to the first checkpoint. They resembled the nearly eighty checkpoints we went through my first night in Cairo, but more menacing. Young men—maybe from six to twelve at a checkpoint—held clubs, pipes, and knives. They motioned for us to stop. Hassan told me he'd take care of it. He showed his ID. I showed them mine. It was enough. They let us go.

But this was just the first. There were others. At one checkpoint one young boy held a machete. Thankfully, he inspected another car. At one of the checkpoints, they asked Hassan to open the trunk. *Oh no*, I thought, *there goes my luggage.* I wondered if they just might help themselves to whatever they wanted. There wasn't much I could do if they did, but thankfully they looked and then closed the trunk.

At one of the vigilante checkpoints, we simply drove through because the "guards" chased down a man on a motor scooter.

The checkpoints ringed Tahrir Square for a certain radius and then disappeared. We thankfully drove on to the airport without stopping.

On the way, Hassan and I talked about his family and the situation. He said people needed food and work. He told me about his children and one daughter who was studying to be a doctor. He was a nice man, one of the many pleasant, kind Egyptians I met during my brief stay. Despite the riot and battle, this visit was often an enjoyable experience.

On the way to the airport, we passed Mubarak's presidential palace heavily fortified with tanks, soldiers, barbed wire, and armored personnel carriers. About ten minutes later, we arrived at the airport. I told him I was flying El Al, and he said they flew out of building number one. We had agreed on a price for the cab ride, however, I decided to give him more. When I offered it to him, he asked me if I had American money instead of Egyptian pounds. After all, Egyptian currency was losing value by the hour. The banks had been closed for days. I gave Hassan American money instead. In fact, I gave him one of the biggest fares I've ever paid for a cab ride. After all, he just ran a gauntlet of vigilante checkpoints for me, any of which potentially threatened my life, limb, and belongings. It was one of the most valuable taxi rides I ever had. He became my unexpected avenue of escape—my way home.

"You prepare a table before me in the presence of my enemies" (Psalm 23:5).

It was also probably one of the biggest fares he ever received. When he saw the money, he smiled broadly, kissed me on both cheeks, and hugged me enthusiastically. I felt like I had just helped send his daughter through medical school!

Building number one was a zoo. Hundreds of people inside and out were leaving Cairo. I didn't have a clue where the El Al counter was. Young Egyptian boys pestered me one after another to carry my luggage and help me through security. Of course you had to pay and they wanted the tip up front. I obliged, but it wasn't enough. They wanted more. I obliged one more time. They wanted even more. Finally I said that was enough and thank you very much, but I'd take care of my own bags.

One of my bags was through the X-ray machine when the security guard gave me the news and the latest bump on my rocky Egyptian road: the flights going to Jerusalem were all cancelled. I retrieved my bags and looked for the El Al office, to do as Ronald Reagan once said, "Trust but verify." I checked with information, British Air, Royal Jordanian, and others. Every direction people sent me ended up in a dead end, no El Al office. I began to wonder if El Al had closed up shop. I even looked into booking flights to Europe—anywhere to get out of Cairo.

After more than an hour, I ran into a British embassy official. She was helping a young English girl who had lost her passport and was trying to leave the country. The girl chirped up and said she heard the Americans were leaving out of building number four. Building number four. That sounded like where I wanted to be. I was on my way.

I left the terminal and confronted the hundreds of people swarming to get in. Like a salmon swimming upstream, I finally wiggled through. A man whispered to me, "Taxi?" It sounded like the same kind of offer when someone on the street says, "Want to buy a watch?" Full of suspicion, I nevertheless decided to accept his offer, though I didn't know if we'd be heading to building four or points unknown. I sat in the front seat. I thought if I needed to leave the cab quickly and jump out the door or if I had to stop the cab, I could slam my foot on the brakes. *Better up front than in the back*, I thought. My trust level had sunk pretty low by then. But he turned out to be an aspiring engineering student. Pretty

soon, I saw reassuring signs to building four. We pulled up to the terminal, and he gave me my bags. I exhorted him to be a good engineer and
hoped the Egypt in his future would permit that.

Building number four exuded a different atmosphere—calm, orderly.
I immediately felt at home. I saw many Americans. After two days of
uncertainty and for the first time in hours, I felt like I might make it. I
wanted to hug someone.

"You anoint my head with oil; my cup runs over" (Psalm 23:5).

I stood in line waiting to be processed for the US evacuation flight
to Frankfurt. It felt comforting, like being in line for a church Sunday
potluck. The lady taking my information could have been asking me if I
had brought a covered dish, salad, or a dessert. One guy at the table wore
a Yankees hat. Even for a Red Sox fan, a Yankees hat was a welcome sight,
though I did ask him if they processed Red Sox fans too.

Later in the day, we finally left the terminal for the plane.

We sat on the tarmac for hours, delayed by several diplomatic and
bureaucratic snafus.

Finally, the wheels lifted off at 10:15 p.m., just more than seventy-
two hours since I had landed.

Again I watched the lights of Cairo below as I had several nights
before. After witnessing Egypt's tumultuous history with more turmoil
yet to come, it seemed abundantly clear how important it is to pray for
this nation, its people, and its spiritual destiny.

What this meant for Israel seemed unclear for the moment, but the
shock waves released in Egypt would certainly crash on Israel's shores
one day. Soon the Jewish state would begin to find the answer to the
question analysts, politicians, and journalists had pondered for years:
What will happen to Egypt after Mubarak leaves, and what will that
mean for the Jewish state? Their answer came quickly.

2 THE ARAB SPRING OR ISLAMIC WINTER

The Arab Spring doesn't lead to democracy, it leads to Jerusalem.

—ANONYMOUS

DATELINE: FRANKFURT, GERMANY

WE ARRIVED IN GERMANY AT ABOUT 2:30 A.M. FRIDAY. LANDING IN Frankfurt was one more stage of decompressing from the pressure in Cairo. The US embassy personnel were terrific. Dare I say angelic, given the circumstances? They were kind, helpful, and considerate. They thought of most everything: water, juices, sodas, snacks, fruit, games for the kids, magazines and books, even Girl Scout cookies! What a relief to see friendly faces, a home away from home.

"He restores my soul" (Psalm 23:3).

After our arrival, I wondered if I had left Cairo prematurely and asked myself why I didn't stay in the heat of the battle. Of course, one powerful argument was that I had no backup. No team, no one to pick me up, as Ecclesiastes says, or watch my back. Then I started hearing stories about the other journalists. One Arabic channel reported that "Mubarak supporters stormed Cairo's Hilton Hotel [the one I was in] searching for journalists."[1] I started to think differently.

The most powerful argument, of course, was the strong sense— confirmed three times—that the Lord had said it was time.

"Surely goodness and mercy shall follow me all the days of my life . . ." (Psalm 23:6).

On a personal note, during this time I gained a profound appreciation and deeper love of life, my wife, children, and family. A renewed appreciation for what really matters. I felt, too, a deeper commitment to fulfill God's calling on my life and a far deeper appreciation for the power of prayer. And a sense that given these tumultuous times we're entering it's vital for all of us to "get it right" and to "get right with God." As we face the future, we need to walk with the One who holds the future.

" . . . and I will dwell in the house of the LORD forever" (Psalm 23:6).

The Cairo experience became my first up-close and personal encounter with the Arab Spring. Much of it I had watched from a distance—like you—but now I was no longer detached. That experience seared into my thinking the profound changes affecting Egypt and the region. It began in Tunisia, shook the entire region, and sent shock waves around the world. The price of oil rose, stock markets plunged, and the world shook with anxiety.

The Egyptian revolution looked in some ways like the Iranian protests of 2009 when a million Iranians took to the streets demanding a corrupt theocracy fall. In Tahrir Square, Egyptians seemed unified around one goal: to bring about the end of an autocratic regime. Egypt's revolution began with a genuine plea by young Egyptians and many others for less corruption and more freedom.

These cries punctuated the revolution. For example, Sharif, a young Egyptian who represented a new generation, told us about the problems he saw. Corruption was number one. Mubarak, his family, and his cabal enjoyed most of Egypt's wealth while most of the country languished. Food was scarce, health care lacking, and education poor. He came to Tahrir

Square as part of the young generation of Egyptians who wanted a better life. They used twenty-first-century technology—Twitter and Facebook—to achieve that ancient human desire—freedom from tyranny.

That cry for freedom rang deep and genuine. The demonstrators knew what they wanted—the removal of Mubarak—but others wondered what would happen next. Would a strong leader emerge? A strong movement? Could, under the surface and behind the scenes, other strata of Egyptian society lead Egypt into even greater bondage than Mubarak ever did? Could this be another plunge into the abyss of an Islamic theocracy like Iran's in 1979? Would an even more oppressive Islamic movement led by the Muslim Brotherhood, who cried out for Sharia law within Egypt and pined for Israel's destruction, rule? We didn't have long to wait.

Just two days after I watched the lights of Cairo fade into the Egyptian night and just eighteen days after the Egyptian revolution began, Egyptian president Hosni Mubarak's reign over Egypt ended. For nearly thirty years, he ruled the largest Arab nation in the Middle East. His fall—something deemed unthinkable just weeks before—stunned the region. Yet in those first heady days of the Arab Spring, it seemed anything was possible. How the mighty fell!

No longer overlooking Tahrir Square, I watched the celebrations and euphoria from Frankfurt, Germany. I watched Andrew Wilson's coverage for Sky News from a balcony high above the street bordering the Nile. Tens of thousands of Egyptians poured into the street and throughout the area. They set off fireworks and reveled in the joy of throwing Mubarak's yoke off their shoulders. He, like most other Western reporters, shared the excitement and euphoria. The promise of democracy seemed at hand. Yet I watched with an uneasy feeling in my stomach, a sense that the revolution Sharif and others longed for would not materialize. I felt an ill wind blowing through Egypt and feared what would come next.

For those concerned that Islamists and the Muslim Brotherhood would pounce on the "revolution," the next signal felt like a shock wave.

Every Friday the revolution fed off Muslim prayers and political speeches from the epicenter of the revolution, Tahrir Square. But the second Friday after Mubarak resigned, I watched from my home in Jerusalem as eighty-six-year-old Sheik Yusuf al-Qaradawi climbed the stage and addressed an estimated one million Egyptians. That uneasy feeling in my stomach grew. His supporters kept the Twitter and Facebook leaders—the ones who spearheaded the revolution—off the stage. Egyptian observers understood the symbolism and significance of al-Qaradawi's appearance and the omission of the social media crowd. An oft-quoted saying by some in those early days rang true: "Revolutions often end up eating their children."

Why was Qaradawi's presence significant? He had left Egypt fifty years before and since then had arguably become the most influential cleric in the Sunni Muslim world. An estimated sixty million Muslims watch his Al-Jazeera TV program *Sharia and Life*. A long history of declarations and Islamic rulings called fatwas trailed Qaradawi. They gave a clue of where he wanted the revolution to go.

For example, in 1995 he declared, "What remains, then is to conquer Rome . . . that means Islam will come back to Europe for the third time. . . . We will conquer Europe, we will conquer America! Not through sword but through Da'wa, (Islamic proselytizing)."[2] In 2002, he outlined his vision of a world under Islam: "The patch of the Muslim state will expand to cover the whole earth and that the strength of this state will grow and become obvious to all. This also denotes good news for the long-cherished hope of revival of Muslims unity and rebirth of [the] Islamic Caliphate."[3]

Now Qaradawi casts a different vision and fixed another tone on Egypt's revolution than the Facebook/Google crowd. During his speech, he exhorted the throng to "continue your revolution and protect it."[4] Then in one of the first indications the revolution would swing against Israel, he declared, "I harbor the hope that just like Allah allowed me to witness the triumph of Egypt, He will allow me to witness the conquest of the Al-Aqsa Mosque [the mosque on Jerusalem's Temple Mount] and will enable me to preach in the Al-Aqsa Mosque."[5]

While Qaradawi pledged cooperation with minorities and the army, his appearance also sent a shiver through many Egyptian Christians. You see, Qaradawi also served as spiritual guide to the Muslim Brotherhood. Could this mean the Muslim Brotherhood was emerging out of Egypt's political shadows? It alarmed many, especially those who knew the history and beliefs of the Brotherhood.

MUSLIM BROTHERHOOD: JIHAD IS THE WAY

Who then is the Muslim Brotherhood?

Their founder, Hassan al-Banna, established the group—Jama'at al-Ikhwan al-Muslimin—in 1928 after the collapse of the Ottoman Empire. He based the Muslim Brotherhood on the premise that Islam is the solution. Its motto is "Allah is our objective. The Prophet is our leader. The Qur'an is our law. Jihad is our way. Dying in the way of the Prophet is our highest hope."

The Palestinian Media Watch (PMW) published a translation of *Jihad Is the Way*, a book by one of the leaders of the Muslim Brotherhood. It reveals a global agenda:

> He [Hassan al-Banna] felt . . . the urgent need and obligation which Islam places on every Muslim, man and woman, to act in order to restore the Islamic Caliphate and to re-establish the Islamic State on strong foundations . . . and to liberate the Muslims and defend them from attack, and to spread the Da'wa [Islamic missionary activity] of Islam in the world and to establish this great religion, which Allah wanted for his servants . . . the banner of Jihad has already been raised in some of its parts, and it shall continue to be raised, with the help of Allah, until every inch of land of Islam will be liberated, the State of Islam will be established, and Allah's Da'wa [Islamic missionary activity] will reach all of mankind.[6]

At its root, the Muslim Brotherhood wants to reestablish the Islamic caliphate that was abolished by the Turkish leader Ataturk in 1924. The caliphate is designed to transcend national borders and rule the Muslim nation, or *ummah*. Eventually the Muslim Brotherhood wants to see the earth submitted to Islam and Sharia law based on the Koran established throughout the world. Sharia controls all aspects of society, from what women can wear to how the state must be run. Since their founding the Muslim Brotherhood spawned most of the major Islamic groups around the globe—including Al-Qaeda—and parented groups like Hamas, the Palestinian branch of the Muslim Brotherhood. They're considered the "grandfathers" of most Islamic terrorist groups today.

Their first step toward establishing the caliphate rested on over-throwing secular Arab regimes, exactly like Mubarak's Egypt, which maintained relations with the West and established a peace treaty with Israel. That's why since 1954 successive Egyptian governments out-lawed them. Mubarak feared them, as did Egypt's president Anwar Sadat before him.

On October 6, 1981, Mubarak stood behind Sadat when they cele-brated Egypt's Armed Forces Day. During the military parade, Muslim Brotherhood members posing as soldiers jumped out of their vehicles, threw grenades, and sprayed the reviewing stand with machine-gun fire. They killed Sadat. Mubarak—then the vice president—survived. The assassination seared his memory about the danger this group represented to his brand of "moderate" Islam. He jailed their leaders and outlawed them as a political group. Yet they continued to spread their influence through a powerful social network throughout the country in schools, clinics, universities, and mosques. In fact, the Muslim Brotherhood became Egypt's most organized group.

He controlled the government, but they won many of the people's hearts.

During the 2011 revolution when the Twitter and Facebook crowd first fomented the country, they waited. But after Mubarak's fall, they sensed a once-in-a-generation opportunity and emerged from the politi-cal netherworld. They knew, however, that they were feared and many suspected their motives, so they moved slowly, cautiously. They camou-flaged themselves under the moniker "moderate." For example, Essam el-Erian, the Muslim Brotherhood's spokesman, said, "We're not in a hurry . . . we need to convince people that we are not the bogeymen that Mubarak talked of."[7]

In June 2011, they formed the Freedom and Justice Party (FJP). When their first political test of strength came following the revolution, they won decisively and outmaneuvered Egypt's liberal political par-ties. First they pledged they would run for a limited number of seats in parliament. But in September 2011, they broke that pledge and ran more candidates than promised. The election results exceeded their expec-tations, and together with the Salafi Al-Nour Party—an even more radical Islamist group—they won more than 70 percent of the seats in Egypt's new parliament.

If Qaradawi's appearance on the stage felt like a shock, the Islamic takeover of Egypt's parliament hit like a tremor. The compass of the Arab Spring that once pointed toward freedom and democracy now swung toward Islam and tyranny. With the overthrow of Ben Ali in Tunisia, Mubarak in Egypt, Gaddafi in Libya, and Ali Abdullah Saleh in Yemen, the Arab Spring had spread the euphoria of democracy through the air. It intoxicated many Westerners who saw these admittedly auto-cratic and hated Arab regimes fall. But they underestimated the savvy, political skill, and ruthlessness possessed by the Muslim Brotherhood.

The Arab Spring set in motion a Muslim Brotherhood takeover of the Sunni Arab world. Here's how several commentators put it:

"So here's the bottom line. There's a new power in the Middle East. It is an alliance of the Muslim Brotherhood groups already ruling the Gaza Strip (Hamas), Egypt and Tunisia (likely to be ruling parties), Libya, Syria, and Jordan. That's pretty impressive. They are all dedi-cated to revolution (even if it has to be achieved through the ballot box) and genocide against the Jews in Israel."[8]

"The voices of those calling for Western-style liberal reforms are invariably crushed by the more ruthless, and better organized, forces of militant Islam and military tyranny."[9]

"Ever since Islamists took office in Tunisia, Libya, and Egypt, they have been trying to convince us that they are advocates of moderation, democracy, women's rights and individual freedoms. And most people in the West, after jubilantly watching the Arab Spring's amazing revolutions last year, wanted to believe them. But now we can see that these Islamic groups are taking us for fools."[10]

A STREETCAR NAMED DEMOCRACY

While the words *democracy* and *Arab Spring* seemed interchangeable during the revolution, the Muslim Brotherhood's idea of democracy differed dramatically from the Western ideal. According to the Meir Amit Intelligence and Terrorism Information Center, "The Muslim Brotherhood does use the term 'democracy.' In its view, however, it has two main connotations: a tactical, instrumental means of taking over countries through the use of democratic process [Some explain this cynical use of democracy as "one man, one vote, one time."]; and an 'Islamic democracy' based on Shari'ah law [Islamic religious law] and a model of internal consultation with the leadership [shura]. These views have nothing in common with the ideas of liberal democracy [including minority rights, personal freedoms, rule of law (and) pluralism]."[11]

Former Israeli ambassador to Egypt Zvi Mazel spent a lot of time in Egypt and understood the mentality of the Muslim Brotherhood. During an interview, he warned us, "They will not go away and will try and stay forever. [The] election was good because it allowed them to reach power by [a] democratic way but I don't think they will continue to be democratic later."[12] Another Islamic leader—Turkish prime minister Recep Tayyip Erdogan—once described democracy like a streetcar: "you ride it until your destination and then you get off."[13]

The Muslim Brotherhood jumped on board the "democracy streetcar."

DÉJÀ VU ALL OVER AGAIN

Some saw the Egyptian revolution as history repeating itself. Marina Nemat did.

She saw the Iranian revolution in 1979 through the eyes of a teenager. She opposed the new and oppressive Islamic regime of Khomeini, wrote articles against the new revolution, and sometimes with her friends played dangerous cat-and-mouse games with the revolutionary police. But one day a knock on the door changed her life forever. At the tender age of sixteen, the police arrested her and the courts sentenced this young antirevolutionary to death. They dispatched her to Iran's infamous Evin prison. Her book *The Prisoner of Tehran* contains her harrowing account. She suffered two years of torture, isolation, and finally the humiliation of being forced to marry the man who tortured her. Even years after experiencing those horrors of Evin prison, it seemed you could hear the nightmarish echoes of Evin haunting this brave soul.

Through a set of remarkable circumstances, Nemat escaped and now lives in the West. She says the Iranian revolution—just like the Egyptian one—started out as a cry for freedom and democracy. But when she watched the TV images coming out of Cairo, it was like watching her past.

"I thought, wow, that looks really like Iran in 1979, and I couldn't help it. You know, you go talk to Iranians. I've been talking to Iranians here in Israel and they agreed with me. It looks identical."[14]

Nemat knew even in the early days of Egypt's revolution that the Muslim Brotherhood outmatched the social media crowd. "Is it going to be the Google guy [to rule Egypt] who started the whole thing, the young man? That would be really promising. But unfortunately, that's not the way it goes. Usually the ones who end up leading the revolution are organized, ones who know how to go for power, how to pounce for it."[15]

The Muslim Brotherhood pounced.

Israeli prime minister Benjamin Netanyahu echoed those warnings when he addressed the US Congress on May 24, 2011, and referred to the Arab Spring.

These extraordinary scenes in Tunis and Cairo evoke those of Berlin and Prague in 1989. Yet as we share their hopes, we must also remember that those hopes could be snuffed out as they were in Tehran in 1979. You remember what happened then. The brief democratic spring in Iran was cut short by a ferocious and unforgiving tyranny. . . . So today, the Middle East stands at a fateful crossroads. Like all of you, I pray that the peoples of the region choose the path less traveled, the path of liberty.[16]

THE PATH MOST TRAVELED

Despite the hope Egypt would choose "the path of liberty," it seemed to cascade toward Islamic tyranny. After the parliamentary elections, Egypt braced itself for the next step toward democracy, the election of a new president. A number of candidates paraded themselves before the Egyptian public, but after a run-off it came down to two candidates who presented fundamentally different choices—and futures—for Egypt. One candidate from the Muslim Brotherhood—Muhammad Mursi—promised a "moderate" Islam. The other candidate—Ahmed Shafiq—served under Mubarak as his prime minister. Many Egyptians dreaded the choice: either an Islamist whom they feared would impose Sharia law or a candidate from the former regime they dreaded and had just overthrown.

On June 24, 2012, Egypt's Election Commission announced the results. Muhammad Mursi won with nearly 52 percent of the vote. When they heard the announcement, tens of thousands of Muslim Brotherhood supporters in Tahrir Square roared their approval. Other Egyptians groaned, mourned, and lamented the direction Egypt was headed.

While Qaradawi's first speech hit like a shock wave and the parliamentary elections vibrated like a tremor, Mursi's election rocked Egypt like an earthquake. For the first time in its history, Egyptians elected an Islamist. In fact, his victory represented the first time any Arab country placed a member of the Muslim Brotherhood in charge. Some felt it represented Islam's greatest victory in the past two to three centuries. While the army still held considerable power and assumed sweeping new powers before the presidential election, many suspected the Muslim Brotherhood might eventually usurp the military. One Egyptian told me he feared what happened in Turkey—when Islamists infiltrated their army and replaced the older generals—might be repeated in Egypt. It took years, but the corrosive strategy worked.

But this time the corrosive strategy took just a few months. In a stunning announcement on August 12, 2012, Mursi sacked Field Marshal Hussein Tantawi and appointed generals of his own choosing. The vaunted Supreme Council of the Armed Forces (SCAF) seemed to simply acquiesce. He then turned his attention to the media and replaced fifty editors who worked for the government's press empire. These brazen moves consolidated Mursi's significant hold on Egypt's political power.

Mursi's victory and political maneuvers put Egypt at a crossroads, and some recognized it. An editor from the Egyptian paper *Al-Sharq Al-Awsat* wrote:

> Following the victory of the Muslim Brotherhood candidate, Muhammad Mursi . . . Egypt and the entire region have entered a new and dangerous stage, whose consequences only Allah can predict. Anyone who feels optimistic . . . and thinks we are watching a movie that is sure to have a happy ending is mistaken, and anyone who watches from the sidelines and thinks this is a purely Egyptian affair . . . is not just mistaken but also negligent.[17]

Christians immediately felt the fallout.

For example, I spoke with a Christian leader soon after the election. He, too, felt Egypt had entered a new era in its history. He said, "From day one things got harder." He noted Christian women, in particular, became targets immediately. Muslim Brotherhood supporters hurled epithets at them like, "It's not like it was before" and "You'll be veiled one day."

He noticed a new boldness among Islamists and heard a harsher tone of the speeches coming out from the mosques. They made Christians feel that this is "our country" and you (Christians) are second-or third-class citizens, *dhimmis*. (The concept of *dhimmis* or *dhimmitude* means "protected," where Jews or Christians living under Islam are protected if they pay the *jizya* tax. The jizya tax constitutes the financial tribute non-Muslims need to pay to Muslims.)

The turn of events in Egypt dazed and confused other Christians. One former ambassador to Egypt told us off camera that Christians "were scared to death."[18] Others decided to leave even in the early days of the revolution. Thousands applied to emigrate. According to *Christian News Today*, "Lawyers who specialize in working with Coptic Egyptians . . . say that in the past few weeks they have received hundreds of calls from Copts wanting to leave Egypt."[19] The Egyptian newspaper *Al-Mary al-Youm* reported, "The Canadian embassy had been swamped by visa requests from Coptic Christians."[20]

Lela Gilbert in her book *Saturday People, Sunday People* questioned if Egypt is on the cusp of another exodus: "Even now tens of thousands of Copts have quietly left Egypt—those with money and connections are able to afford airfare, relocation, legal assistance and other costly but necessary services to begin their lives again elsewhere.

"As for the others—those with few resources and even fewer options, except perhaps to flee on foot someday—where will a potential eight to ten million fleeing Copts and other Christians go? Will there be a future refugee crisis of enormous proportions? Is another Egyptian exodus yet to come?"[21]

Yet many are holding fast, believing, as one leader said, "God is in control!"

Meanwhile, some Christian leaders in the West strategized how to help their persecuted brethren and alert Western leaders and governments to the plight of Christians in Egypt. A meeting at Hudson Institute's Center for Religious Freedom in June 2012 asked, "Can Mideast Christians survive under surging Islamist movements, especially now that Egypt's Coptic Church must live under the Muslim Brotherhood?"[22] Lebanese professor Habib Malik observed, "'A persistent plague' of dictatorships collapsing, creating a 'jumble of disturbing outcomes.'" Malik "urged the West to 'draw a thick red line to protect meager freedoms' in the Mideast."[23]

MURSI AND HIS POWER GRAB

Yet those freedoms seemed to ebb drastically in the Middle East's largest Arab country. Mursi stunned Egypt and the region when on November 22, 2012, he assumed sweeping new powers as president. He declared he would be the final arbiter "on all constitutional amendments, decisions and laws."[24] He even set himself above Egypt's constitutional court. Opponents branded him the "new pharaoh." Spiegel Online interviewed a former Muslim Brotherhood member who sent out an alarm:

> Abd al-Galil al-Sharnubi says he can only laugh at the thought that there are people in the West who still see the Muslim Brotherhood as "moderate Islamists." Sharnubi is a journalist and a Muslim—and he was a member of the Brotherhood for 23 years. He's been familiar with the movement since he was 14, and he says that the Brotherhood could be the kiss of death for democracy in Egypt . . . As the former editor in chief of Ikhwan Online, the brotherhood's website, Sharnubi went public shortly after his resignation. In talk shows he warned his fellow Egyptians that the movement was undemocratic and authoritarian, and that leading Muslim Brothers were no less corrupt than politicians from the old regime . . . the former member of the Brotherhood says that last week's events show that he's been right all along. The president's "coup," says Sharnubi, provides just an inkling of the Brotherhood's obsession with power.[25]

The next month—along with help from Salafists—Mursi took his next step for power. He directed the constitutional committee—now almost exclusively run by Islamists—to finish their work on the new constitution. After they hastily cobbled the new document together, Egypt's new "Magna Carta" was put to a national referendum. The vote put Egypt at another profound crossroads: "[T]he election wasn't purely about approving or rejecting a proposed constitution. Instead, the battle over Egypt's proposed constitution is a function of the larger battle unfolding over ownership of the 2011 revolution and the very identity of the country."[26]

Though only one-third of Egyptians voted, the new constitution passed by a huge majority. Its articles began to steer Egypt's ship of state toward Sharia law.

For example, Egyptian analyst Samual Tadros concluded, "In Article 81, it is explained that constitutional rights and freedoms shall be exercised only insofar as they do not contradict the principles in the section of the constitution on state and society (that is, the Sharia). In effect, all the articles backing religious freedom, freedom of the press, and freedom of thought have thus been limited."[27]

But opposition grew. The National Salvation Front—a group that included many of the original opponents to Mubarak—now set their sights on Mursi. They coalesced around Mursi's brazen power grab and accused him of replacing one dictatorship with another. Once again, crowds took to the streets and even rushed to the gates of the presidential palace. Demonstrations mushroomed throughout Egypt. Dozens of Egyptians died in the riots and Egypt's future and fate once again seemed to be hanging in the balance.

New evidence also emerged to show what kind of future Mursi and the Muslim Brotherhood envisioned for Egypt, Israel, and the Jews. It lifted the veil on his real beliefs. In a 2010 video published by MEMRI (Middle East Media Research Institute), Mursi exhorted Muslims to forsake all dealings with Israel:

> Dear Brothers, we must not forget to nurse our children and grandchildren on hatred towards those Zionists and Jews, and all who support them.[28]

Again in 2010, Mursi ranted:

No reasonable person can expect any progress on this track. Either [you accept] the Zionists and everything they want, or else it is war. This is what these occupiers of the land of Palestine know—these blood-suckers, who attack the Palestinians, these warmongers, the descendants of apes and pigs. We should employ all forms of resistance against them.[29]

He went on to rail against the United States:

All products from countries supporting this entity—from the U.S. and others—must be boycotted. We want a country for the Palestinians on the entire land of Palestine, on the basis of [Palestinian] citizenship. All the talk about a two-state solution and about peace is nothing but an illusion, which the Arabs have been chasing for a long time now. They will not get from the Zionists anything but this illusion. They have been fanning the flames of civil strife wherever they were throughout history. They are hostile by nature. We should employ all forms of resistance against them.[30]

These diatribes by the president of Egypt raised serious questions about the future of Egypt's three-decades-long peace treaty with Israel and its relationship with the United States and the West. It also sounded the alarm on Capitol Hill where the US Congress had to decide whether to approve military aid to a nation led by a man with such profound anti-Semitic beliefs.

DESTINATION JERUSALEM

So where will this Arab Spring end up? Where will what started in January 2011 go? The Arab Spring rearranged the Middle East and seemed to set up the region for its next season of history, a season when seventh-century Islam would once again dominate the Fertile Crescent and make its way to Jerusalem.

Israel itself took a direct hit from the Arab Spring.

A series of incidents unmasked the deep hostility toward Israel brewing under the surface in Egypt. On September 11, 2011, a mob attacked Israel's embassy in Cairo. The Muslim Brotherhood called it "justified."[31] Islamists also threatened to end Israel's thirty-year peace treaty with Egypt. Egypt's southern border morphed from a concern to a crisis for Israeli leaders. The Sinai Peninsula degenerated into a Wild West state within a state. Egypt appeared unable or unwilling to control weapons smuggling or terror attacks from this desert home that housed a pantheon of Bedouin tribes and terror groups. It also threatened to open up the Gaza Strip—now controlled by Hamas, the Palestinian version of the Muslim Brotherhood—that could serve as a gateway for potentially game-changing weapons. Israeli defense planners included the distinct possibility of a potential war with Egypt into its strategic calculus.

And what's the ultimate destination of the Arab Spring?

Mursi and his supporters made that clear on May 1, 2012. Safwat Higazi, a cleric, led one of Mursi's campaign rallies. He declared:

> We can see how the dream of the Islamic Caliphate is being realized, Allah willing, by Dr. Muhammad Mursi and his brothers, his support-ers, and his political party. We can see how the great dream, shared by us all—that of the United States of the Arabs—the United States of the Arabs will be restored, Allah willing. The United States of the Arabs will be restored by this man and his supporters. The capital of the Caliphate—the capital of the United States of the Arabs—will be Jerusalem—Allah willing. . . .
>
> Our capital shall not be Cairo, Mecca, or Medina. It shall be Jerusalem, Allah willing. Our cry shall be: "Millions of martyrs march toward Jerusalem." Millions of martyrs march toward Jerusalem.[32]

He then led the crowd in a chant: "Banish the sleep from the eyes of all Jews. Come on, you lovers of martyrdom, you are all Hamas . . . we say it loud and clear: Yes, Jerusalem is our goal. We shall pray in Jerusalem, or else we shall die as martyrs on its threshold. Millions of martyrs march toward Jerusalem."[33]

On April 13, 2011, NBC reporter Richard Engel analyzed the state of the nascent Arab Spring to *Nightly News* anchor Brian Williams. His analysis was remarkably prescient:

This whole movement in the Middle East, and I'm worried about it because while people in the region deserve more rights, and they want more rights, and they're embracing more of "the will of the Arab street." Well, "the will of the Arab street" is also ferociously anti-Israel, against Israel. And there's many people who believe that if you empower the Arab street, and the Arab street wants to see a war, or wants to see more justice for the Palestinians, that down the road, three to five years, this could lead to a major war with Israel. It could also force a negotiated settlement, but I think over time, this thing ends in Jerusalem.[34]

3 TURKEY: THE RISE OF THE CALIPHATE

Remember Khaibar, Khaibar, oh Jews! The army of Muhammad will return![1]

—CHANT BY MEMBERS OF THE TURKISH FLOTILLA

DATELINE: TAKSIM SQUARE, ISTANBUL, TURKEY

FIVE MONTHS AFTER BEING EMBROILED IN EGYPT'S REVOLUTION in Cairo's Tahrir Square, and nearly eight hundred miles to the north, I stood in Istanbul's Taksim Square. This time, however, we found ourselves not in the heat of a revolution but in the heart of one of Turkey's most pivotal modern political campaigns. We came to cover Turkey's national elections. Those elections would be crucial for the future not just of Turkey but of Israel and the Middle East.

Just like Tahrir Square in Cairo, Taksim Square stands as the public venue where citizens protest or celebrate. It's Istanbul's hub. A statue of Ataturk, Turkey's modern founder, stands at one end of the square, commemorating the birth of the Turkish Republic in the early 1920s. Sultan

Mahmud I once used the square as a place where water lines from the northern part of Istanbul merged and then divided to other parts of the city, hence the name *taksim*, which means "division." It also seemed to reflect the divisions in Turkey's electorate.

Independence Avenue—a wide, long street—runs out from the square. Pedestrians jam the boulevard and enjoy the dozens of cafes, restaurants, and shops. A tram runs down the middle and ends near the Tunel, the world's second oldest subway, built in 1875, twelve years after the London Underground.

When we arrived, antinuclear demonstrators filled one section of the square but banners of Turkey's prime minister Erdogan covered several nearby buildings. In fact, Erdogan's image appeared all over the city. He led the AKP (Justice and Democratic Party) that had held power since 2002. We arrived during the final days of the campaign. The polls pointed to a sizable victory for the AKP, their third straight election triumph. This campaign for his reelection and the AKP centered, however, not just on their victory but on the margin. What they desperately wanted was a super majority of seats—more than 330—in Turkey's parliament.

If they achieved that goal, they could rewrite Turkey's constitution, set up a presidential system, and consolidate their power without the interference of other political parties. The election outcome—one way or the other—would have a profound impact on the future of the Middle East. You see, the AKP had worked hard to make one of the most secular Muslim nations on earth Islamic. The fear many Turks—and others— had was that this election could shut the door on democracy and open the door to an Islamic dictatorship.

One of those nuclear protesters cautioned us, "I don't think we're going to go to Sharia law, but many people fear we are going more and more to our Middle Eastern roots."[2] Translation: a more Islam, less secular society.

We came to the square just moments before one of Erdogan's main political adversaries, Gursel Tekin, the number two man in the AKP's main opposition party, the CHP, arrived. Our Turkish fixer—I'll call him "M" for security reasons—arranged a quick interview. We rushed over and, as a crowd gathered in the Turkish sun, Tekin told us the world is now finally seeing the real Erdogan: "The dear prime minister [Erdogan] in America and Europe was very popular and they supported him in 2004 and 2007, and his mask looked very liberal. But now they see that he's not liberal. He's restricted freedom, and the journalists can't express themselves because of the prime minister. Therefore, the mind of Erdogan is fascist and it's a dictatorial regime."[3]

Tekin had a point. At that time, the Turkish government imprisoned more journalists than China.

Later in the day M snagged another interview for us, this time with Erdogan's number two man, Egemen Bagis. We asked him about Tekin's accusation: that the AKP used democracy to gain power and then limit freedoms. He countered, "Turkey has never been as democratic as she is today. Some people might not enjoy the fact that Turkey's becoming a stronger country. We can understand their feelings, but Turkey's becoming more and more democratic every day."[4]

Yet Bagis's explanation contradicted a statement his leader Erdogan had made years earlier, in 1996, the comment mentioned earlier: "Democracy is like a streetcar. You ride it until you arrive at your destination and then you step off."[5]

Many suspected Erdogan—and Turkey—would step off democracy's "streetcar."

BACK TO THE FUTURE

But when did Turkey get on democracy's "streetcar"? To find out, you need to go back to that statue in Taksim Square, the one of Ataturk.

His full name was Mustafa Kemal Ataturk. He ruled Turkey after World War I and the fall of the Ottoman Empire. As the first president of the Republic of Turkey, he served from 1923 to 1938 and implemented sweeping reforms. He succeeded in bringing Turkey out of its Ottoman Empire past and into the twentieth century. He transformed Turkey into a modern, secular, and yet Muslim nation. In every strata of society—education, the judiciary, and the military—Turkey left its Ottoman Empire roots and entered the modern—Western—world. He even encouraged Turks to wear Western dress. The Hat Law of 1925 introduced Western-style hats instead of the fez.

In March 1924, Ataturk undertook what might have been his most important change. He abolished the caliphate, the institution of Islamic rule over the Muslim nation called the Ummah. Since the time of Muhammad's death, various caliphs—literally "successors," sometimes called "Commander of the Believers"—ruled over the ummah. The Ottoman Empire established the last caliphate in Istanbul in 1517 when they defeated the Mamluks. For more than four hundred years, caliphs—sometimes called sultans—had lorded over the vast expanse of the Ottoman Empire.

From the Topkapi Palace on the shore of the Bosporus Strait, their edicts affected the Muslim masses (and those living under their dominion) from the Arabian Peninsula to the gates of Vienna. But Ataturk's ruling brought an end to this Muslim marriage of religion and state. He turned the Topkapi Palace into a museum, and for most of the twentieth century Turkey became the prime example that a Muslim nation could be both Islamic and democratic.

Turkey seems to sit on a pendulum swinging east or west. It straddles two continents, and you can see that most clearly in Istanbul. On one side of the Bosporus Straights sits Asia, and on the other side stands Europe. Turkey's geography often mirrors its history and affiliations. Sometimes it turns to the west, sometimes to the east. In the 1920s, under Ataturk it turned west. In the 2000s, under Erdogan it swung east.

In 2002, Erdogan and the AKP began an assault on Ataturk's secular foundations. Almost imperceptibly, those institutions he built started to disintegrate. Janet Levy in an article called "Turkey and the Restoration of the Caliphate" in the *American Thinker* described some of those attacks:

The Erdogan government publicly claims to be democratizing Turkey but has curtailed freedom of the press, jailed and sued journalists for criticizing the government and confiscated newspapers and sold them to AKP sympathizers. AKP supporters have infiltrated the military and are suspected of wiretapping and evidence fabrication against retired military officers. Erdogan lowered the age for judgeships in order to replace nearly half of all judges with his younger AKP sympathizers. He also removed banking regulatory board members and replaced them with Islamic banking officials and is reported to have received significant financing from Saudi Arabia, including a known Al Qaeda financier.[6]

From the media to the military, finances, and beyond, the AKP undermined the secular nature of modern Turkey. Levy added, "What actually exists is the *veneer* of a democratic republic overlaying an insidious, percolating revival of the Ottoman Empire by way of Islamic fundamentalism and Turkish nationalism."[7]

Many other Middle East experts agreed. "There's a new order, the Erdogan order, which is an Islamist order."[8] That's how Daniel Pipes explained the "new" Turkey when he visited our CBN News Jerusalem studio. Pipes, the director of the Middle East Forum and one of the most informed and prescient Middle East analysts, told us he believes the recent changes in Turkey outweighed even the so-called Arab Spring. He said,

> The most significant [event] of the past year has not been the overthrow of Mubarak or Ben Ali or Gaddafi. I think it's been the overthrow of the Ataturk order in Turkey. Last June and July [2011], there were a couple of events, an election, a series of resignations, which point me to the fact that the old, secular, military-dominated order in Turkey established by Turkey in the twenties and thirties is now on the way to becoming defunct. . . . It took Ataturk about fifteen years to establish his order; Erdogan took about ten to reassert his own order.[9]

Bernard Lewis, perhaps the world's leading Muslim expert, also warned about Turkey's transformation: "In Turkey, the movement is getting more and more toward re-Islamization. The government has that as its intention; and it has been taking over, very skillfully, one part after another of Turkish society. The economy, the business community, the academic community, the media. And now they're taking over the judiciary, which in the past has been the stronghold of the republican regime."[10]

Boaz Ganor, the executive director of the International Institute of Counter Terrorism, confirmed Pipe's and Lewis's conclusions. Although Ganor's center is based near Tel Aviv, we ran into Ganor in one of Jerusalem's outdoor cafes and invited him up to our bureau. He told us he believes the unfolding revolution in Turkey has global implications:

> The Middle East is witnessing two opposite revolutions right now: a pragmatic revolution in Iran [the often suppressed uprising against the Iranian regime] and the dogmatic revolution in Turkey. And I've answered that the future of the Middle East, the future of the world, will be influenced on answering the question, which revolution will materialize first? Unfortunately, it seems to me right now, the dogmatic revolution in Turkey is much faster than the pragmatic revolution in Iran.[11]

DRAMA ON THE HIGH SEAS

Turkey's dogmatic revolution dramatically transformed its relationship with Israel, one that for years had been marked by close military, economic, and political cooperation. That was seen no more clearly than on Memorial Day 2010.

I had just opened the door to our Jerusalem bureau and expected a quiet day. After all, the United States celebrated Memorial Day, and I wanted to catch up on some work.

But that did not happen on May 31, 2010.

"Did you hear the news?" asked Tzippe, our CBNNews.com Internet producer.

"No, what happened?"

The news struck like a thunderclap. Like many other times in Jerusalem, news can suddenly and immediately change your day, your week, and sometimes your life.

For several days we tracked the progress of a small fleet of nine ships called the "freedom flotilla." They embarked out of Istanbul, Turkey, and plowed through the Mediterranean on their way to the Gaza Strip. Their goal? They wanted to break Israel's naval blockade of Gaza, a blockade they claimed was illegal. It seemed Israel's navy would safely turn the flotilla away before they reached Gaza. But few expected things to turn so bad, so fast. The initial reports sounded ominous for Israel. Several Turkish civilians died—who knew exactly how many at first—while others lay wounded after Israeli commandos stormed the lead ship of the flotilla. The first reports made it sound like another example of Israeli brutality, another reason for Israel's enemies to defame the Jewish state.

We rushed to the Foreign Ministry for a hastily arranged briefing with Deputy Foreign Minister Danny Ayalon. Press from Israel and around the world gathered to hear Israel's explanation. Yet Israel—and Ayalon—needed to hurry. Israel's side of the story fell several hours behind the relentless 24/7 news cycle. Al-Jazeera and other media already flashed live reports with their version to the world. This saddled Israel's shoulders with a PR nightmare and initially portrayed the commando raid as another of Israel's brutal, inexcusable acts against innocent, peaceful citizens who simply wanted to bring relief supplies to the suffering people of Gaza. One reporter beside me reflected the mood of the room: How would Turkey—a NATO member no less—react to Israel killing its citizens? It looked like a botched raid with catastrophic results to Israel's image and uncertain and potentially volatile ramifications.

Ayalon—Israel's former ambassador to the United States—began. He called the incident a "premeditated provocation."[12] He said that "weapons were prepared and used." He stated the flotilla members were "connected to global jihad." He made the case the flotilla "chose not to use appropriate humanitarian means of distribution" and that the "blockade [was] justified [and] if [the flotilla was] successful, it would have opened up a corridor of weapons and terrorists" into Hamas-controlled Gaza. Maritime law, he asserted, "gave Israel the right" to board the vessels and "no [other] sovereign country would tolerate this."[13]

Ayalon made a strong case. But it wasn't until video of the raid came out that the PR tide began to turn. Israel released grainy, black-and-white IDF (Israel Defense Forces) video of the predawn raid. It clearly showed Israeli commandos rappelling down by helicopter on to the deck of the flotilla's largest ship, the *Mavi Marmara*. Once on deck, the demonstrators ambushed the commandos and brutally attacked them with clubs, knives, pipes, guns, and other weapons. Two threw an Israeli soldier over the railing from one deck to the deck below. They captured other soldiers and dragged them away.

The ambush startled the commandos, armed originally only with paint ball guns and sidearms. They anticipated "peaceful" activists. Other video—in color—showed part of the desperate skirmish between the Israeli soldiers and the "activists." One clip showed an "activist" stabbing a soldier. The soldiers feared for their lives and, unable to locate some fellow soldiers, responded with deadly force.

After the tense battle concluded, the commandos secured the ship and sailed it into the Israeli port of Ashdod. Nine Turkish demonstrators died in the melee and a full-blown international incident between Turkey and Israel shattered already strained relations between the two former allies.

In the aftermath of the "freedom flotilla," Turkish-Israeli relations crumbled. Turkish prime minister Erdogan bellowed the Israeli commando raid was a *casus belli*, a cause for war.[14] After a UN commission exonerated Israel's action during the raid, Erdogan took a number of bellicose steps:

- He threatened Turkish warships would join the next flotilla to Gaza.
- He shut down Turkish air space to Israeli military planes.
- He ended joint Israeli-Turkish military exercises.
- He suspended all military agreements with Israel and froze billions of dollars of mutual defense contracts.
- He downgraded diplomatic relations.

The flotilla and its aftermath marked the end of a long Israeli-Turkish alliance. They had formalized diplomatic relations in 1949, which made Turkey the first Muslim nation to recognize the state of Israel. Throughout the years, Israel and Turkey enjoyed robust economic relations, participated in joint military exercises, and shared intelligence information. Turkey used to be a prime tourist destination for Israelis. But that recognition of Israel in 1949 and much of those bilateral relations took place under a Turkey eager to establish ties with the West. But as Barry Rubin pointed out, "Before the 'Arab Spring' began, the 'Israeli-Turkish Spring' had already ended."[15]

The next source of friction between Turkey and Israel could lead to a catastrophic collision. Israel and Cyprus discovered mammoth natural gas and oil reserves off their shores and signed an agreement to facilitate offshore exploration. But Turkey warned it "will stop Israel from unilaterally exploiting gas resources in the eastern Mediterranean." Erdogan defiantly stated, "Israel has begun to declare that it has the right to act in exclusive economic areas in the Mediterranean. . . . [Israel] . . . will not be the owner of this right."[16] "When the government of Cyprus announced its plans to drill, Erdogan responded with threats to send 'frigates, gunboats and . . . air force.' This dispute, just in its infancy, contains the potential elements of a huge crisis."[17]

One commentator said, "This is very high-stakes poker. It's very, very dangerous."[18]

Another said, "The latest threat is not only diplomatically difficult, but may even require direct U.S. involvement if Israel and Turkey come to face each other in the Eastern Mediterranean. And the only one capable of coming between them is the United States, and the U.S. Sixth Fleet."[19]

GLOBAL JIHAD

Many of the flotilla participants included a coterie of "peace activists." For example, one elderly couple told their story to Sky News. They insisted they came peacefully. They looked like a pair of grandparents. Harmless. They—and others in the flotilla—felt compelled to free the people of Gaza from Israel's naval blockade. They sailed on one of the many smaller vessels. But the largest ship and the scene of the deadly confrontation—the *Mavi Marmara*—and at least one other vessel sailed under a different flag with a different agenda.

Then more video came out that told the "rest of the story." One participant told Al Jazeera, "Right now, we face one of two happy endings: either martyrdom or reaching Gaza."[20] Not quite the "grandparents" side of the story.

Al Jazeera also reported, "The flotilla includes hundreds of Arab and foreign solidarity activists from more than 40 countries . . . they have announced their determination to use resistance to any attempt at piracy by the Israeli occupation."[21] Most telling, it showed some flotilla members hearkening back to another conflict battle before sailing into their own. Al Jazeera broadcast demonstrators stoking the pre-skirmish atmosphere with chants about a clash fourteen hundred years ago. The video later released by the Palestinian Media Watch (PMW) showed participants chanting, "Remember Khaibar, Khaibar, oh Jews, the army of Muhammad will return."[22]

Why would they chant about Khaibar? They evoked the memory of a campaign Muhammad fought in AD 629 against the last Jewish village in Arabia, Khaibar. Muhammad defeated the Jews and then forced the survivors to pay one-half of their income to the Muslims. This precedent set up the jizya tax where non-Muslims pay a tribute to Muslims. According to PMW, "There are Muslims who see that [Khaibar] as a precursor for future wars against Jews. At gatherings and rallies of extremists, this chant is often heard as a threat to Jews to expect to be defeated and killed again by Muslims."[23]

More investigation revealed the real flotilla organizers masqueraded as peaceful activists in order to embarrass and delegitimize Israel.[24] Steven Merley of the Jerusalem Center for Public Affairs (JCPA) discovered the Free Gaza Movement grew out of the International Solidarity Movement (ISM) that acted "in concert with the Turkish/MB network and the Global Muslim Brotherhood in a massive effort to demonize and delegitimize Israel by leveling accusations of serious crimes, such as massacres and genocides, and by invoking Nazi imagery such as concentration camps in connection with Israeli actions and policies."[25] They provoked the crisis.

Israel also demonstrated the humanitarian crisis was a ruse. Every day Israel allowed tons of supplies, equipment, and food through regulated checkpoints from Israel into Gaza. The naval blockade existed to keep massive supplies of weapons from getting into the hands of Hamas. In fact, Israel seized ships through the years with massive amounts of weapons for either the Yasser Arafat–controlled Palestinian Authority or Hezbollah, the Lebanese Shiite Muslim group allied with Iran. Just one ship with the right kind of sophisticated arms sailing into Gaza would shift the military balance of power between Israel and Hamas. Since 2007, when Hamas overthrew their rival Fatah faction, they set up a brutal theocracy. Terrorists also attacked Christian organizations and martyred a Christian worker named Rami Ayad.

But even more information came out. According to Merley, "There is strong evidence for Turkish involvement in the Gaza flotilla incident, including the office of Prime Minister Tayyip Erdogan."[26] This so-called "peace flotilla" traced its roots back to the Turkish government itself and into the office of its prime minister, Erdogan. It raised new questions about Turkey's leader and his agenda. As mentioned, since coming to power in 2002, his government slowly transformed the nature of Turkey.

Those changes alarmed Israeli and Western observers who knew Turkey's transformation meant the geopolitics of the eastern Mediterranean might never be the same. It led some to look to Turkey—not Iran—as the power to watch in the "new" Middle East.

By the time the *Mavi Marmara* sailed back to its mooring in Istanbul harbor and after its showdown with IDF commandos, the mask began coming off Erdogan's Turkey. Just as Ayalon warned, the flotilla—and Erdogan himself—didn't just undermine Turkey's secular revolution. They had global ambitions and connections.

An exhaustive investigation by the Jerusalem Center for Public Affairs provided compelling evidence of the connection between the Erdogan government and the Global Muslim Brotherhood:

> The Gaza flotilla incident brought into sharp focus an even more significant long-term development: the growing relationship between the Erdogan government and the Global Muslim Brotherhood, which has given rise to some of the most notorious Islamist terrorist groups— from al-Qaeda to Hamas. Since 2006, Turkey has become a new center for the Global Muslim Brotherhood, while the Hamas regime in the Gaza Strip acted as the main axis for this activity. The AKP allowed key elements of the Global Muslim Brotherhood, and above all the International union of Muslim Scholars, led by Sheik Youssef Qaradawi [remember him—Yusuf al-Qaradawi—from Cairo's Tahrir Square?], to operate freely on Turkish territory with its active support.[27]

The report also cited a US State Department cable that stated Turkey's foreign minister Ahmet Davutoglu labored under "'neo-Ottoman fantasies' of regaining lost Muslim lands and avenging Muslim defeats. Like the Muslim Brotherhood, which envisions a restoration of Islamic rule, at an initial stage, in parts of Europe that were once under the banner of Islam, a participant at an AKP think tank meeting expressed the reportedly widespread belief that a neo-Ottoman Turkey would want to take back Andalusia and avenge the defeat of the siege of Vienna in 1683."[28]

By the way, if you don't recognize the country Andalusia, it's the Arabic name for most of the Iberian Peninsula. For centuries—from 711 to 1492—Muslims controlled parts of this land. The 1961 movie *El Cid* dramatizes some of the battles in which Spaniards began to drive out the Muslims. Even more than six hundred years after they lost control, however, some Muslims still dream of reconquering Spain.

This dream reveals one of Islam's driving principles. If Muslims once control land—called a *Waqf*—and then lost it, it's the duty of Muslims to regain that land and put it—once again—under the dominion of Islam. Waqf lasts forever. While Muslims might temporarily allow land to be controlled by "infidels," their long-term goal remains to regain that land. Many in the West simply don't know this principle or may dismiss it. But it's the underlying drive beneath much of Islam today and why it continues to spawn "holy wars."

For example, it's one of the principles driving the Palestinian Authority when negotiating with Israel and why there may never be a negotiated settlement. Because of their Muslim beliefs, they cannot give up on reclaiming all of "Palestine." During the 1683 siege of Vienna, a combination of Polish, German, and Austrian forces defeated an Ottoman army. It represented the farthest Islamic penetration into Europe. But now these State Department cables show the dream of a neo-Ottoman revival throughout Europe is stirring not only in the hearts of al-Qaeda operatives in the Afghan mountains but in the halls of power in Ankara and Istanbul.

You don't have to look far in Istanbul to see the remnants of the last caliphate. The day before those national elections, we climbed to the top of the Galata Tower. It's the oldest standing tower in the world still open to visitors. For more than four centuries it stood as a silent witness to Turkey's history. It's seen days of glory, decline, and now once again resurgence into world affairs. It overlooks some of the most important and famous waterways in the world, the Bosporus Straights, coming out from the Black Sea and the Sea of Marmara. On the spit of land called the Golden Horn sits the Topkapi Palace where Turkish sultans ruled the

Ottoman Empire. Other landmarks include the Blue Mosque, and the Sophia Mosque, once the largest church in Christendom that became a mosque and now sits as a museum.

World history was made here. Sultan Melmet "the Conqueror" defeated Constantinople—which became Istanbul—in 1453 and changed the face of world history. This defeat affected the destiny of nations, the region, and untold millions of both Christians and Muslims. A Christian empire met its end here, and a Muslim empire rose at this crossroad of history. Now, while the remnants of the last caliphate stand today as museums, its resurrection is a dream getting closer to reality.

RESURRECTING THE CALIPHATE

But an even greater dream than Andalusia or Europe animates many Muslims: the restoration of the caliphate. Will Erdogan himself resurrect the glory of the Ottoman Empire? Will he reestablish a form of the Muslim caliphate that dominated a large swath of the earth for four hundred years? The caliphate's resurrection is not an idle notion but a fervent goal. And what exactly is the caliphate? Andrew McCarthy, author of *The Grand Jihad*, gave this definition:

> The caliphate is an institution of imperial Islamic rule under sharia, Muslim law. Not content with empire, Islam anticipates global hegemony. Indeed, mainstream Islamic ideology declares that such hegemony is inevitable. . . For Muslims, the failure of Allah's creation to submit to the system He has prescribed is a blasphemy that cannot stand.[29]

This leads us back to Turkey's election. Many feared if the AKP got its super majority, it would be one step closer to its dream of reestablishing the caliphate. The election results disappointed Erdogan. They fell several seats short of their super majority. But in his victory speech,

Erdogan claimed the vote reverberated throughout the Middle East, alluding to his dreams of a revived Ottoman Empire.

But there's another layer to the unfolding drama of Turkey's new leaders, a man behind the scenes called by some "the most dangerous Islamist on planet earth." Unless you've watched some of the reports by my CBN News colleague Erick Stakelbeck, you might never have heard of Fethullah Gülen. While Erdogan is the face of the AKP, Gülen is its heart. Gülen began a movement in the 1970s with ties to the Muslim Brotherhood. He wants to reconnect the state and religion as part of an Islamic theocracy.

His achievements are impressive:

Beginning in the 1970s, Gulen began establishing a worldwide network to promote Islam and Turkish nationalism. His followers have since established hundreds of schools in over 110 countries. Gulenists operate an Islamic bank with over $5 billion in assets and own significant print and broadcast media properties, NGOs, think tanks and a publishing company. Gulen recruits Turkish youth by providing housing and education and grooms them for careers in the legal, political and academic professions. In recent years, the AKP passed legislation allowing graduates of Islamic high schools entry into Turkey's universities, guaranteeing Islamist leadership in the future. Gulen controls the majority of schools, universities and dormitories throughout Turkey. His followers remain loyal and donate up to one-third of their income to the movement. In Turkey, Gulen and the AKP together control the police, the intelligence services and the media and actively recruit diplomats for their utility as foreign intelligence satellites. Overall, the holdings are valued at up to $50 billion.[30]

While his achievements are impressive, his goals are no less ambitious. He wants to "restore the Ottoman Empire and . . . establish a universal caliphate."[31] Under his tutelage, the AKP "has transformed [Turkey] from a secular state into an Islamic country with 85,000 active mosques—one for every 350 citizens—the highest number per capita in the world, 90,000 imams, more imams than teachers and physicians—and thousands of state-run Islamic schools."[32]

While his goals are ambitious, his methods are subdued and stealthy. Here's how he described how to overthrow the existing order to restore the old: "You must move in the arteries of the system without anyone noticing your existence until you reach all the power centers. . . . You must wait until such time as you have gotten all the state power, until you have brought to your side all the power of the constitutional institutions in Turkey."[33]

Ironically, Gülen now lives in Saylorsburg, Pennsylvania, and maintains permanent US resident status. In 1998, Gülen voluntarily moved to the United States after the Turkish government (before the rise of the AKP) convicted him of "trying to undermine the country's secular institutions, concealing his methods behind a democratic and moderate image."[34]

Through Gülen's influence and Erdogan's power, Turkey has allied itself with Hamas, becoming more anti–United States, anti-Christian, and anti-Semitic. They have succeeded in overthrowing the Ataturk order and establishing their own. Turkey's transformation, "could precipitate a precarious shift in the balance of power in the world."[35]

But what does this mean for Israel? It not only lost one of its most stable allies in the Middle East but also added to its list of enemies one of the region's most formidable foes.

This might well be true even after US President Obama pressured Israeli Prime Minister Benjamin Netanyahu to make a highly publicized apology to Turkey's Erdogan about the Mavi Marmara incident. Many felt Turkey owed the apology not Israel. Daniel Pipes like some other commentators professed skepticism the apology would change the relationship. He wrote, "Now that the deed is done, can we expect a change in Turkish policy toward Israel, an end to its aggressive statements and support for its enemies? That would surprise me. Rather, I expect the AKP government to pocket this apology and use it as a building block for its neo-Ottoman empire."[36]

4 THE TWELFTH IMAM: IRAN'S AMBITION

Oh mighty Lord, I pray to you to hasten the emergence of your last repository, the promised one, that perfect and pure human being, the one that will fill this world with justice and peace.[1]
—IRANIAN PRESIDENT MAHMOUD AHMADINEJAD'S SPEECH BEFORE THE UNITED NATIONS GENERAL ASSEMBLY, SEPTEMBER 17, 2005

DATELINE: SOMEWHERE IN ISRAEL'S NEGEV DESERT

WE DROVE A FEW HOURS FROM JERUSALEM BEFORE ARRIVING AT the IAF (Israel Air Force) air base. It sat somewhere in the middle of Israel's Negev Desert, miles from civilization, barren, desolate, and remote. Scrub brush littered the landscape. Even after we entered the gates, we took a number of turns and several minutes to get to where the IAF had prepared a rare and unusual briefing. We drove down a broad ramp leading to a number of underground hangers. I wondered what this looked like from a spy satellite. Each hanger housed one of Israel's premier means of defense—and offense—the F-16I fighter/bomber. The

I stood for Israel. Nicknamed the "Sufa" or "Storm," these planes were manufactured by the US-based Lockheed Martin and modified by Israel to meet their unique needs.

We could videotape the planes (except the cockpit) and interview the pilots, but there were rules. We weren't allowed to ask their names, nor could we videotape their faces. That was easy since the pilots wore their flying helmets with the visors pulled down. We also couldn't ask about the range of the F-16I. They pointed out, however, that the F-16I was outfitted with external fuel tanks. Without saying it, their message came through clear: yes, they could reach Iran and its nuclear facilities.

The planes and pilots impressed me. I wondered if any of these pilots might someday be streaking their way across the Persian Gulf to Natanz, Isfahan, Qom, or any one of Iran's far-flung nuclear facilities. Would they attack those facilities in a preemptive strike like Israeli pilots struck Egyptian airfields in the first hours of the 1967 Six Day War a generation ago? Then Israeli leaders saw Egypt as a threat to the existence of the nascent Jewish state. Egyptian president Nasser thundered that his goal was "the destruction of Israel."[2] Now, Iranian leaders like President Ahmadinejad promised to "wipe Israel off the map."[3]

Separated by more than forty years and a thousand miles, the venom and threats from Egypt's Nasser or Iran's Ahmadinejad came from the same poisoned well and meant the same thing for Israel: the need to defend itself. In 1967, the conventional might of the Soviet-supplied Egyptian army arrayed against Israel posed a considerable threat. Nasser's threat was not an idle one. But Iran's nuclear ambitions exponentially raised the threat to Israel. If they got a nuclear bomb, Iran could do what author Joel Rosenberg once pointed out, "Finish in six minutes what Hitler took six years to do; kill six million Jews."[4]

But Israel's arsenal against Iran contained more than just one of the most sophisticated planes in the world. They also possessed a fleet of F-15s and midair refueling tankers. Israel maintained three Dolphin-class submarines plowing through secret waters somewhere in the region. Many military analysts suspected they contained nuclear-tipped cruise missiles. Iran—if it ever got "the bomb"—could be assured Israel could strike back with a nuclear capability of its own. Military expert Eli Lake also revealed in 2011 that "for much of the last decade, as Iran methodically built its nuclear program, Israel has been assembling a multibillion dollar array of high-tech weapons that would allow it to jam, blind, and deafen Tehran's defenses in the case of a pre-emptive strike."[5]

Yet another Israeli weapon fit simply on a thumb drive. That's where Israel fired one of the opening salvos against Iran in the new era of cyber wars. According to the *New York Times*, Israeli and American computer programmers developed two sets of malicious software known as malware.[6] The first program dubbed "Stuxnet" sabotaged Iran's uranium enrichment facilities. In a brilliant move worthy of any *Mission Impossible* movie, they surreptitiously wormed into Iran's computers at the Natanz uranium enrichment plant and programmed the centrifuges to destroy themselves. Another malware called "Flame" didn't destroy but spied. The program took espionage to a new dimension. Some called it "the most complex computer spying program ever discovered."[7]

> It has the ability to log key strokes from an infected user's computer, use the computer's sensors such as the microphone and Web cam to record what is being said around it, and take screenshots. It can also sniff a network to steal passwords. . . . In a nutshell: Flame can control almost every aspect of the computer, disappear without a trace, encrypt its own communications, and organize the data it collects. That is one smart virus.[8]

These computer programs added one more facet in Israel's elaborate arsenal to stop Iran's mullahs from getting the means to annihilate Israel.

HEZBOLLAH: MISSILES OVER METULLA

But if Israel attacks Iran's nuclear program—the question overhanging the Middle East for years—it's likely that Hezbollah, Iran's Shiite ally in Lebanon, will enter the fray. In 2006, Israel got a taste of what that would look like. It began as a border skirmish on July 12, 2006, and swelled into a full-scale battle on Israel's northern border. Then CBN News—like most of the world's media—raced to the front lines. We spent most of our time in the small Israeli town of Metulla on Israel's border with Lebanon.

Metulla—one of Israel's most beautiful towns—is nestled on a finger of land jutting into southern Lebanon. Below Metulla sweeps the Hula Valley, one of Israel's most scenic and fertile agricultural breadbaskets. The Golan Heights on one side of the valley runs majestically all the way down to the Sea of Galilee. Mount Hermon, thought by some Bible scholars to be the site of the transfiguration of Jesus, looms in the distance. But Metulla—called the Switzerland of Israel—was anything but neutral in the summer heat of 2006. Instead, it sat at the center of a pivotal and historic battle between Israel and its Islamic nemesis Hezbollah.

Hezbollah, a Shiite militia group, operated for years as an independent entity within southern Lebanon. In fact, it acted more like a "state within a state." It takes orders not from the Lebanese government in Beirut but from Iran's government in Tehran. This led to a unique situation where Israel fought Hezbollah, an Iranian-backed proxy operating within Lebanese territory, but not the state of Lebanon itself. In May 2000, they declared victory over the Israeli Army when Israel unilaterally abandoned its security zone. Israel had established this security zone eighteen years earlier as a buffer against cross border attacks by Palestinian Liberation Organization (PLO) terror groups and later Hezbollah provocations. But incessant Hezbollah attacks finally bullied Israel to forsake this twelve-mile strategic buffer. Hezbollah seized advantage of Israel's retreat. For the next six years, Hezbollah erected an elaborate and sophisticated network of bunkers, tunnels, and fortifications on Israel's northern border. They also assembled a formidable arsenal of more than fourteen thousand short- and long-range rockets.

During the war, Hezbollah unleashed those rockets. The Katyusha made up the bulk of its arsenal. This weapon first hit the battlefield during World War II when the Red Army used it successfully against German troops. Russian soldiers nicknamed the easy-to-produce rocket "Katyusha," after a popular wartime song. That song told of a girl, Katyusha—the Russian equivalent of Katie—pining for her lover on the battlefield. But this Katyusha in the summer of 2006 bore no love for Israelis. Hezbollah used this inaccurate but devastating rocket to virtually shut down northern Israel. When they fired larger and longer-range rockets, Israeli planes could regularly pinpoint their location by air within minutes and destroy their launchers and crews. But the advantage of the smaller Katyusha lay in Hezbollah's ability to launch the rocket undetected from virtually anywhere at a moment's notice. This mobility and stealth provided Hezbollah with a huge advantage. Their rocket teams launched Katyushas from homes, schools, and orchards throughout southern Lebanon. The results shifted the tide of the war.

More than a million Israeli residents in northern Israel either fled the area altogether or sought the safety of bomb shelters. Not since the London blitz during World War II more than sixty years earlier had a civilian population endured a rocket barrage of this magnitude. Almost every day for thirty-four days, an average of more than one hundred rockets rained down on northern Israel. By the end of the war, nearly four thousand rockets had landed in Israel. The rockets killed dozens, wounded hundreds, and damaged thousands of buildings.

For most of the war we stayed in Metulla. For the remainder of the war, it served as our base and offered a unique vantage point to watch this war—and Israel's history—unfold. Journalists from around the world flocked to Metulla. In fact, the reporters, producers, cameramen, and technicians outnumbered the few remaining residents. The Israeli Army used Metulla as a staging area before launching into southern Lebanon against Hezbollah strongholds. In the early morning, Israeli soldiers patrolled the streets on foot while Humvees carried other troops through the town. Merkeva tanks, considered by some the best battle tanks in the world, lined up on the road just outside town. Massive D-9 armored bulldozers, big and strong enough to push over a house, joined the armored columns. Israeli artillery batteries positioned themselves throughout the area and pounded Hezbollah positions either deep within Lebanon or the hills nearby Metulla.

During the war, we traveled several times back to Jerusalem, just a three-hour drive away. Jerusalem in those days seemed like another world, with little to remind you that desperate life-and-death battles were being fought just more than 160 miles to the north. I remember vividly those times driving back to the north. We passed through some of Israel's most beautiful countryside, but now it lay under a cloud of war. The whole of northern Israel experienced what it was like to have rockets raining down.

Both Haifa and Tiberius were major casualties of the war: Haifa because it was Israel's busiest port and Tiberius because it's one of the major centers for Israeli tourism. On the shores of the Sea of Galilee, Tiberius resembled a ghost town. Rockets hit that far south, and it's hard to expect Christian pilgrims to visit Capernaum where Peter lived or the Mount of Beatitudes where Jesus delivered the Sermon on the Mount when a Hezbollah rocket could fall from the sky. As we drove farther north, most of the traffic lights were out. Driving through Kiryat Shmona, the site where most of the rockets fell during the war, felt like running through a gauntlet. What traffic did fill the roads were either military vehicles or journalists.

We could tell when we got within range of the Katyusha rockets because you could see the fires they started in the fields on either side of Route 90 North. Despite that realization, you could also sense coming under a divine canopy, under His protection. We felt an incredible sense of peace. The words of Psalm 91 rang true once again while we nestled "under the shadow of the Almighty." We felt the impact of the words penned by King David three thousand years before:

> I will say of the LORD, "He is my refuge and my fortress; my God, in whom I trust." Surely he will save you from the fowler's snare and from the deadly pestilence. He will cover you with his feathers, and under his wings you will find refuge; his faithfulness will be your shield

and rampart. You will not fear the terror of night, nor the arrow [or Katyusha rocket] that flies by day. (Psalm 91:2–5 NIV)

During this war, we experienced life under missile attack. It was surreal. We often sat writing our stories or preparing for our live satellite shots under palm trees kissed by a warm and pleasant breeze. Yet death could rain down at any moment. Perhaps journalists carry a false sense of security, but few if any headed for the bomb shelters when the sirens went off. One time I was on the phone with my wife when the siren started to wail. I immediately hung up hoping she didn't hear the alarm. I hoped to shield her from unnecessary worry. Too late. Next time we talked she said she had figured it out.

The battle raged all around the hamlet. This tiny, quaint town found itself awash in the sounds of war, like being in a kettledrum. My dad served in North Africa, Sicily, and the Italian campaign during World War II. I finally realized what he meant when he said you could tell the difference between "outgoing" and "incoming." After a few days, you knew the difference between Israeli artillery going out and Katyusha rockets coming in. Locals would say that you don't want to hear the whistling sound of the Katyusha but rather the boom of Israeli artillery. The incessant artillery like rolling thunder was deafening, and the concussion from the volley could be felt for an incredibly long distance. Above it all you could hear both the roar of jets and the monotone sound of Israeli drones scanning the battlefield.

Down below, Katyusha rockets often hit the fields of the Hula Valley and the forests surrounding the hills of Kiryat Shmona. More rockets hit that area than any other within Israel during the war. Kiryat Shmona— just five miles below Metulla—got hit with more than one thousand missiles. The fires these rockets started often sent plumes of smoke billowing hundreds of feet in the air. At times, the contorted and twisted smoke made the area look like a scene out of Dante's *Inferno*. But the hellish sights and sounds marked just the visible signs of an extraordinary struggle going on between the forces of freedom and tyranny.

During the war, CBN founder Pat Robertson came to the front lines to see the fighting firsthand and to show the support of millions of evangelical Christians for Israel during its crisis. He interviewed one of Israel's top generals—Major General Benny Gantz—in Metulla. With the sound of artillery in the background, he asked Gantz about the Iranian influence on Hezbollah. Gantz noted Iran's influence permeated the conflict:

> Up to the necks; their heads. They are all over the place. They have munitions, weapons. If you ask me all the way to directions, order. It's a war against Hezbollah, Iran, elements of Syrian support that this access was given in the last few years. As a matter of fact, not against Lebanon as a people but maybe Lebanon as a state host [for] this very negative, negative NGO, I would say. This is the only semi-state terror organization that posses[es] strategic capabilities and we have to fight it.[9]

Gantz added that Iran—like ancient Persia once did—wants to annihilate the Jews: "It sounds strange—the year 2006—and people still think that they can destroy Israel as a people and as a nation . . . Ahmadinejad who simply talks about trying to destroy the Jewish people, complaining to the Germans why they didn't finish the Second World War. We're going to fight."[10]

Israel's battlefield against Hezbollah had at one time served as a platform for Christian ministries to transmit the gospel throughout the region. High Adventure is a Christian radio ministry transmitted from a hill just behind the border town of Metulla. Just a few miles up the road inside Lebanon, CBN's own Middle East Television broadcasted the good news to a spiritually dry and thirsty land for years. While the hope and prayer of many believers is that Lebanon will one day become what Isaiah the prophet declared "a fruitful field," for now, the ideology of radical Islam spews forth from this region.

A few minutes after his interview with Gantz, Robertson walked across the street and went live via satellite in Metulla back to a nationwide US audience. He warned, "This might be the front line of a war that one day might come to the United States." CBN president Michael Little, an audience throughout the United States, and I joined Robertson as he prayed, "On this eighth day of the eighth month, we pray for the nation of Israel. The gospel went forth from Marjyoun of Middle East Television for eighteen years and we pray, Lord, that those seeds that have been planted will bear fruit."[11]

That prayer has yet to be answered in its fullness, but many believe that those gospel seeds will indeed spring forth. In the meantime, the 2006 Second Lebanon War ended without a significant victory for Israel over its nemesis Hezbollah. But how did the world see the conflict? Was it just one more Mideast war between Israel and its many enemies? Could it be dismissed as their—not our—problem? And did history provide any lessons to learn?

While Israel stood on the front lines, Benjamin Netanyahu warned of Iran's global agenda. After all, Israel represented just the "little Satan" while the United States was the "great Satan." In Iran's view, both had to be defeated. Netanyahu drew a clear history lesson and parallel from the war. He compared the ominous threat coming out of Iran to 1938, the year before the outbreak of World War II. Then, the world failed to act against Nazi Germany. Now, the world is failing the test to stand against Shiite Iran.

At a speech before the Jewish General Assembly, he warned that Iran's nuclear program represented another Holocaust in the making. "It's 1938 and Iran is Germany. And Iran is racing to arm itself with atomic bombs," Netanyahu told the assembly. "Believe him [Iranian president Mahmoud Ahmadinejad] and stop him. . . . This is what we must do. Everything else pales before this." He noted Israel would be Iran's first, not last stop: "Israel would certainly be the first stop on Iran's tour of destruction, but at the planned production rate of 25 nuclear bombs a year . . . [the arsenal] will be directed against 'the big Satan,' the U.S., and the 'moderate Satan,' Europe. . . . Iran is developing ballistic missiles that would reach America, and now they prepare missiles with an adequate range to cover the whole of Europe."[12]

Netanyahu criticized the world for not being more forceful against this Iranian nuclear threat much like the world avoided confronting the rising power of Nazi Germany in 1938: "No one cared then and no one seems to care now." He warned of Tehran's nuclear and missile program: "[It] goes way beyond the destruction of Israel—it is directed to achieve world-wide range. It's a global program in the service of a mad ideology."[13]

IRAN'S TICKING NUCLEAR CLOCK

Yet, despite Netanyahu's warning of Iran's clear and present danger, its nuclear clock keeps ticking.

Iran insisted it wanted to develop a civilian nuclear program for its own energy needs. But with one of the largest reserves of oil in the world, Iran's protestations rang hollow and disingenuous. Throughout the decade, numerous reports—both official and unofficial—pointed to a robust Iranian nuclear program and an accelerated ballistic missile program to deliver a nuclear weapon. The UN nuclear watchdog group— the IAEA (International Atomic Energy Agency)—released a 2011 report with stunning clarity that Iran pursued a nuclear bomb. It stated, "The Agency has serious concerns regarding possible military dimensions to Iran's nuclear programme. After assessing carefully and critically the extensive information available to it, the Agency finds the information to be, overall, credible. The information indicates that Iran has carried out activities relevant to the development of a nuclear explosive device."[14]

Yet while the world negotiated with Iran and implemented more sanctions, Iran's centrifuges enriching uranium kept spinning ever closer to the nuclear threshold. The sanctions may have hurt the Iranian people, but they failed to dissuade the Mullahs from their drive for nuclear weapons. Amos Yadlin, the director of Israel's Institute for National Strategic Studies (INSS) and the former head of IDF Military Intelligence, told a briefing of foreign journalists of his sober analysis of Iran's progress toward a nuclear bomb:

They have enough fissile material for 5 to 7 bombs. They have the knowledge. They haven't decided to go the last tactical mile, but strategically they are ready for the bomb. Why are they not breaking out tonight? Or yesterday? Because it will take them about 4 to 6 months to enrich the uranium which is now in the low level of enrichment or medium level of enrichment to a military grade. And in the eye of the Iranians 4 to 6 months is too long a time and the situation in the world is not such they think that they can get away with it. They want the time of the break out to be much shorter and they are waiting for an international crisis that the attention will be moved from them. This can happen in 2013 and if Iran will decide to break out, it will be a huge challenge for Israel and the international community.[15]

But making an Iranian bomb is just one side of their nuclear equation. Putting it on a ballistic missile is the other side. In that arena, Deputy Prime Minister Moshe Ya'alon warned Iran is developing a missile with a six-thousand-mile (ten-thousand-kilometer) range. Missile expert Uzi Rubin told us those missiles advance not just their regional aspirations but a global agenda. He added Iran now has about four hundred Shahab Three Ballistic missiles. Ominously, he told us, "You only need one."

Again Israeli prime minister Benjamin Netanyahu put this all in historical perspective when he told the German newspaper *WELT am SONNTAG,*

Is there such a thing as a suicidal regime? You can't rule it out. I would say the greatest threat; the greatest challenge right now to world peace is the marriage of [a] militant Islamic regime with nuclear weapons. Either that a militant Islamic regime will meet up with nuclear weapons or the nuclear weapons will meet up with a militant Islamic regime. The first danger is called Iran and the second danger is called a Taliban takeover of Pakistan. Either way, it will be a hinge of history: history will change, and for the worse.[16]

He also spelled it out to the world in simple terms when he addressed the United Nations on September 27, 2012. He brought out a rudimentary diagram of a bomb. It could have been drawn for a third-grade class. But it worked.

> This is a bomb; this is a fuse. In the case of Iran's nuclear plans to build a bomb, this bomb has to be filled with enough enriched uranium . . . Ladies and Gentlemen, The relevant question is not when Iran will get the bomb. The relevant question is at what stage can we no longer stop Iran from getting the bomb. The red line must be drawn on Iran's nuclear enrichment program because these enrichment facilities are the only nuclear installations that we can definitely see and credibly target. I believe that faced with a clear red line, Iran will back down. This will give more time for sanctions and diplomacy to convince Iran to dismantle its nuclear weapons program altogether.[17]

But will sanctions work or will Israel launch a military strike against Iran? This has been the question hanging over the entire Middle East for years. I've heard Israeli officials—on and off the record—make it clear that one, Iran's nuclear program represented a threat to the world, not just Israel, and two, they won't allow it to happen. For Israel it's a matter of survival, life and death. They're in the nuclear crosshairs and the target of Iran's deadly end-times theology spewing out of their leaders. For many the bottom line continues to be that the only thing worse than a strike on Iran's nuclear facilities would be a nuclear Iran. History has shown that when faced with a nuclear neighbor, Israel responded. In 1981, Israeli planes destroyed Saddam Hussein's Osirak nuclear reactor. Then again in 2007, Israeli warplanes decimated a Syrian reactor. Would they do it a third time? Given their memories of the Holocaust, it's likely when the time comes they will act.

While the world knew what Iran was doing, they often didn't know why. For example, a majority of Americans see Iran as the number one threat to its national security. What many do not realize are the religious and spiritual roots to Iran's relentless pursuit of nuclear weapons.

THE COMING IS NEAR

On September 17, 2005, Iranian president Mahmoud Ahmadinejad addressed the annual meeting of the United Nations General Assembly.

During his speech, he said, "Oh mighty Lord, I pray to you to hasten the emergence of your last repository, the promised one, that perfect and pure human being, the one that will fill this world with justice and peace."[18] After the speech he said he "opened their eyes to the message of the Islamic Republic."[19] What was this "message of the Islamic Republic" and who was this "promised one, that perfect and pure human being"?

The message and the man are one and the same: the Mahdi or the Twelfth Imam.

CBN News international correspondent George Thomas provided a rare look into who the Mahdi is and this belief driving Iran's president and his regime. Thomas may be one of the few—if not the only—Western journalists to travel inside Iran to the small village of Jamkaran, near the city of Qom. In Jamkaran stands a mosque that draws the attention—and affection—of millions of Shiite Muslims. Behind the mosque sits a well.

Thomas's firsthand account reads:

On a recent Tuesday afternoon, CBN News made [the] journey heading south out of Iran's capital, Tehran. Some 95 miles and a couple of wrong turns later, we arrived at the Jamkaran mosque on the outskirts of Qom. The night begins with a visit to the sacred well. CBN News is given a rare opportunity to visit with people praying there. The opening of the well is covered by a green-like metal box to prevent people from jumping in. Most of the time here is spent praying and kissing the metal box. Others scribble prayer requests to the Mahdi on pieces of paper that are then dropped into the well. Many believe the Mahdi is actually hiding at the bottom of the well reading the prayer requests. . . . Shiite Muslims [believe] out of that well will emerge one day their version of an Islamic savior. . . . I stood at the entrance to the Jamkaran mosque; and I've been told that as a non-Muslim I am not allowed to go inside the mosque. The truth is every day, tens of thousands of men and women come through this mosque to say their prayers but also to pray that one day soon the Mahdi would return.[20]

Those who believe in the Mahdi or the Twelfth Imam are sometimes called "Twelvers." But where did the belief of the Mahdi come from? According to Ron Cantrell, author of *The Mahdi: Hijacked Messiah*, the Mahdi descended from the Prophet Muhammad himself but vanished in the middle of the ninth century. Now more than eleven hundred years later, Shiites anxiously expect the Twelfth Imam to come back at the end of the age.

Cantrell explained the Mahdi comes "with a promise that he would return and he would bring Islam to its total fruition as the world's last standing religion. The Mahdi is a personage that is expected to come on the scene by Islam as a messiah figure. He is slotted to come in the end of time according to their writings, very much like how we think of the return of Jesus, although there are some staggering differences between our Messiah and the Islamic expected Messiah."[21]

A 2012 Pew Research poll showed a huge number of Sunni and Shiite Muslims believe Islam's Mahdi will return "in their lifetime." In the research 83 percent in Afghanistan, 72 percent in Iraq, 67 percent in Tunisia, and 62 percent in Malaysia anticipate his appearance. While the percentage in other countries like Indonesia (23 percent) is far less, the percentages worldwide translate to more than 600 million Muslims who expect Islam's messiah in their lifetime.[22] Sunnis and Shiites both agree the earth will eventually become an Islamic world, but Shiites have a particular, and some say alarming, view of the end-times.

In Shiite eschatology, chaos precedes the return of the Mahdi and marks the end of the age. This is an apocalyptic time marked by wars, plagues, and famines, followed by the Day of Judgment. Cantrell says, "This is an important situation that we are heading into with the nation of Iran. Chaos and worldwide turmoil is a prerequisite for the coming of the Mahdi. Now Ahmadinejad has stated that this chaos must take place before the Mahdi can come on the scene. He is willing to make this situation take place."[23]

Since Ahmadinejad has made such a prominent public display of his intention to prepare the way of the Mahdi, it presents a unique situation. It straddles the worlds of public policy and spiritual warfare. The implications for public policy and the response of the West are staggering, and the spiritual ramifications profound. While Ahmadinejad's second and final term ended in June 2013, the ideology of the Twelfth Imam permeates Iran's ruling mullahs.

When you mix this messianic theology with nuclear weapons, Iran's current foreign policy becomes a toxic brew with regional and global ramifications. If Iran got the bomb it would change the face of the Middle East. Iran could cast its nuclear shadow over the region and especially its Sunni rivals like Saudi Arabia and their Gulf neighbors. It would put themselves off limits to any credible military intervention unless their adversary—whomever that might be—wanted to risk nuclear retaliation. Any one of many terror groups—most likely Hezbollah—would be emboldened knowing that their patron had their "nuclear" back. Iran with its ballistic missiles—possibly nuclear tipped—could pose a constant existential threat to Israel.

THE ARAB SPRING, IRAN, AND THE MAHDI

While the Arab Spring swept through and transformed the Middle East, Iran watched the unfolding events. What did they think of the fall of governments in Tunisia, Libya, and Egypt? How did they interpret those "signs of the times"? Did the Arab Spring fit Shiite eschatology? Early in

2011, CBN News terrorism analyst Erick Stakelbeck found out. He broke the story of an Iranian video not yet seen in the West. The smuggled video revealed Iran's regime viewed the unfolding Middle East events through the prism of the Mahdi.

Here's his report:

New evidence has emerged that the Iranian government sees the current unrest in the Middle East as a signal that the Mahdi—or Islamic messiah—is about to appear. CBN News has obtained a never-before-seen video produced by the Iranian regime that says all the signs are moving into place—and that Iran will soon help usher in the end-times. While the revolutionary movements gripping the Middle East have created uncertainty throughout the region, the video shows that the Iranian regime believes the chaos is divine proof that their ultimate victory is at hand.

The video is called "The Coming Is Near" and it describes current events in the Middle East as a prelude to the arrival of the mythical twelfth Imam or Mahdi—the messiah figure who Islamic scriptures say will lead the armies of Islam to victory over all non-Muslims in the last days.[24]

The video also noted Iran was destined to defeat America and Israel. Iran's Supreme Leader, Ayatollah Khamenei, Hezbollah leader Hassan Nasrallah, and President Mahmoud Ahmadinejad are all "hailed as pivotal end times players," and Khamenei is the Shiite's mythical "*Seyed Khorasani*," the person who creates the atmosphere for the Twelfth Imam to appear and "passes the flag to the last Imam."[25]

Stakelbeck's report brings to light Iran's current religious thinking and explains their incessant and up-to-now unstoppable drive to obtain the atom bomb. Since his report and after the 2011 IAEA report came out, Iranian expert Michael Segall ominously reported, "Of all the [recent] Iranian statements, one made by Ahmadinejad stands out. During a meeting with supporters . . . he added in an apocalyptic-messianic spirit the conditions taking shape in the region are not normal [a hint at Imam Mahdi] and that 'we are nearing the point of final confrontation.'"[26]

DESTINATION JERUSALEM . . . AGAIN

The polestar of Shiite eschatology lands in Jerusalem. For example, in *The Coming Is Near* video, "Ahmadinejad will conquer Jerusalem prior to the Mahdi's coming." While the Mahdi comes back to "save" humanity, before his appearance Israel—and America—must be destroyed. One pivotal aspect of this Shiite end-time's theology centers on the destruction of Israel as a precondition for the return of the Mahdi—and like spiritual heirs to Hitler, the death of the Jews:

> One of Iran's leading hard-line clerics who supported speculation about the Mahdi was Grand Ayatollah Nouri-Hamedani from Qom. He explicitly asserted in one of his sermons that one of the preconditions for the Mahdi's appearance is the killing of the Jews: "One should fight the Jews and vanquish them so that conditions for the advent of the Hidden Imam can be met." This might help explain how in Ahmadinejad's circles, the preoccupation with the arrival of the Mahdi and the destruction of Israel appeared at times to be mutually supportive.[27]

It explains the venomous Iranian anti-Semitism.

Joel Richardson, in his book *The Islamic Antichrist*, documented Jerusalem as the "location of the Mahdi's rule over the earth."[28] He wrote, "Rasulullah [Muhammad] said, 'Armies carrying black flags will come from Khurasan. No power will be able to stop them and they will finally reach Eela [Baitul Maqdas in Jerusalem] where they will erect their flags.'"[29] Baitul Maqdas is the Dome of the Rock.

Richardson cited Islamic scholars Muhammad ibn Izzat and Muhammad Arif.

The Mahdi will be victorious and eradicate those pigs and dogs and the idols of this time so that there will once more be a caliphate based on prophethood as the hadith states. . . . *Jerusalem will be the location of the rightly guided caliphate and the center of Islamic rule, which will be headed by Imam al-Mahdi* . . . That will abolish the leadership of the Jews . . . and put an end to the domination of the Satans who spit evil into people and cause corruption in the earth, making them slaves of false idols and ruling the world by laws other than the Sharia [Islamic law] of the Lord of the worlds.[30]

It's clear Iran's regime and its messianic theology pose a "clear and present danger" to the Middle East and the world, but especially to Israel. For Israel, this deadly end-time's theology poses an existential threat and once again emphasizes that Islam's final destination remains the city of Jerusalem.

5 ISRAEL: PRESSED ON EVERY SIDE

[This] leads us to the conclusion that through a long-term process, the likelihood of an all-out war is increasingly growing.[1]
—ISRAELI GENERAL EYAL EISENBERG

DATELINE: ISRAEL'S NORTHERN BORDER

I DROVE THE SEVERAL HOURS NORTH FROM JERUSALEM AND watched Israel's varied topography change along the way. From the flat coastal plain with the Mediterranean to the west, I turned northeast through the rolling hills near Megiddo and the Jezreel Valley, then onward toward the steep mountains of the Upper Galilee. The biblical battles of days past echoed in my imagination when the armies of Egypt, Assyria, or Babylon once came to conquer these lands of ancient Israel. The sound of chariots, soldiers, swords, and shields once clanged on this ground.

Now, the echoes of epic struggles yet to come wafted through the valley the book of Revelation calls Armageddon. Part of the Great Rift Valley, it sat at the crossroads of ancient civilizations and will lie at the bull's-eye of a future constellation of hostile nations. It forms part of the Via Maris—the "way of the sea"—one of the ancient world's most important trade routes. Isaiah mentioned this route when he wrote, "And afterward more heavily oppressed her, by the way of the sea, beyond the Jordan, in Galilee of the Gentiles" (Isaiah 9:1).

But today it was quiet, unassuming, and at the crossroads of modern-day traffic, commerce, and construction. Honking horns, delays, detours, and traffic jams didn't seem very "biblical," nor did the fertile farmland—Israel's breadbasket—intersected by Route 65. Yet this day I journeyed to hear about not ancient battles or future conflicts but the pressing clashes just days, weeks, months, or even a few years away. The ones already pulsating on Israel's radar screen.

The late afternoon sun glinted on Israel's northern mountains in terrain that reminded me of Virginia's Appalachians. I got closer to an IDF-arranged off-the-record briefing with one of Israel's northern commanders. He could only be identified as a "senior military official." We met at one of the IDF northernmost bases, just a few feet from the Lebanese border. As my golfing brother would say, "About a nine iron away." I told the soldiers at the gate about my meeting.

As they let me in, I was again struck by the nonchalant manner of Israeli soldiers. It's a citizen's army with an esprit de corps unlike the more formal US military but with a worldwide reputation for excellence and being the most feared army in the Middle East. The base too—as usual—looked Spartan. Perhaps it reflected the same disdain those ancient Greeks once had for military bluster without military prowess. Perhaps, too, these IDF soldiers felt like the three hundred Spartans who once stood against the hordes of a Persian empire.

After all, Israel by now was "pressed on every side."

I joined only one other reporter, from England's *Daily Telegraph* newspaper. We greeted the "senior military official" and sat down for an hour-long briefing. He explained the situation on the border six years after Israel's 2006 Second Lebanon War. Since then, with the exception of one major incident, the border remained quiet. But beneath the quiet, war lurked, and our official predicted, "One day it will come!"

He noted Hezbollah—Iran's proxy and Israel's adversary—had made a "significant" increase in its military capability in the last six years. By "significant," he meant in two specific ways. They now possessed ground-to-air missiles. This revelation meant a great deal for any Israeli helicopter or jet pilot venturing over Lebanese airspace in the future. They also secured shore-to-ship missiles, which meant any Israeli naval ship off the Lebanese coast plied through dangerous, potentially deadly waters.

Despite the placid countryside across the valley and up and down the forty-nine-mile (seventy-nine kilometer) border with Lebanon, he emphasized Hezbollah prepared "all the time" for "the next round." They stockpiled weapons, built underground bunkers, stored more rockets, and trained constantly. He indicated Hezbollah infiltrated the villages along the border and established their headquarters and set up their weapons depots and observation points inside. They honeycombed its military infrastructure within their streets and near schools, hospitals, and homes. In March 2011, the IDF released classified information quantifying that massive military buildup. They identified nearly one thousand military sites including five hundred and fifty underground bunkers, three hundred surveillance sites, and one hundred other facilities belonging to Hezbollah.[2]

In 2006, Israel found itself embroiled in a thirty-four-day war when nearly four thousand rockets and missiles rained down into northern Israel. This briefing—six years later—felt like getting an updated weather report. Now Hezbollah had more rockets and missiles with longer ranges and greater accuracy. In fact, Israeli intelligence estimated Hezbollah stockpiled as many as fifty thousand missiles and rockets. He added with emphasis that Hezbollah's new capabilities put population centers like Tel Aviv in range and under threat for the first time since 1948.

With the situation in Syria so precarious at the time, he said they watched very carefully President Bashar Assad's deadly stash of chemical weapons. Dubbed "the chemical superpower of the Middle East," Syria possessed a formidable arsenal. If Hezbollah gained control of these internationally banned substances, it would be a game changer.

Finally, our official warned Israel would not fight the next war the way they fought the last. He reminded us the IDF fought the Second Intifada (the Palestinian Uprising) since 2000 and employed urban warfare tactics. The nature of that war demanded those methods. But tragically they incorporated those same tactics in 2006 with deadly results. Hezbollah booby-trapped many homes throughout southern Lebanon, which put Israeli soldiers in great peril. They would not repeat those experiences. The next time they would set clear and decisive rules of engagement.

First, they would warn civilians to leave combat areas. Then they would move swiftly, powerfully. He added those civilians may not have homes to return to, and it might take ten years for the villages to rebuild. The more missiles Hezbollah fired into Israeli cities, he countered, the more they would attack Lebanese villages. He made it clear he couldn't allow Israeli cities to be under missile fire even with the threat of international condemnation from a UN commission.

He said war is unpleasant, but after it starts, "it's a war."

DATELINE: TEL HAZEKA, THE GOLAN HEIGHTS

A blustery winter wind buffeted our small group at Tel Hazeka on Israel's Golan Heights. We came for another background "off the record" briefing on Syria's bitter civil war. This took place on Israel's border with Syria and potentially represented an even greater threat than its border with Lebanon. Tel Hazeka means "Mount Strength" and it's a strong link in Israel's electronic listening and observation posts on its northern frontier. The IDF listening post sat up on a hill above us. It commanded the area while it scanned the horizon and beyond for digital communications inside Syria. From the ridge, you could see why the "strategic" Golan Heights was so strategic.

The bluff overlooks a flat plain that runs all the way to Damascus. Whoever controlled the high ground controlled the area and the advantage in any potential future battle. It reminded me of the famous scene in the movie *Gettysburg*, the pivotal battle in America's civil war. Colonel John Buford rides onto Seminary Ridge on the outskirts of Gettysburg. He realizes he's found the tactical and vital high ground. He tells his men, "We can deprive the enemy of the high ground . . . we hang onto the high ground, we have a good chance to win this fight that's coming." The next day his brigade held the high ground for several hours in a pivotal military action. Many credit his decisiveness with setting the stage for a Union victory. "Buford's keen eye for terrain and tactical awareness on July 1 secured for the Union the position from which they would win the Battle of Gettysburg and turn the tide of the war."[3]

Now another war splashed up on Israel's northern shoreline and its strategic high ground. Since March 2011, Syrian president Bashar Assad fought a desperate battle to survive an uprising spawned by the Arab Spring. To keep his despotic regime alive, he employed some of the most barbaric tactics in modern history. He fired Scud missiles into his own cities, indiscriminately shelled civilian areas, tortured and imprisoned thousands.

One refugee from the Syrian city of Homs told us some of the horrors when we visited Jordan. Through tears she told us that Assad's troops set up a tent at one of the city's traffic circles. There Assad's soldiers tortured men from the city whose screams could be heard throughout the area. Then often those men would be driven away never to be seen again. By early 2013 more than seventy thousand Syrians had died in the conflict. The conflict represented a geo-political struggle of immense proportions but the world often grew numb to the fighting, the killing, and the enormous human toll.

From Tel Hazeka to the north, Mt. Hermon stood in its wintery splendor, draped in a white blanket. It dominated the region. Below was the Syrian village of Bir Ajam. It was a stone's throw away and only the border fence separated us from one of the front lines of Syria's civil war. The fence marked the 1974 Alpha cease line established after the 1973 Yom Kippur War. Then men fought and died over this land. Not far from our spot lay the Valley of Tears where Syrian and Israeli soldiers fought one of the greatest tank battles in history. Less than forty Israeli tanks faced and fought nearly five hundred Syrian tanks. The battle became one of the turning points of the war. The Valley of Tears earned its name because of the number of burning tanks.

Yet for forty years, this border remained Israel's quietest.

No longer. Now the sounds of war punctuated the silence.

During our briefing, sporadic gunfire split the sound of the howling wind. Relics of the bitter and desperate fighting from years before littered the area. An abandoned Syrian bunker lay in ruins behind us and a destroyed Israeli tank sat nearby. Our IDF officer told us that just a few weeks before our front lines briefing, the fighting in Bir Ajam spilled over into Israel. After several mortar shells landed within Israel, Israeli tanks hit Syrian positions in the village.

But while the fighting in Bir Ajam spilled over the border, Israel had even more serious questions to answer. What might happen to Assad's huge stockpile of chemical and biological weapons of mass destruction? Could they fall into the hands of either Hezbollah or the many jihadist groups now operating in Syria? His nonconventional stockpile included the deadly nerve agents sarin and VX. Would Assad transfer strategic weapons like the SA-17 ground to air missile system to Hezbollah? If they did, would Israel respond? Israel answered that question in January 2013 when it launched an air strike deep inside Syria and destroyed trucks loaded with SA-17 ground-to-air missiles on their way to Hezbollah. Their message was clear. Israel had its "red lines" and would not allow any "game-changing" weapons systems into the hands of Hezbollah.

Yet one question remained unanswered: If Assad fell, what impact would the many jihadist groups that infiltrated Syria during the fog of war have on Israel? For decades Israel knew who they were dealing with in Syria. Assad was a ferociously anti-Israel dictatorship but for strategic reasons allowed his border with Israel to remain quiet for a generation.

Now as Assad's control waned, the status quo changed. For months a coterie of Islamist interlopers sneaked through Syria's porous border, filled a waiting vacuum, and heavily infiltrated the rebel forces. Their grand strategy was to overthrow Assad, destroy Israel, and establish a caliphate. Syria could become their forward operating base for such an Islamist dream. Now the day after Assad—if and when it came—meant Israel might have to deal with a radicalized Syria.

MEMRI released a video from Aleppo, Syria, featuring what some of these fighters have in mind:

> Syrian Mujahid: "We will move on. When, Allah willing, we cleanse Syria. We won't stop there. We will continue to the Sheeba Farms and Kafr Shuba (areas of the Golan Heights), and we will pass through the Golan Heights all the way to Jerusalem. (Other Syrian Mujahid) . . . and then . . . all the way to Persia." Syrian Mujahid: "Then we will make and an about-turn, cleanse Iraq, where there is still some filth. After we are done with Iraq, we will move on to Constantinople, and then Cordoba and Andalusia. That's it. Now that we have weapons, we don't intend to ever lay them down."[4]

It's the fact these groups won't lay their weapons down after Assad falls that concerns Israeli strategists.

The prospects for a good resolution to this civil war are bleak. Experts at Israel's BESA Center speculated on prospective scenarios. None seemed promising: "A Muslim Brotherhood dictatorship might emerge." "A total collapse of all government and economic systems, and the emergence of hundreds of militias, including radical Islamic ones—meaning anarchy for years." Or "Iran could yet send real troops to Syria."[5]

In the meantime, Israel announced plans to build a forty-three-mile-long, fifteen-foot-high fence to shore up its northern border. One more barricade to keep out the "barbarians at the gate."

PRESSED ON EVERY SIDE

But our "senior official" identified only one of Israel's threats. At every point of the compass now, Israel faces potentially devastating threats. Several months after the Arab Spring began, the IDF's Home Front command chief Major General Eyal Eisenberg delivered an uncommonly frank address and discussed those threats. During a speech to the Institute for National Security Studies in Tel Aviv, he offered a bleak analysis of the shifting Middle East. He said it "leads us to the conclusion that through a long-term process, the likelihood of an all-out war is increasingly growing."[6]

Every direction Eisenberg looked, he saw trouble:

Iran has not abandoned its nuclear program. The opposite is true; it continues full steam ahead. In Egypt, the army is collapsing under the burden of regular security operations, and this is reflected in the loss of control in the Sinai and the turning of the border with Israel into a terror border, with the possibility that Sinai will fall under the control of an Islamic entity. In Lebanon, Hezbollah is growing stronger within government arms, but it has not lost its desire to harm Israel and ties with Turkey aren't at their best.[7]

He concluded the Arab Spring could also be a "radical Islamic winter," which "raises the likelihood of an all-out, total war, with the possibility of weapons of mass destruction being used."[8] While the general warned of literal bombshells, his message dropped a public relations bombshell. His speech infuriated some defense and security officials for "provoking regional tensions." But Eisenberg's candor lifted the veil on how some Israeli officials see the increasingly unstable Middle East.

That's why Israel's home front command regularly holds drills simulating missile, chemical, biological, or other unconventional attacks. Sometimes Israel's public gets little warning. So the residents in towns like Ramat Gan, Givat Shmuel, or Or Yehuda might suddenly hear an air-raid siren.[9] CBN News has reported on a number of these drills like "Orange Flame Six" in Haifa. It simulated "a silent bioterrorism event" where terrorists secretly attack a shopping mall. The manager of the exercise said they have to deal with potential bioterrorism attacks. That presents all sorts of dilemmas: What to do with hospitals? Do we quarantine? Do we not quarantine? Do we close shops? What about transportation?

Dr. Aziz Darawsha told us, "We are fortunate that we are more experienced, maybe better than others to manage mass casualty events."[10] Those who grew up in the Cold War and under the shadow of a nuclear Soviet Union may remember similar school drills in case of a nuclear attack. In Israel today, its citizens live under the shadow of a potential nuclear Iran but also Hezbollah, Syrian, or Hamas rockets, Turkish warships, and terrorists out of the Sinai Peninsula.

TO THE WORLD: ISRAEL'S RIGHT TO EXIST

While military threats, advanced munitions, nuclear weapons, and isolated terror attacks fill Israel's portfolio on every point of its compass, yet another threat might be the greatest one of all. It's one that undermines Israel's very existence and one that could be the biggest weapon facing Israel. It's not just from one point on the compass but from all directions. It's a worldwide campaign to undermine the existence of Israel, to erode its legitimacy and delegitimize the state of Israel. It's a goal to so impugn Israel's motives, its actions, and its very reason for being.

The front lines of this battle lie on college campuses, YouTube, the Internet, the editorial page. It's spreading the notion that Israel is so bad, so racist, and so evil it no longer has a right to exist. It's an attempt to wipe Israel off the map, not with a nuclear bomb, but with slander and to promulgate the idea of a world without Israel. Supporters of Israel see this as a very real and growing threat, a campaign—often coordinated—to delegitimize Israel, to undermine the very existence of the Jewish state.

You can see it expressed in different forms and forums:

- Muslim students at the University of California's Irvine campus shouting down Israeli ambassador to the United States Michael Oren eleven times.
- Turkey's national television broadcasting a fictitious prime time special spreading the libel that Israeli soldiers execute Palestinian women and children in cold blood.
- Former Israel defense forces Chief Moshe Ya'alon canceling his trip to Spain out of fear he'd be arrested on charges of war crimes.
- Dozens of cities holding "Israel Apartheid Week," comparing the Jewish nation to the former apartheid state of South Africa.
- The BDS campaign to "Boycott, Divest and Sanction" Israel.

It's happening from the US West Coast to the West Bank and around the world. It's a formidable weapon in the hands of Israel's enemies. When Israel was founded in 1948, its enemies outnumbered and out-gunned tiny Israel on the battlefield. But more than sixty years later, Israel boasts the strongest military in the Middle East. No longer able to defeat Israel militarily, some say Israel's enemies have shifted to another battlefield: the worldwide court of public opinion.

Much of the campaign is waged by a Red/Green Alliance. "You have an alliance of what many have called the Red/Green Alliance where you have on the one hand the leftists—political movements both in the United States and in Europe and throughout the western world joining forces very openly with Islamists—with radical Muslims and even moderate Muslims for that matter, saying that Israel has not a right to exist," Caroline Glick, managing editor of the *Jerusalem Post*, told CBN News.[11]

Former Israeli ambassador to the United Nations Dore Gold told us, "The state of Israel can win all the wars in the world, but if they have all the nations against them, the way it's becoming, it's very difficult. It's going to be very, very difficult for the state of Israel to survive and to defend its borders and just to defend its right to exist."[12] How well Israel fights on this battlefield may well determine its own survival and may also be a bellwether for other democracies like Israel around the world. Shmuel Ben-Shmuel, the director of World Jewish Affairs in Israel's Foreign Ministry, told us, "My concern is that other people—liberals, people of good will, people who don't know much about this area—will fall into this trap and slowly accept the notion that Israel is the new pariah."[13]

THE FIDDLER ON THE ROOF

With the added layer of fighting in the court of worldwide public opinion, Israel finds itself a target from all points of the compass. To the south, it views an Egypt where the Muslim Brotherhood genie is out of the bottle and finds its thirty-year peace treaty hanging in the balance. While Egypt's new rulers appear moderate to some, others see them as a chameleon covertly dedicated to a worldwide caliphate with Jerusalem as its capital.

To the east they gaze on Iran and the spectacle of a country dedicated to establishing regional hegemony based on its brand of messianic Islam. They want to produce the circumstances to bring about the return of the Mahdi, their Islamic messiah. They continue to develop nuclear weapons and ballistic missiles to deliver them while calling for Israel to be "wiped off the map."

To the north they watch Iran's proxy Hezbollah arming themselves with enough rockets to smother Israel for weeks if not months. To the east, they scout a Turkey—once an ally—now a foe that threatens war over either a flotilla or Israel's own natural resources.

It's no wonder then Defense Minister Ehud Barak said in February 2012 Israeli leaders are facing the most important decisions of their lives and described the dangers facing Israel "no less critical than those challenges faced by the founders of the state, no less important than those challenges faced by our cabinet during the waiting period before the

Six Day War, and no less significant than those challenges facing the decision makers in those days before the breakout of the Yom Kippur War."[14]

Israel's precarious situation today reminds some of the movie *Fiddler on the Roof*. In that classic film, the small town of Anatevka in early twentieth-century Russia finds itself surrounded by anti-Semitism, pogroms, physical danger, and modernity eroding its way of life.

Tevya, the main character, explains the people of their small town are like a "fiddler on the roof." He explains:

> A fiddler on the roof. Sounds crazy, no? But here in our little town of Anatevka, you say every one of us is a fiddler on the roof trying to scratch out a pleasant, simple tune without breaking his neck. It isn't easy. You may ask, why do we stay up there if it's so dangerous? Well, we stay because Anatevka is our home. And how do we keep our balance? That I can tell you in one word: Tradition![15]

At the end of the movie, the Jews of Anatevka had to leave their homes. But they survived and now through a modern-day odyssey and exodus unknown in human history the Jewish people have migrated back to their ancient homeland. Why do they stay there? They would answer—like Tevya—"because Israel's our home." Ultimately, the Jewish people survived those pogroms of Russia, the later gas chambers of Nazi Germany, and the incessant terror attacks through the years. Given their remarkable history, they will survive the threats facing them today as they balance like a "fiddler on the roof."

6 THE HOUSE OF WAR AND THE HOUSE OF PEACE

"What are the stakes, professor?"
"The survival of our civilization."[1]
—PROFESSOR BERNARD LEWIS, WORLD-
LEADING ISLAMIC SCHOLAR

DATELINE: FRENCH HILL, JERUSALEM

WE DROVE PAST THE WALLS OF THE OLD CITY, THE DAMASCUS
Gate, and up the hill toward the famous Mandelbaum Gate. From 1949
to 1967, the gate provided the only access between Jordan and the nascent
state of Israel. At that time the area lay as a no-man's-land marked by
barbed wire and land mines. Now it's Route One and one of Jerusalem's
busiest roads. We headed for French Hill, a neighborhood in northeast
Jerusalem. Hebrew University dominates French Hill and straddles
Mount Scopus next to the Mount of Olives and offers a commanding
view of Jerusalem's Old City.

We came to French Hill to interview once again Professor Moshe Sharon, one of the world's leading scholars on Islam. I first heard Professor Sharon speak many years before. His message on Islam moved and startled me so much I got copies and sent them to then President George W. Bush. I held little hope President Bush would actually receive the videotapes, but I felt I had to do something to alert the leader of the free world about the dangers posed by radical Islam. Unfortunately President Bush, the United States, and the world would soon learn a tragic lesson in the capabilities of radical Islam on 9/11.

Throughout the years, Sharon provided invaluable insight into the tenets of Islam, its history, and its way of thinking. These insights proved particularly useful in understanding current events like the war in Iraq, the Iranian threat, or the Israeli-Palestinian conflict. His tussled hair, wired glasses, brilliant mind, and irrepressible good humor made me think being in one of Sharon's classes would have been a great student experience.

Although I graduated from Regent University many years ago, I felt like our interviews with Professor Sharon became one-on-one tutorials and a unique opportunity to learn from one of the world's leading Islamic scholars. Except now it wasn't just me but the whole world going to school. It's vital the world learns the lessons it needs to know in fighting radical Islam and the dangers it poses to our way of life. The grades in this class are more like pass or fail. The question is, will Western civilization pass this great test of our time?

ISLAM 101

Professor Sharon has been warning of Islam's ascendant ambitions for more than thirty years. So when the Muslim Brotherhood aims at "mastership of the world" with Jerusalem as its capital, Turkey dreams of a resurrected neo-Ottoman caliphate, and Iran pledges to "wipe Israel off the map," he can help explain what's behind these dreams, goals, and ambitions. One of the first things he explained is that this growing phenomenon is an ancient enemy:

One has got to understand, America is, with all its might, it is fighting against something . . . back into the Middle Ages, we are back into a situation, which [then] President [George W. Bush] might be very right by saying, we are talking about in many ways, some new kind of crusade, but this is not one-sided crusade, it is crusade also on the other side. So in other ways we are talking about holy war.[2]

Sharon explained the first doctrine to understand in this holy war is how Islam looks at the world. In Islamic theology, Islam divides the world into two parts. The part of the world already under the rule of Islam is called the House of Peace or "*dar-al-Islam*." The other part of the world not under the rule of Islam is called the House of War or "*dar-al-Harb*." Islam's goal is to conquer the House of War, bring it under its dominion, and make the entire world Islamic. While many Muslims love peace and abhor radical Islam, millions of others throughout the world embrace jihad and want to make the House of War submit to Islam. The House of War includes the United States, Europe, Israel, and any other part of the world not under Islam. According to their view, we can either come to Islam willingly or be conquered by Islam. If you take a look at a map of the world today, you'll see that many—if not most—of the wars being fought today fall on this fault line between the House of War and the House of Peace. Israel itself stands on the front line.

In our discussion with Professor Sharon, he made four illuminating points along with some "extra credit" quotes. Remember, we're in the House of War and we need to know why there are many people in the world—some trying to get nuclear weapons—who want to defeat us and make us submit to their religion. It's why American troops are fighting and dying in Afghanistan and Iraq; why 9/11 scarred our lives forever; and why every time you get on a flight you go through a thorough TSA screening. Our clash with radical Islam has changed our lives forever.

First, Sharon explained, we're in a war without end:

To make the whole world Islamic is the responsibility of every Muslim. That's why they are trying to Islamize Europe and the United States. Since the world must be all Muslim, this is a war that can never cease until the final goal is realized. Islamists cannot stop, they are accountable to God. The end of the war comes when the other side accepts Islamic rule. However, Islam is allowed to make peace with its enemy as long as the Muslims are weaker, but are obligated to fight when they become stronger.[3]

Second, Sharon said the world is the battlefield. Putting it another way, it's not the kind of war my father fought during World War II.

Because it is not a normal story—you are not hitting at an enemy, you are not on a battlefield. If it was a battlefield between two armies, you'd finish the story, but the battlefield is the world, and the victims are not soldiers, the victims are housewives; the victims can be just clerks that go to their offices. As we have seen, the victims are people that board airplanes. So you are in a different story altogether . . . because almost every imam anywhere and the mosque is speaking in this language . . . this war is also all over the Islamic world: Pakistan, Iraq, Egypt, Saudi Arabia, the Philippines. And these views are not coming from the streets, they're not coming from the bus drivers and from the lorry drivers, and from the street sweepers, they're coming from the universities, they're coming from the centers of learning.[4]

Third, Sharon said Muslims see this as a cosmic end-times struggle between the true believers, the unbelievers, and the misbelievers. In the end of days, they see a world totally Muslim, complete and final victory. According to many Islamic traditions, the Muslims who are in hell will have to be replaced by somebody and they'll be replaced by Christians. Christians will not exist. The fate of Jews is grim too. Sharon explained,

It says very quickly that in the end of the days there's going to be a great war between the Muslims and the Jews, and the Muslims would kill the Jews and the Jews would hide behind the trees and behind the stones, and behind the rocks, but Allah in those days will give a mouth to the trees and a mouth to the rocks, and they would say, "Oh, Muslim, come here, there is a Jew behind me, kill him." And the end of the world, mainly the time in which the divine power would be the reigning power in the world, basically through the establishment of Islam, cannot happen before the extermination of the Jews altogether, and this would be with the help, of course, of the trees and of the rocks.[5]

This helps explain the unnatural hatred toward Jews and the venom and vitriol directed toward Israel and the Jews. It also helps explain why Ahmadinejad's threats to exterminate the Jews and "wipe Israel off the map" need to be taken seriously.

Sharon also illustrated why the concept "land for peace" slavishly followed by the West does not work:

While Judaism and Christianity are personal and appeal to the individual, Islam is territorial. Allah wants to rule over the world and its territory. That's why it is so important that land once under the rule of Islam—according to their beliefs—it must come back under the rule of Islam. This explains in part the ferocious struggle over the land of Israel. It's why when Jews talk peace, Muslims talk territory. It also helps explain why the Western concept of "land for peace" championed for the last fifteen years is counterproductive. It encourages Muslim leaders that Allah is on their side. When unilateral withdrawals like Gaza in the summer of 2005 take place, it's seen as a reward for their terror tactics. To the Muslim way of thinking, land given back that was once under the control of Islam is a reward for their terror tactics and does not diminish their hunger for land, but increases their hunger for more.[6]

Sharon emphasized this Muslim thirst for land to come back under Islamic sway is compounded with Israel. "The establishment of the State of Israel on Islamic land is regarded [as] a double reverse of history because it does not only involve the loss of land but also the unacceptable situation where Jews, who are *dhimmis* [second-class citizens], rule over Muslims. It cannot be tolerated and it must be changed."

It's important to note not all Muslims believe these ideas and teachings. Most do not. In fact, many fear the power of those following classical Islam. Another Islamic scholar, Bernard Lewis, said it's "a curse to its own people even before it's a threat to the rest of us."[7]

But Sharon pointed to the bottom line: Who has the power? "The so-called moderate people, like the moderate state, and so on, you've got to understand one thing—they themselves are afraid."[8] The important point is who sets the tone and who has the ability to harm. Many of these groups have a tremendous ability and willingness to harm. For example, Sharon has no doubt that as soon as a radical Moslem power gets atomic, chemical, or biological weapons, they will use them.

It's also why the Western drive for democracy and free elections in predominantly Muslim lands often backfires, especially after the Arab Spring. When given the choice between democracy and the caliphate, the choice of the "new" Middle East is often the caliphate. Why? "Because the idea is that in the end, the whole world will be under the rule of Islam and they will use the means at their disposal to achieve their goal."[9]

EXTRA CREDIT

Adding on to Sharon's lesson, there are a few points to emphasize. For example, this battle with Islam did not begin on 9/11. The United States faced Islam in the infancy of the new republic. In 1785, just a few short years after 1776, John Adams and Thomas Jefferson met with Abd al-Rahman, the emissary of Tripoli. Tripoli demanded a million-dollar tribute from the United States to guarantee their Barbary pirates would not raid American shipping in the Mediterranean. During their diplomatic rendezvous, Al-Rahman told his American guests two hundred years ago something that sounds like it came from the latest Al-Qaeda diatribe:

> It was . . . written in the Koran, that all Nations who should not have acknowledged their [the Muslims'] authority were sinners, that it was their right and duty to make war upon whoever they could find and to make Slaves of all they could take as prisoners, and that every Mussulman [Muslim] who should be slain in battle was sure to go to Paradise.[10]

In addition, while Islamists may see Israel as the "Little Satan" to be destroyed; they view America as the "Great Satan" to also be overthrown. The Muslim Brotherhood laid out that plan in a stunning document discovered during an FBI raid: "The Ikhwan [Arabic for "brothers"] must understand that their work in America is a kind of *grand jihad* in eliminating and destroying the Western civilization from within and 'sabotaging' its miserable house by their hands and the hands of the believers so that it is eliminated and God's religion is made victorious over all other religions."[11]

Also, it's important to emphasize they want to overthrow the United States because their ambitions are global. Muhammad Badi, the Supreme Leader of the Muslim Brotherhood, said, "The Brotherhood is getting closer to achieving its greatest goal as envisioned by its founder, Imam Hassan al-Banna. This will be accomplished by establishing a righteous and fair ruling system [based on Islamic Sharia], with all its institutions and associations, including a government evolving into *a rightly guided caliphate and mastership of the world*."[12]

Islamists state their goals clearly and often. But are we listening? Raphael Shore, the producer of *Obsession*—a documentary on radical Islam's war against the West, sees a striking parallel between our days and the times before World War II: "The parallel of the time before World War II and today is very striking for a number of reasons. Number one, because just as the radical Islamists have declared war on the West but most people don't want to appreciate it, so also the Nazis declared war on the West and said their intentions very explicitly and people didn't want to believe it until it was too late."[13]

It seems too many Westerners—and particularly Americans—continue to see this Islamic threat as if it's something out of a cartoon. Years ago, my son used to watch a cartoon called *Pinky and the Brain*. The cartoon characters Pinky and the Brain are genetically enhanced laboratory mice that live in the Acme Labs research facility. Pinky, the dim-witted sidekick to the Brain—a rodent with an enormous brain—asks the same question every episode to his genius master: "Gee, Brain, what do you want to do tonight?" Brain answers, "The same thing we do every night, Pinky. Try to take over the world!" Pinky and the Brain then spend the rest of the cartoon devising outlandish schemes to do just that. But not unlike the cartoon, the reality in the world today is that Islamists are out to do just that: take over the world.

Finally, it should be noted, too, that with the world of Islam there are two main camps, the Sunnis and the Shiites. The Sunnis make up the larger of the two. Some of those nations include Egypt, Turkey, the Gulf States, Yemen, Saudi Arabia, and Indonesia. The Shiite camp is led by Iran with its proxy Hezbollah and its ally Syria. The difference goes back to the beginning of Islam. Sharon explained,

> The Sunni Muslims are the majority of Islam and the Shiites are the minority, a very small minority in Islam. The Shiites believe that Islam should have been led from the very beginning by a caliph who came from the prophet himself. In fact from the family of the cousin of Ali and to this very day they believe that one of the descendants of Ali is in hiding. He is the Mahdi and he is the messiah of Islam and he is going to appear one day and to lead the Shiite world to rule the world and create a real Islamic world. These are the Shiites. The Sunnis believe the caliph, namely the leader of the Islamic community—the Commander of the Faithful—should be chosen by the community.[14]

While this division is deep and Sunnis and Shiites often clash as bitter enemies, they will unite if necessary to fight the House of War and fulfill their ultimate goal to kill the Jews, eliminate Israel, and rule the world.

ONE MORE CLASS

Besides Sharon, we were given a rare opportunity to speak with another world-leading Islamic scholar, Professor Bernard Lewis of Princeton University. In this rare interview, Lewis explained after a lifetime of studying Islam the main message he's trying to communicate to the West. "I'm trying to communicate that we are engaged in a struggle, comparable with the two great struggles of the twentieth century, against Nazism [Nazi Germany] and against Bolshevism [Soviet Union]. But it would improve our chances of winning if we understood who they are and who we are, and what it's all about."[15]

Lewis went on to warn,

Now the only obstacle that remains for the worldwide triumph of Islam is the US. So that is the next target, and that is very clear. . . .

I think the main weakness from our side is the failure to appreciate the nature of the conflict in which we are engaged. I mean, this was true for dealing with the Nazis for a while. [Neville] Chamberlain really believed that by going to Munich [in 1938] and reaching an agreement with Hitler, he could establish peace in our time and so on. All that he succeeded in doing was to postpone the war for a few months and weaken our side. We see something of the same error nowadays with the tendency in the Western world to blame ourselves. If I may quote another saying, "my country right or wrong," a great saying, with limitations, but now it's been shortened, "my country—wrong." That's the general view of many people in the media and in the public debate, I mean, this tendency to self-abasement, to say oh yes, we have been wrong. For example, as I said before the struggle between Islam and Christendom has been going on for fourteen centuries. . . . [16]

But for these people, with their apocalyptic mind-set, they believe the end of the world is now, that this is the messianic age. For them, mutual assured destruction is not a deterrent, it's an inducement, and the catalyst to bring the messianic age and the final triumph of the true faith closer.

At the end of our interview, we asked Lewis what then are the stakes in this battle between Islam and the West. His sobering answer: "The survival of our civilization."[17]

7 THINKING THE UNTHINKABLE

*Application of an atomic bomb would not leave
anything in Israel, but the same thing would just
produce damages in the Muslim world.[1]*

—HASHEMI RAFSANJANI, FORMER IRANIAN PRESIDENT, 2001

WITH WAR MORE OF A CERTAINTY THAN A POSSIBILITY AND growing threats on every side, Israelis are preparing for the inevitable. Israel's home front command has issued gas masks by the tens of thousands to prepare their population for chemical or biological attack. They regularly conduct drills for missile strikes, and Israel's military is poised to respond to a number of scenarios. War is not a question of "if" but "when." While it's hard to know exactly what will happen and when, here is one possible scenario through the eyes of one Israeli soldier.

DATELINE: ISRAEL'S GREEN PINE RADAR STATION, THE NEGEV DESERT

Avi Mizrachi, an Israeli radar operator, sat stunned. He spent months in training and nearly a year at his position scanning Israel's eastern sky.

But all his training and experience didn't prepare Mizrachi for what he saw. Frozen by the sight, he knew immediately what it meant.

Mizrachi served on Israel's radar unit called the Green Pine tracking system. It formed one part of a multibillion-dollar joint US-Israeli project called the "Arrow," the world's premier antimissile system. His radar unit complemented an American radar complex called "X Band" hidden deep in Israel's Negev Desert. Israeli and American engineers developed a system the technological equivalent of "hitting a bullet with a bullet." Their chief engineer claimed if you had the money and didn't violate the laws of physics, it would work. It did. For years, well-publicized tests demonstrated over and over, the Arrow could hit a missile going more than nine times the speed of sound hundreds of thousands of feet in the stratosphere.

The Arrow stood as Israel's frontline defense against ballistic missile attack. Its designers planned for a worst-case scenario: a huge salvo of enemy missiles simultaneously coming from several directions. American satellites played a key role. They detected the flare of an enemy missile, calculated where and when it was launched, and relayed that information to Israel. While it represented the apex of Israeli and American technology, the Arrow system also depended on human operators like Mizrachi. He evaluated the trajectory, speed, and direction of any incoming missile. Those missiles might be carrying chemical, biological, or even nuclear warheads. The fate of several million people—and the future of the state of Israel—depended on their split-second decisions.

Mizrachi knew the dangers. As a boy, he lived through the 1991 Gulf War when Iraq's Sadaam Hussein pounded Israel with more than thirty Scud missiles. He knew the sound of the air-raid sirens, the smell of sealed rooms designed to protect against chemical weapons, and the sight of the ubiquitous gas masks the home front command required his family and the rest of Israel to carry. Sadaam's missiles didn't do significant damage then but reinforced the need for Israel's Arrow antimissile system it began developing in the mid-1980s. Now that technology stood between Israel and possible annihilation.

What Mizrachi didn't know because of security reasons, but suspected, was that Israeli F16I fighter/bombers had earlier screamed into Iranian airspace to deliver their payloads on Iran's nuclear facilities. But despite a massive electronic jamming campaign, Israel failed to stop the communications of at least two Iranian missile batteries deep inside Iran's Lut Desert, the hottest place on earth. According to the US Geological Survey, the Lut Desert set the highest temperature ever recorded, an astounding 159 degrees Fahrenheit in 2005. Now the heat of Iranian missile engines added to the heat of this unfolding Mideast conflagration.

He also didn't know Hezbollah, Iran's Lebanese proxy, began launching their own missiles from bases all along Israel's northern border. Hezbollah's leader, Sheik Hassan Nasrallah, promised to unleash ten thousand rockets whenever Israel attacked Iran. He kept his promise. Now with a refurbished and robust arsenal of more than fifty thousand rockets and missiles, he could hit Israeli targets as far south as Tel Aviv.

Thousands of residents in Kiryat Shmona scurried to bomb shelters just a few miles from the Lebanese border when smaller Katyusha- and larger Iranian-built Farj rockets began to rain down. Farther south, the people of Netanya heard air-raid sirens for the first time in seven years. Deep underground in Tel Aviv, Israeli home front commanders monitored the incoming missiles from east and north and sprang their home front operational plan into action. Down the hall, the IDF's chief of staff, along with his top aides, watched the next major war unfold in their command and control center. They carefully watched for reactions from Egypt to the south and Turkey to the north.

In the meantime, Mizrachi sat in the Arrow's fire control and battle management center, Israel's defensive front line. But this front line didn't look like the twentieth-century front lines of pill boxes, observation towers, and sentries. This "Maginot" line existed on the edge of space. Satellites and state-of-the-art radar systems monitored this twenty-first-century battlefield where ballistic missiles would duel in a battle of technological superiority. It was a ballistic cat-and-mouse game, the enemy's offensive system against Israel's defensive system, or as one engineer called it "a technological wizard war." But could one missile shoot down another? What about dozens? The lives of tens of thousands—maybe hundreds of thousands, even millions—depended on the answer.

The scientists felt sure it would work. After all, in their minds, the system rested on engineering, not magic. They designed Arrow to detect and track incoming missiles from 500 kilometers (310 miles), engage them from between 16 to 48 kilometers (10–30 miles) away, and then explode its warhead within 50 meters (150 feet) of the incoming missile. Following a recent test of the Arrow, a senior defense official told reporters it proved Israel could defend itself against Iran's nuclear threat. One Israeli Knesset member boasted the Arrow could bring down any kind of ballistic missile, a capability no other power in the world possessed.

Now the world would soon discover if his boast was true.

Syria's missile program, though far less visible than Iran's, followed closely behind. After the 1973 Yom Kippur war, then Syrian president Hafez Assad saw the Israeli Air Force once again decimate his fleet of Soviet-bought Migs as it had in the 1967 Six Day War. He vowed then that while the last war with Israel may have been a war with aircraft, the next war would be a war with missiles.

First he invested heavily in Russian-made missiles during the Soviet era. Later, he switched his missile procurements to North Korean–made Scud Cs and Ds. He spent the rest of his life building enormous missile bases in the Syrian Desert near cities like Homs. His son Bashar continued the massive construction projects. Concrete-hardened bunkers deep in Syria's interior hid hundreds of Scud C and D missiles. Syria boasted they could hit a target anywhere in Israel, from Metulla on its northern border to the southern Israeli resort of Eilat on the Red Sea. Syrian legislator Mohammed Habash once warned their missiles could even hit Israel's Dimona nuclear reactor. Their missiles potentially came armed with chemical weapons from a weapons program that earned Syria the unofficial title of "chemical superpower of the Middle East."

Now in one last desperate act, Syrian president Assad unleashed his own substantial missile cache. Weakened by months of fighting Syrian opposition forces, he barely held on to power. But he still did control several hundred of those Scud missiles. Mizrachi could see a number of rockets streaking from Israel's northeast. He knew Assad was taking a stand with Iran, perhaps his last.

For years, Mizrachi—and Israel—expected a major missile attack from their arch enemies, Syria and Iran. Iran, driven by its messianic president and their ruling mullahs, regularly promised to "wipe Israel off the map." Syria stood beside Iran in a mutual defense pact. Mizrachi knew both nations boasted the most formidable missile arsenals in the Middle East. For decades, Iran manufactured its line of Shahab missiles. *Shahab* means "meteor" in Persian, and it constituted part of what one Israeli missile expert called "the most ambitious missile program in the world." For years, much of the world focused on Iran's irrepressible pursuit of nuclear weapons.

But behind the nuclear headlines, Iran pursued a missile program with similar vigor. It answered the question: Once you have a nuclear bomb, how do you deliver it? One Israeli engineer noted, "The missile is just a bus to take the nuclear bomb. If the nuclear people did a good job, it will work." Iran strove to make Israel the first bus stop on their way to dominating the Middle East.

Now, dozens of targets filled Mizrachi's screen. He knew this was not a test, simulation, or computer war game. These green targets represented some of the most sophisticated ballistic missiles in the Middle East. Screaming in the upper reaches of the stratosphere and skirting the edges of space, they raced at Mach 9.5, more than nine times the speed of sound. With epitaphs like "Death to Israel" emblazoned on the missile casings, they represented a strike at the heart—and future—of the Jewish state.

Suddenly, the radar room exploded with sound. The cacophony jolted Mizrachi. Other radar operators and their officer in charge burst out with exclamations and instructions. For the next two minutes, the fate of Israel rested in the decisions these operators would make. Any longer would be too late. Even though the Arrow traveled nearly two miles a second, it needed those precious moments to hit the incoming missiles.

Mizrachi knew those missiles represented the height of Iranian, Syrian, and North Korean technology. Reduced to its simplest terms, they represented a one-thousand-mile slingshot at hypersonic speed. He remembered the time he spent patrolling the streets of Hebron. A Palestinian Arab with a good slingshot could send a rock flying a couple of hundred feet. But these weren't rocks. They possibly carried warheads of several hundred pounds of high explosives, enough to destroy a city block. Worse, they carried chemical weapons. Or Israel's nightmare scenario, they came roaring at the Jewish state tipped with nuclear weapons. No one knew. What he did know is that they were likely aimed at the port of Haifa, the population center of Tel Aviv, or Dimona, Israel's nuclear power plant.

The Arrow batteries lifted into position.

Mizrachi's mind raced with different scenarios of the bigger Middle East picture. He knew other operators, this time in control of Israel's own nuclear arsenal, had their own decisions to make. Would they be instructed to fire Israel's nuclear-tipped cruise missiles? He knew at least one of Israel's three Dolphin class submarines silently and stealthily patrolled the Persian Gulf, well within range of Iranian cities like Teheran, Qazvin, and Esfahan. He knew Israeli F16I fighter-bombers—equipped with extra fuel tanks—flew on their missions to take out Syria's remaining missile sites and Iran's own nuclear facilities.

He wondered if the United States would join the attack. How would Europe respond? Or the UN? What about Russia since it had given nuclear fuel and technology to both Iran and Syria? Would it stay out of the war Mizrachi saw starting on his radar screen? He could easily presume Israel's prime minister, the US president, and the capitals of the world were now abuzz with encrypted communications.

On Israel's southern flank, he wondered if Egypt would join the attack. Now that Egyptian president Hosni Mubarak had been deposed in early 2011, it remained unclear what Egypt's military or its new leaders would do. Influenced by the Muslim Brotherhood, would Egypt be tempted to join the fray and eliminate once and for all "the Zionist entity"? But they knew the risks too. Israel could launch missile strikes against Cairo or destroy Egypt's Aswan Dam. They might strike south through the Sinai Peninsula with armored divisions and once again, as they had in 1967 and 1973, nearly capture Egypt's capital.

He knew Syria would pay a high price too. When Syria's president Bashar Assad made his military pact with Iran years before, he sealed his fate. Would Damascus be destroyed as the prophet Isaiah once wrote, "Behold, Damascus will cease from being a city, and it will be a ruinous heap" (Isaiah 17:1)?

He knew the targets on his radar screen threatened the existence of the state of Israel. They also marked the beginning of the next world war. Mizrachi wondered if this could be the start of the battle prophesied by Ezekiel, the great and fearsome battle of Gog and Magog.

He heard the roar of the Arrows. The war had begun.

———

Avi Mizrachi is an imaginary character, but the preceding scenario falls well within the realm of plausibility. There will be another war in the Middle East. Many experts warn it will be a war of missiles and could be catastrophic. In fact, one report published by the Center for Strategic and International Studies (CSIS) concluded a potential nuclear war between Israel and Iran would kill as many as 16 to 20 million Iranians and between 200,000 and 800,000 Israelis.[2]

The report called "Iran, Israel and Nuclear War" from the Center for Strategic and International Studies envisions a doomsday scenario. What would happen if Iran does acquire nuclear weapons and then attacks the Jewish state? Their analysis concluded Iran might develop as many as thirty nuclear weapons between 2010 and 2020. Given the range of its ballistic missile arsenal, they could hit anywhere in Israel. But they might not deliver a lethal blow or "wipe Israel off the map" as

Iran's president had hoped. Why? The report noted Iran's nuclear weapons would not be as powerful as Israel's, their missiles were less accurate, and Israel's Arrow antimissile system would be able to intercept most of Iran's incoming missiles.

Israel's retaliation, they predicted, would be overwhelming. The reasons: Israel's nuclear arsenal—which they presumed to be about two hundred nuclear bombs—carried a far greater "yield" than Iran; their offensive missiles were far more accurate and could hit Iran's population centers with devastating power. The report concluded, "Iranian recovery is not possible in the normal sense of the term, though Israeli recovery is theoretically possible in population and economic terms."[3]

Their conclusion soberly contradicted the boast of Iran's ayatollah Hashemi Rafsanjani in 2001. He said then, "If a day comes when the world of Islam is duly equipped with the arms Israel has in possession, the strategy of colonialism would face a stalemate because application of an atomic bomb would not leave anything in Israel but the same thing would just produce damages in the Muslim world."[4]

These apocalyptic scenarios might sound far-fetched but given the current realities in the Middle East, they seem all too plausible. A storm is stirring in the Middle East.

8 THE ISRAEL YOU NEVER KNEW

Anybody who had spent time here realizes mostly it's a very peaceful, wonderful country.[1]

—MARTIN FLETCHER, NBC CORRESPONDENT

DATELINE: HERZYLIYA, OVERLOOKING THE MEDITERRANEAN

WE RENDEZVOUSED AT ONE OF ISRAEL'S MANY OUTDOOR CAFES. About a dozen Israelis spent a relaxed morning at small tables over espresso or *café afouk*, an Israeli cappuccino. Martin Fletcher offered me coffee. Tempting. But we were already were behind schedule. We tried to catch up with a morning getting away from us and keep ahead of the harsh noonday sun that always presents a problem when shooting an outdoor interview. Fletcher knew a good spot for the interview. I jumped into his car and our cameraman followed. I had never met Fletcher. Just saw him on TV. Delightful character. Nice guy.

He took us to an overlook just behind the US ambassador's residence in Herzliya. Security didn't seem to mind, so we set up our camera and audio. The bluff offered a commanding view of the Mediterranean,

Israel's coastline, and the beach more than one hundred feet below. Perfect. We met Fletcher—NBC's veteran Middle East correspondent of more than thirty years—to talk about his book *Walking Israel: A Personal Search for the Soul of a Nation.* The book traces his step-by-step personal odyssey of walking Israel's coastline. He started on Israel's northern border with Lebanon and traversed all the way down to the Gaza Strip. By the time he reached Gaza, he discovered an Israel he never knew existed.

In fact, Fletcher found an Israel few people know. With a brilliant sky as a canopy and a refreshing breeze off the sea, he shared his discoveries. "I wanted to show it's a great place that has made tremendous contributions to the world, that has tremendous problems that need to be solved very urgently, but we don't need to focus only on the problems. We should focus also on the good things about Israel."[2]

Fletcher came to Israel years ago, and he's heard over and over the same question. It's the same one I've heard too: "Is it safe?"

He explained, "So many people used to call me up and say, 'Hey, is it safe to come to Israel?' And I'd say, 'Of course it is.' And then they'd call me back a week later after they've arrived and say, 'Wow, it's a great place. I had no idea.' And I wanted to write a book about that great place which people often don't have any idea."[3]

Despite the fact I just documented the many ominous threats facing Israel, when tourists come they almost always say how safe they feel. In fact, it's a nearly universal refrain. They feel safe. Many feel "at home." Most come in spite of the protests of family and friends. "Are you crazy?" is one of the most common questions fired at potential visitors. But I've watched Christian pilgrims weep over the joy of sailing on the Sea of Galilee or walking the streets of Jerusalem, "walking where Jesus walked," and grateful they made the journey.

But why don't some people have any idea Israel is a great place? Fletcher puts much of the blame on the media, which often portrays a one-sided story. "We [the media] present a country that is always in conflict and therefore the story of Israel is the war, the brutality, the occupation, the

Jewish settlers, the fighting, the bombs, the killings. That's the Israel the world knows." But he says there's much more. "Anybody who has spent time here realizes mostly it's a very peaceful, wonderful country and that peaceful, wonderful country rarely gets shown. And that's what I wanted to do with the book, is show that peaceful, wonderful place."[4]

In the meantime, Fletcher believes Israel gets a raw deal in the world's court of public opinion and fired back at the smear campaign that Israel shouldn't exist:

> I think Israel is the only country in the world whose very existence is in question. Its right to exist is in question. I mean, nobody says about Zimbabwe or North Korea: hey, should that country exist? Israel is the only country in the world that people say, should that country exist? Israel has a right to exist and I love the country personally, and I was hoping to show in the book that it is a great place that should continue to exist. It's got terrible problems that need to be solved. But the process of delegitimization of Israel that is taking hold in some parts of Europe especially I think is wrong.[5]

After living in Israel for thirteen years, I know Fletcher's right. It is a wonderful country. It does have tremendous problems, but it's neither a pariah nor an apartheid country. The delegitimization sticks sometimes because people don't know the other side of the story. For example, here are a few things you might not realize if you didn't live here. You might not know Jews and Arabs walk side by side on the streets of Jerusalem. You might be startled to see a Muslim mother and father pushing their baby stroller through a Jewish and Arab neighborhood like Abu Tor with toddlers straggling along. You might be surprised to hear the Muslim call by the muezzin from dozens of mosques in Jerusalem. You might not imagine a Jerusalem park in west Jerusalem filled with Arab families on a Friday afternoon. Or you might not see thousands of Muslims flood Jerusalem during their celebration of the Islamic holy month of Ramadan.

On the other hand, you won't see a synagogue in the Palestinian-controlled West Bank or Gaza Strip. Nor do Jews celebrate Passover in Ramallah. It's too dangerous.

In addition, most Israeli Arabs don't want to leave Israel and migrate to a Palestinian state. In fact, many Arabs moved to Israeli-controlled Jerusalem when the threat of a Palestinian state became more real. This doesn't mean Israeli Arabs are Zionists. Some see the Jewish state as a temporary stage in history, and there's deep resentment percolating under the surface. But many believe it's better to live in Israel with all its faults than in a future Palestinian state with its shortcomings.

On the Palestinian side, they wait in long lines and suffer profound inconvenience because of Israel's security barrier designed to prevent terror and suicide attacks. Some criticize the security barrier separating Israel and Palestinian areas. About 95 percent of the barrier is a fence; about 5 percent is a wall. The wall gets most of the press. It's formidable looking. The barrier itself makes life for Palestinian Arabs very difficult. But the barrier exists for a reason: to keep suicide bombers away from Israeli shops, streets, and buses.

From late 2000 to 2004, Palestinian terrorists killed hundreds of Israelis and wounded thousands. The barrier became one part of Israel's solution. It's worked. For Israel, the choice became one of inconvenience for some or life and death for others. If the threat was eliminated, the wall would fall. In addition, Israeli border police and the IDF have been caught on camera guilty of police brutality. The issue is not that bad things like that don't happen in Israel but what happens when bad things do happen. Most often investigations, discipline, or dismissal follow those incidents. I've lived here long enough to see Israel's warts. It's not perfect, but it's no pariah. In fact, some of the strongest defenses of Israel in the past few years have come from Arabs themselves.

For example, Mosab Yousef, the famed "Son of Hamas," drew the stark difference between Israel, the Palestinian Authority, and the Arab world. He courageously told a Jerusalem press conference:

Show me how many Jewish organizations are registered in the Palestinian Authority or Arab countries. How many Jewish movements we have? None! But look at Israel. How many radical, Islamic movements live in Israel legally and they are protected by the constitution. This is what we are talking about. This is why I stand by Israel and I want the entire region to learn from this experience. . . . Israel represents the values of the Western Civilization of democracy, liberty, personal freedom, the authority of the constitution. . . . I love Israel because Israel is a democratic country. I love Israel because I love democracy. I love Israel because I love a country that respects and protects personal and religious freedom and protects people from the absolute control of religion. That's the reason why I stand by Israel. . . . It's not stand by Israel against Palestinians. It's to stand with democracy against dictatorship and against absolute control of religion over people's lives.[6]

THE REST OF THE STORY

Many of Israel's good stories simply don't get heard. For example, twenty-five hundred miles south of where Fletcher and I shot our interview is one such story. That's where nine-year-old Esther—a Christian girl from the Massai tribe in Tanzania—lay dying. Esther suffered from congestive heart failure. Her diagnosis gave the young girl only a few months to live. Sister Angelika, a Catholic nun overseeing Esther in a children's home, heard about an Israeli program called Save a Child's Heart. Coincidentally, she learned a team from the organization had recently landed in Tanzania to climb Mount Kilimanjaro. Sister Angelika contacted the team and they examined Esther. Dr. Lior Sasson, one member of the team, said, "Her heart was huge, so she was very limited in very simple tasks. Even simple walking was difficult for her."[7] He recommended surgery.

Two months later, Esther landed in Israel.

Dr. Sasson operated for several hours reconstructing Esther's heart. After the successful surgery, Sasson explained, "Now she can live a normal life [but] she has to take preventive medicine so that her valve will not be affected."[8] Two weeks after her surgery, CBN News videotaped a happy, healthy Esther dancing and singing with new friends at Tel Aviv's Tel Hashomer Hospital.

Esther became the twenty-five-hundredth patient of Save a Child's Heart. Simon Fisher, its executive director, told us, "The idea behind Save a Child's Heart is to provide life-saving surgery for children from developing countries. We believe that Save a Child's Heart is a very positive message, which it sends out from the Middle East, from Israel about people working together from different nationalities and different religions for the best of our children." Palestinian children from the West Bank and the Gaza Strip make up more than half of all the patients treated by Save a Child's Heart.[9]

The program trains doctors from developing countries like Dr. Goedgrey, a Tanzanian professional who assisted with Esther's surgery. He told us, "This training will be one of its kind for my country. So hopefully when I go back I will actually start the open-heart surgery also for the young children. Actually for me, it looks like a miracle."[10]

It's just one of the many "miracles" coming out of Israel. For example, when farmers around the world grow their crops using drip irrigation, they can thank Israel. Israeli Daniel Hillel won the 2012 World Food Prize for developing this groundbreaking system. It allows small amounts of water to nourish plants in some of the world's driest countries. Hillel has spread drip irrigation technology to as many as forty other countries.[11]

Another Israeli scientist, Professor Pedro Berliner of Ben Gurion University, travels the world "showing researchers and farmers in countries such as Kenya, Turkmenistan, Uzbekistan, India and Mexico how they can fight against desertification" by reviving ancient water techniques.[12]

But agriculture just scratches the surface of Israel's contributions to the world. For example, Israeli engineers from Motorola helped develop the cell phone. Microsoft-Israel programmers wrote the Windows NT and XP operating systems. Israeli Intel engineers invented the Pentium MMX Chip technology, the Pentium-4 microprocessor, and the Centrino processor. AOL Instant Messenger ICQ started in Israel. Some other Israeli innovations include the Pill Cam developed by Given Imaging, an ingestible video camera that detects damage or disease to the small intestine. Seambiotics develops biofuels made of algae.[13] Benny Landa pioneered a revolutionary method of printing called nanography. Landa—called "the Steve Jobs of the printing world"—said it provided "a whole new way to apply ink, Israel is now positioned to usurp Germany as the king of the multi-billion dollar digital printing industry."[14]

In other areas, Israelis won ten Nobel Prizes, and Jews worldwide have accrued an astounding 20 percent of all Nobel Prizes since they were first awarded in 1902.

Israeli search, rescue, and medical teams were some of the first who responded to the 2010 Haiti earthquake and the 2011 Japanese tsunami. According to CNN, Israel set up the first field hospitals in both Haiti and Japan.

Israel is also a world leader in desalination, turning seawater into drinking water.

Dan Senor and Saul Singer's book *Start Up Nation* documents that there are more start-up businesses per capita in Israel than any other nation in the world. Senor told CBN founder Pat Robertson on the *700 Club*, "Israel has been in a state of war since its founding, has had no access to energy but Israelis haven't left. A state of mind, sense of survival, sense of commitment, sense of business success as a form or patriotism" has made "tiny Israel into a technological giant."[15]

In fact, Israel per capita has the largest number of biotech start-ups; the highest ratio of university degrees; more scientific papers than any other nation; more home computers per capita; the second highest publication of new books; and more museums. It's also the largest immigrant-absorbing nation on earth.

Nonprofit organization Israel21c reports on Israel's innovations and concludes,

> When Israel was founded . . . it was a barren country with no natural resources, little water, and more than half of its land mass desert. The only thing the new country had going for it was the natural creativity of its people. More than six decades later, the Israelis have turned their country into an oasis of technology and innovation. With the most startups per capita worldwide, and the third highest number of patents per head, Israel has become one of the leading players in the world of high-tech innovation, attracting international giants to its shores. From health breakthroughs to technology, agriculture, the environment and the arts, the country's innovations are transforming and enriching lives everywhere. Israel today is playing a significant role in some of the most important challenges facing our planet. Not bad for a country the size of New Jersey.[16]

When you consider Israel's contributions to the world, it's astounding. While his numbers differ a bit, Mark Twain discovered the same phenomenon way back in 1899:

> If statistics are right, the Jews constitute but one percent of the human race. It suggests a nebulous dim puff of stardust lost in the blaze of the Milky Way. Properly the Jew ought hardly to be heard of, but he is heard of, has always been heard of. He is as prominent on the planet as any other people, and his commercial importance is extravagantly out of proportion to the smallness of his bulk. His contributions to the world's list of great names in literature, science, art, music, finance, medicine, and abstruse learning are also away out of proportion to the weakness of his numbers. He has made a marvelous fight in this world, in all the ages; and has done it with his hands tied behind him. He could be vain of himself and be excused of it.[17]

THE DESERT BLOOMING

But thirty-two years before Twain penned his impressions about the immortality of the Jew, he visited Palestine and described a wasteland in *Innocents Abroad*: "It is a hopeless, dreary, heart-broken land. . . . Palestine sits in sackcloth and ashes. Over it broods the spell of a curse that has withered its fields and fettered its energies. . . . Palestine is desolate and unlovely."[18]

When many Jews began to return to the land of Israel, like Twain they discovered a barren desert land. Yet today Israeli farmers have transformed that sparse land into a land flowing—as the Bible says—with "milk and honey." CBN News reporter Julie Stahl found that to be true—literally. The expression—found nearly two dozen times in the Scriptures—promised Israel would be a land flowing with "milk and honey." In her report, she stated that despite the heat, humidity, and limited resources, Israeli cows now produce more milk per year than most cows in the world, including those in the United States, the European Union, and Australia. CBN News visited the Kibbutz Yotvata dairy that developed a high-tech operation where—according to its manager, Ronen Gal—the milk production keeps "going up."[19]

And the honey? Most believe the honey in Bible times came from date trees. CBN News found thousands of those trees on Kibbutz Ketura, actually not far from the cows in Kibbutz Yotvata. Botanist Dr. Elaine Solowey emigrated from the United States in 1974 and oversees the date palm orchards. She said, "Actually I started out here as the head of the orchard branch and of course that was kind of funny because at that time we didn't have any orchards." But since then Solowey planted three thousand date trees, just a fraction of the tens of thousands of acres now planted throughout Israel.

Soloway even managed to sprout a two-thousand-year-old date seed found by archeologists at Massada. Now she's looking for more trees to plant. "I'm looking for trees that love to live in the desert, that rejoice to live in the desert—not the ones I have to keep on life support." To do that, she found clues in the Bible. "Well, the biblical trees, if they grew here in the old days, why shouldn't they grow here now?" She's also pioneering other biblical items. "We reintroduced frankincense and myrrh, which had probably been introduced at the time of King Solomon. According to what we can tell from folk tales and from the Bible, there was already an incense and medicinal tree being cultivated here called the Balm of Gilead."[20]

To some, it seems the very earth of Israel is experiencing a revival. "Since Israel attained its independence in 1948 . . . agricultural production has expanded 16 fold, more than three times the rate of the population grown."[21] "Israel is the only country in the world where the desert is receding, and a . . . statement from the U.N. Development Programme called the Jewish state 'one of the driest, but agriculturally most successful, countries of the world. Israel's knowledge of drylands agriculture could be of great value to some of the world's poorest people . . .'"[22]

Jewish commentator Moshe Kempinski sees the cows, dates, and trees as signs of biblical redemption. According to Kempinski, the revival of trees in the land is the first sign: "Ezekiel 36 says 'mountains shoot forth your branches, give forth your fruit because My children are coming home' . . . that's an unusual thing for God to tell a tree. That's what He created a tree to do, except God is saying in Leviticus, it's going to be a desolate land when I kick you out . . . but watch when I bring My people back home the land is going to come forth with blossoms and trees and fruits."[23]

So he says when you're in Israel, every date you eat or every glass of milk you drink is like prophecy being fulfilled. "God says I'm going to do something miraculous. I'm going to create a land that even though those climate issues don't call for it, it's going to be a land that's going to be filled with dates and honey and also with milk so that you know that nothing comes here, nothing in this land comes here except when it's from Me."[24]

ISRAEL: THE LAND OF MIRACLES

Israel's first prime minister, David Ben Gurion, once reportedly said, "In Israel, to be a realist, you have to believe in miracles."

It's hard to describe modern-day Israel as anything other than a miracle. Never before in human history had a nation been displaced and scattered to the four corners of the world and then regathered. After being dispersed to the winds during the Roman conquest of Israel two thousand years ago, they hung tenaciously to their faith, customs, and culture. They cried, prayed, sang, and whispered, "Next year in Jerusalem." And then one year it began. Slowly as a trickle and then a torrent, then it ebbed and flowed with the world's conditions. It slowed tragically when the British Empire dramatically restricted immigration before World War II and gushed when the former Soviet Union collapsed. That condemned thousands of Jews to the Nazi gas chambers. But like a Phoenix rising out of the ashes, they came together. To many it signaled a divine migration and calling. They point to Ezekiel's prophecy in the valley of the dry bones and see a picture of modern Israel coming to life:

> The hand of the LORD came upon me and brought me out in the Spirit of the LORD, and set me down in the midst of the valley; and it was full of bones. Then He caused me to pass by them all around, and behold, there were very many in the open valley; and indeed they were very dry. And He said to me, "Son of man, can these bones live?"
>
> So I answered, "O Lord GOD, You know."
>
> Again He said to me, "Prophesy to these bones, and say to them, 'O dry bones, hear the word of the LORD! Thus says the Lord GOD to these bones: "Surely I will cause breath to enter into you, and you shall live. I will put sinews on you and bring flesh upon you, cover you with skin and put breath in you; and you shall live. Then you shall know that I am the LORD."'"
>
> So I prophesied as I was commanded; and as I prophesied, there was a noise, and suddenly a rattling; and the bones came together,

bone to bone. Indeed, as I looked, the sinews and the flesh came upon them, and the skin covered them over; but there was no breath in them.

Also He said to me, "Prophesy to the breath, prophesy, son of man, and say to the breath, 'Thus says the Lord GOD: "Come from the four winds, O breath, and breathe on these slain, that they may live."'" So I prophesied as He commanded me, and breath came into them, and they lived, and stood upon their feet, an exceedingly great army.

Then He said to me, "Son of man, these bones are the whole house of Israel. They indeed say, 'Our bones are dry, our hope is lost, and we ourselves are cut off!' Therefore prophecy and say to them, 'Thus says the Lord GOD: "Behold, O My people, I will open your graves and cause you to come up from your graves, and bring you into the land of Israel."'" (Ezekiel 37:1–12)

Now the land of Israel teems with Jews from the ends of the earth, from Morocco, Yemen, China, India, America, and beyond. For centuries, Israel was but a dream and a prayer. Now, despite overwhelming odds, pogroms, an Inquisition, the Crusades, persecution, and discrimination, it's a reality. The Jews survived, but the nations that attacked them are no more. Once again Twain captured the essence of Jewish history:

The Egyptian, the Babylonian, and the Persian rose, filled the planet with sound and splendor, then faded to dream-stuff and passed away; the Greek and the Roman followed; and made a vast noise, and they are gone; other people have sprung up and held their torch high for a time, but it burned out, and they sit in twilight now, or have vanished. The Jew saw them all, beat them all, and is now what he always was, exhibiting no decadence, no infirmities of age, no weakening of his parts, no slowing of his energies, no dulling of his alert and aggressive mind. All things are mortal but the Jews; all other forces pass, but he remains. What is the secret of his immortality?[25]

THE SECRET OF THE JEWS

Twain asked, "What is the secret of the immortality" of the Jews? Thousands of years before, Jeremiah answered Twain's query: "Thus says the LORD, who gives the sun for a light by day, the ordinances of the moon and the stars for a light by night, who disturbs the sea, and its waves roar (The LORD of hosts is His name): 'If those ordinances depart from before Me, says the LORD, then the seed of Israel shall also cease from being a nation before Me forever'" (Jeremiah 31:35–36).

Jeremiah continued: "Thus says the LORD: 'If heaven above can be measured, and the foundations of the earth searched out beneath, I will also cast off all the seed of Israel for all that they have done, says the LORD'" (Jeremiah 31:37).

If you believe the Bible, the secret of the Jews is God Himself. He promised the sun would stop shining before Israel ceases to be a nation. "A Friend in the highest places" indeed—and it's in writing.

While it's hard to describe the modern state of Israel without using the word *miracle*, it's impossible to explain Israel without the Bible. According to the Bible, the Jews hold a special place in God's heart. He warned, "For he who touches you [Israel] touches the apple of His eye" (Zechariah 2:8). He also said that "the LORD did not set His love on you [Israel] nor choose you because you were more in number than any other people, for you were the least of all peoples" (Deuteronomy 7:7). That's why the Jews are the chosen people. Of course, it's not an easy calling. In fact, Tevya in *Fiddler on the Roof* tells God: "It's nice that we're the chosen people. But could you choose somebody else."[26]

The Bible also says He has something in mind—His own purpose in choosing the Jews: "'And I will sanctify My great name, which has been profaned among the nations, which you have profaned in their midst; and the nations shall know that I am the LORD,' says the Lord GOD, 'when I am hallowed in you before their eyes. For I will take you from among the nations, gather you out of all countries, and bring you into your own land'" (Ezekiel 36:23–24).

Despite Israel's size, God has a special calling for the Jewish people and the nation of Israel *and declarations that have never been rescinded.* First Chronicles 17:21 says, "Who is like Your people Israel, the one nation on the earth whom God went to redeem for Himself *as* a people—to make for Yourself a name by great and awesome deeds, by driving out nations from before Your people whom You redeemed from Egypt?"

God knows they are not always right, but they are *always* His people. The famous Bible teacher Derek Prince emphasized that point in one of the first interviews I ever did in Israel. We met in Jerusalem's Yemin Moshe neighborhood in 1996. With the walls of Jerusalem's Old City and the Jaffa Gate in the background, the first question I asked Prince was, "Why care about Israel?" He simply replied, "Because God cares about Israel."[27]

In one of his teachings called "Why Israel?" Prince cites a number of Bible facts about Israel:

- "Israel is the name for the nation descended from Abraham, Isaac and Jacob."
- "The name Israel or Israelite occurs in the Old Covenant more than 2500 times."
- "You cannot fully understand the Bible until you know something about Israel."
- "Israel is mentioned 79 times in the New Covenant."
- "The word Jew occurs 84 times in the Old Covenant and 192 times in the New Covenant."
- "Their whole history was told through prophecy. That's not true of any other nation."[28]

He said you could say the Bible is Israel-centric and holds a sacred place for Christians. He notes John 4:22 says, "You worship what you do not know; we know what we worship, for salvation is of the Jews." He exclaimed: "Five breathtaking words: salvation is of the Jews!" ... "Every spiritual blessing I've ever enjoyed I owe to one people, the Jewish people:

without them, no patriarchs, no apostles, no Bible and no Saviour. How much salvation would you or I have without those five things . . . everyone one of us who is blessed in Jesus Christ owes all our spiritual blessings to one nation, the Jewish people."[29] As it says in Romans 9:4–5: "Who are Israelites, to whom pertain the adoption, the glory, the covenants, the giving of the law, the service of God, and the promises; of whom are the fathers and from whom, according to the flesh, Christ came, who is over all, the eternally blessed God. Amen."[30]

Prince says Revelation 5:5 shows a remarkable fact: "But one of the elders said to me, 'Do not weep. Behold, the Lion of the tribe of Judah, the Root of David, has prevailed to open the scroll and to loose its seven seals.'" He expounded, "I want to point out to you that the identification of Jesus to the Jewish people was not temporary. It was not just for the few years of His earthly life and ministry but it was eternal. Many years later in Heaven, after His Resurrection and Ascension, He is still called the Lion of the Tribe of Judah. Not only was He a Jew, He's still a Jew. To me that's breathtaking. That's astounding. You see we need to remember there's a Lion up there and He's a Jew and one day that Lion will roar."[31]

But despite the spiritual, technological, and material contributions by the Jewish people and the state of Israel and the world, many nations clamor for a Middle East devoid of a Jewish presence. The legitimacy of the only democracy in the Middle East still stands in the docket of the world's court of public opinion. But long ago and far away from the dawn of the twenty-first century, twentieth-century leaders staked out the legal rights for Israel and Jerusalem. That story is part of Israel's forgotten history.

9 SAN REMO: JERUSALEM'S FORGOTTEN HISTORY

Because if the agenda is to divide up the land and if the agenda is to internationalize Jerusalem, this goes completely contrary to what was pledged here ninety years ago.[1]
—TOMAS SANDELL, EUROPEAN COALITION FOR ISRAEL

DATELINE: SAN REMO, THE ITALIAN RIVIERA

"WOULD YOU COME TO SAN REMO AND COVER THIS EVENT NEXT month?"

San Remo? I thought, *That's on the Italian Riviera, isn't it?* Sounded a bit extravagant. Certainly didn't seem like a hardship assignment. I wrestled over the invitation. Should I go? What about the expense? There're always pressing things to do here in Israel. It's not easy to get to San Remo. You have to fly into Nice, France, rent a car, and drive to San Remo. Why was this anniversary so important anyway? Then factor in Iceland's Eyjafjallajökull volcanic eruption in April 2010 that grounded or disrupted most air traffic in and out of Europe for days, and the trip seemed unlikely. But after a few days of deliberation, discussion, and prayer, we made the call. Okay, let's go.

The invitation came from Tomas Sandell from the European Coalition for Israel. They planned a ceremony marking the ninetieth anniversary of the signing of the San Remo resolution. But what was it about San Remo that was so intriguing? And what was the significance about a villa overlooking the Mediterranean in one of the world's playgrounds? I knew enough to know I didn't know enough. That helped prod me to go. I went, however, not fully comprehending or appreciating the import of San Remo.

Sandell explained to me San Remo was where Israel got its legitimacy under international law. For years, I've heard Palestinian spokespeople use the terms *occupied territories* and *illegal settlements*. They tossed around the word *settler* with a pejorative, kind of "dirty" connotation. Jews living in the "occupied territories" or the "West Bank" violated "international law." They cited UN Resolutions 181 and 242. Palestinian poetry, editorials, and schoolbooks claim the Jews stole their land.[2] They used these mantras like a cudgel to bludgeon any opposing argument. Said over and over, it took on a profound, near-universal legitimacy. The psychological impact was significant. The world believed, and the press for the most part agreed. Of course the West Bank was "occupied territory" and the Jews didn't belong. "Everybody knows that."

But did they?

For years, I've wrestled with those terms. To me, it felt like being in an argument when you believe you're right but don't know exactly why or how to defend your point of view. It reminded me of a shopkeeper who one time in Jerusalem's Old City invited me into his shop. I said no. But he retorted, "But you promised the last time you would come in." His line dazed me. *Did I?* I thought to myself. I didn't think I did, but maybe I did. I couldn't remember. Because I didn't remember I went into his shop. The next time he gave me the same line, however, I knew I'd been "had."

I felt there must be some legitimacy more than their biblical attachment—as profound and sacred as that is—to the Jews living in the West Bank, what they call by their biblical names Judea and Samaria. I wondered, did time hide a deeper law, one slid into the folds of history's files; one that explained a different side of the story? Could there be a secret? What if a sleuth could find the answer to this question? How would Charlie Chan, Nancy Drew, or the Hardy Boys investigate this? But this wasn't fiction; this was serious, and this was history.

The answer to these questions holds the key to the biggest prize of all: Jerusalem. Who really "owns" Jerusalem and who had the legal rights to the city and the ancient Old City itself? What about the so-called West Bank? These questions penetrate the heart of the controversy surrounding the Israeli-Palestinian conflict. They're pregnant with global implications.

For example, when a Jewish developer wanted to build a hotel on land he acquired in East Jerusalem, it created an international crisis. When Vice President Joe Biden visited Jerusalem and a local zoning board approved hundreds of apartments in a contested part of the city, it sparked a major diplomatic fallout between the United States and Israel. The fallout arose because US policy does not recognize Jerusalem as the capital of the Jewish state and opposes Israel establishing "facts on the ground" like building or expanding neighborhoods in contested "East Jerusalem." Israel, however, maintains Jerusalem is their capital and affirms their right to build anywhere in the city. The zoning board's decision exposed this deep diplomatic divide.

Conventional wisdom about the struggle rests on a few widely accepted dogmas. One of them says the West Bank is "occupied territory," including East Jerusalem. Another dogma insists the Palestinians, not Israelis, have a historic right to the land of Palestine. The Jews constitute usurpers or European colonists while the Palestinians settled the land since "time immemorial." Therefore, many consider the Jewish settlements in the West Bank illegitimate, if not illegal. World leaders from the UN secretary general, the European Union foreign affairs chief, and the US secretary of state often claim the settlements are an "obstacle to peace." Journalists from around the world usually echo this "truth."

But there's a deeper history behind the land, a history that started long ago and far away. That's what we began to find out in San Remo.

THE CITY OF FLOWERS

San Remo sits on the Italian Riviera coast and is called the City of Flowers. Tourists flock to this picturesque town perched over a crystal Mediterranean. Because of its beauty, for years the rich and famous came here, including Czar Nicolas II of Russia and Alfred Nobel, the inventor of dynamite and the man behind the Nobel prizes. Today many still migrate annually to this jewel, but nearly one hundred years ago, the great statesmen of their era congregated in San Remo. Those political giants included David Lloyd George, Great Britain's prime minister. They came in 1920 in the aftermath of World War I and decided nothing less than the future and fate of the Middle East.

For four hundred years, the Ottoman Empire ruled an empire that at one time stretched from the gates of Vienna to the tip of the Arabian Peninsula. But during World War I, the Allied powers vanquished the Ottoman Empire. Now the European victors met to divide up one of history's largest empires.

From April 18 to 26, 1920, the representatives of Great Britain, France, Italy, and Japan, along with the United States as an observer, met at the Villa Devachan in San Remo. They debated the various claims throughout the former Ottoman Empire, and on April 25, 1920, they signed the San Remo resolution. The significance of this document is hard to underestimate. It created the Middle East we know today.

But this history that seemed lost is being revived.

Ninety years to the day after the signing of the San Remo Resolution and in the very same Villa Devachan, representatives from many of those same nations that signed the original resolution gathered to commemorate this historic document. CBN News came to document the gathering and report on the significance of this resolution.

The European Coalition for Israel hosted the commemoration. Its president, Tomas Sandell, explained the reason for the gathering: "At a time when even the core existence of Israel as a Jewish state is being challenged by its enemies it is of vital importance that we take a closer look at international law. The purpose is simply to go back in history and to show to the Christians and to Europeans in general what already happened 90 years ago in San Remo."[3]

We sat down with Sandell for an interview just a few feet away from where the representatives of the Supreme Council signed the resolution.

> On the 25th of April 1920 you had the Allied powers, the supreme council of the Allied powers, meeting in this very place, for the first time in international law incorporating the Balfour Declaration. So as Chaim Weizman said at the time, you can say that the Israeli state was born on the 25th of April in San Remo because that was the significance of it. . . . It was agreed here in San Remo that there is a historical, religious, and cultural connection and continuity between the people and the land, the Jewish people and the land of Israel. So this was the basis for granting the Jewish state.[4]

SOVEREIGNTY OVER THE OLD CITY OF JERUSALEM

Sandell and various representatives—including a Knesset member from Israel—commemorated the landmark signing of the San Remo resolution. But Iceland's volcano prevented one world-class legal expert from attending. Two years later, however, we met Dr. Jacques Gautier from Canada. Gautier produced a landmark document called "Sovereignty over the Old City of Jerusalem." It's a mammoth work.

It is thirteen hundred pages long with thirty-two hundred footnotes and weighs about ten pounds! Gautier spent more than twenty-five years researching the subject through the Graduate Institute of International Studies in Geneva. He's arguably one of the world's leading experts—if not the leading expert—on this topic. Gautier came to Jerusalem in 2012 to sponsor a conference on this issue and present his work to Jerusalem mayor Nir Barkat. Behind Jerusalem's landmark hotel, the King David, we sat down with Gautier and discussed the conclusions to his quarter century of research.

He knows to get the conclusion right you have to get the history right.

He said the history behind San Remo began in the late nineteenth century when Theodore Herzl first wrote his book *The Jewish State* in 1896. Herzl later conferred the Basel Conference in 1897. These twin actions unified the global Jewish movement of its day and established modern Zionism, the dream of the return of the Jews to their former homeland. After the death of Herzl, Chaim Weizmann championed the Zionist cause and helped lobby for Great Britain's Balfour Declaration of 1917. That declaration said in part:

> His Majesty's Government view with favour the establishment in Palestine of a national home for the Jewish people, and will use their best endeavours to facilitate the achievement of this object, it being clearly understood that nothing shall be done which may prejudice the civil and religious rights of existing non-Jewish communities in Palestine, or the rights and political status enjoyed by Jews in any other country.[5]

The Balfour Declaration written by British foreign secretary James Balfour was a landmark political document. For the first time, a major power publicly declared its support for a Jewish "national home" in Palestine. While the Balfour Declaration committed Britain to a solemn pledge to help the Jewish people establish a national homeland, it did not carry the weight of international law. Britain released the 1917 declaration during World War I, the "war to end all wars." That conflict embroiled not only the European powers but the Middle East too.

When the war ended, the victorious nations met in Paris for the 1919 Peace Conference. Gautier sees that conference as a defining moment in history:

> This is the time, this is the place on the one hand the Jewish people, the Zionist organization led by Weizmann presented the political claim, like a statement of claim in a court of law. They said this is what we

want recognized. They wanted recognition of the Jewish people as a people in international law. They wanted recognition of their historic connection to the land then known as Palestine. And they wanted, and this is crucial, the right to reconstitute what they used to have.[6]

The word *reconstitute* denotes Israel's prior connection to the land. It's a crucial point because some claim Israel is a twentieth-century interloper whose "right" to the land is based purely on the pity of the nations following the Holocaust.

Winston Churchill not only endorsed the Balfour Declaration but agreed history had tethered the Jews to the land of Palestine. On March 28, 1921, he stated, "It is manifestly right that the Jews who are scattered all over the world should have a national centre and a national home where some of them may be reunited. And where else could that be but in the land of Palestine, with which for more than 3000 years they have been intimately and profoundly associated?"[7]

During that conference the Arabs—through Faisal Hussein—also presented their claims. "They were seeking legal standing as well and asking for recognition of their right to establish an independent Arab state." The Arabs and Jews presented these two political claims to the Supreme Council of the Principal Allied Powers, the United States, the United Kingdom, France, Italy, and Japan. Gautier said their role was pivotal since they held legal authority. "These five nations . . . had the legal power of disposition. They're the key victorious nations and they have legal title by way of peace treaties and they can turn around and give it to others. You can't give rights to others unless you have the right to give them territorial sovereignty."[8]

But how did those nations decide to transfer that sovereignty? One of the cornerstones for both Jewish and Arab claims rested on Article 22 of the Covenant of the League of Nations. Since the war obliterated the Ottoman Empire, the League adopted a mandate system to put those lands and peoples under the tutelage of more advanced nations. You could think of it like the "big brothers" of the world helping their "little brothers" until they grew up and started life on their own. Article 22 of the Covenant put it this way:

> To those colonies and territories which as a consequence of the late war have ceased to be under the sovereignty of the States which for-merly governed them and which are inhabited by peoples not yet able to stand by themselves under the strenuous conditions of the modern world, there should be applied the principle that the well-being and development of such peoples *form a sacred trust of civilization.* . . . The best method of giving practical effect to this principle is that the tute-lage of such peoples should be entrusted to advanced nations . . . as Mandatories on behalf of the League.[9]

The mandate system entrusted the major powers to oversee their "little brothers." The 1919 Paris Conference ended, however, without addressing the claims of the Jews or Arabs. Those claims waited until the next year and the Italian Riviera.

SAN REMO: THE TURNING POINT

That's where San Remo comes in. Representatives of the Great Powers listened to the claims of the Jews and the claims of the Arabs for several days in the City of Flowers. Their final answer? They said yes to both.

First they declared the Jews could reconstitute what they used to have in that land. Then they also allowed the Arabs to establish new states in that part of the world. "So this is the turning point," Gautier exclaimed. Chaim Weizmann himself declared, "This is the most momentous political event in the whole history of our [Zionist] movement, and it is perhaps, no exaggeration to say in the whole history of our people since the Exile. [The San Remo Resolution] crowns the British [Balfour] dec-laration by enacting it as part of the law of nations on the world."[10]

The San Remo Resolution codified into international law the Balfour Declaration of 1917. While the Balfour Declaration carried political weight, now the San Remo resolution carried the clout of international law with profound implications. One British diplomat—Lord Curzon—called the San Remo Resolution Israel's "Magna Carta." Those original signers faded long ago, but their decisions made history. Now for the first time in nearly two thousand years they called for the establishment—with the force of international law—of a Jewish homeland in the area called Palestine.

Both France and Great Britain undertook the mandates, this "sacred trust of civilization" Article 22 stipulated. They accepted three separate mandates for the Middle East. France would oversee the Syrian (and later Lebanon) mandates while Great Britain would oversee the mandates of Iraq and Palestine. The mandate originally included territory on both sides of the Jordan River. To settle a dispute between the French and British, however, Winston Churchill at the Cairo Conference in 1921 gave Transjordan to Faisal Hussein. This decision eliminated more than three-quarters of the territory originally given to the Jewish homeland and created one more Arab state in the region.

Under its mandate for Palestine, Great Britain was given certain charges. One of them was article 6, and in light of today's debate, it's a stunning paragraph. It says, "The Administration of Palestine, while ensuring that the rights and position of other sections of the population are not prejudiced, shall facilitate Jewish immigration under suitable conditions and *shall encourage, in co-operation with the Jewish agency referred to in Article 4, close settlement by Jews on the land*, including State lands and waste lands not required for public purposes."[11]

Article 6 therefore commands the British government to encourage "settlement" on the land of Palestine from the Mediterranean to the Jordan, including the West Bank. This legal right of Jews to build in the West Bank or Jerusalem is little known or understood in the world today. Eli Hertz of www.MythsAndFacts.org told us in San Remo, "Again the legal document of the mandate for Palestine and [it] clearly says that not only the Jews have the right to settlement [but] that the world has the obligation to help them to settle."[12]

This raises the question of the "occupied territories" and who's occupying whose land. If the region of Palestine was given to the Jews, then how can they "occupy" someone else's land?

The San Remo Resolution went on to be internationally recognized. On July 24, 1922, fifty-one nations of the League of Nations ratified it with this key clause: "Whereas recognition has been given to the historical connection of the Jewish people with Palestine and to the grounds for reconstituting their national home in that country."[13]

Six days later, both US Houses of Congress unanimously endorsed the "Mandate for Palestine":

> *Resolved by the Senate and House of Representatives of the United States of America in Congress assembled.* That the United States of America favors the establishment in Palestine of a national home for the Jewish people, it being clearly understood that nothing shall be done which should prejudice the civil and religious right of Christian and all other non-Jewish communities in Palestine, and that the holy places and religious buildings and sites in Palestine shall be adequately protected.[14]

Yet two crucial questions remain. One of them is, what about the rights of the Arabs? Isn't there a powerful argument for the Palestinians since, after all, the land is called Palestine? Cynthia Wallace, in her work "Foundations of the International Legal Rights of the Jewish People and the State of Israel," wrote:

> In actual fact, the land called "Palestine" covers territory that the Jews have called the "Holy Land" well before the name "Palestine" was first used by the Greeks and Romans. In a word, the territory known as "Palestine" has never—either since this name has been applied before—been an Arab nation or been designated to be an Arab nation. But this nomenclature carries great psychological impact with the inference that is the former Arab inhabitants of Palestine that are true "Palestinians," that they belong in "Palestine" and that

they have been displaced from territory that was their ancestral heritage, rather than that of the Jewish "Palestinians" who in actual fact had no other "home."[15]

Palestine then defines a geographical area, not a culture or people. *Palestine* was a term used by the Romans. In fact, before the establishment of the state of Israel, Jews were called Palestinians. For example, the Jewish newspaper the *Jerusalem Post* used to be called the *Palestine Post*.

While the mandate applied to Jews living in the region in Palestine, the Arabs got the lion's share of the Middle East and most of the political rights throughout the former Ottoman Empire. Howard Grief, the author of *Legal Foundation and Borders of Israel under International Law*, said:

I mean they got Syria which was subsequently divided between Syria and Lebanon. They got all of Mesopotamia and all of Arabia. This is what Balfour himself said. He said, "Why are you complaining? You are getting all these lands and we're granting a niche—he called it a niche—to the Jewish people who were going to get Palestine. . . . In the mandate itself, there are no national and political rights granted to the local Arabs or the Arabs of Palestine. All national and political rights were granted to the Jewish people exclusively.[16]

That is, exclusive legal and political rights in Palestine went to the Jews while those rights in the rest of the Middle East went to the Arabs.

Yet another question remains. Despite this international recognition, what about future decisions—decades later—by either the United Nations General Assembly or the Security Council? Don't they supersede the San Remo resolution? How about UN General Assembly Resolution 181, the 1947 Partition Plan, or the UN Security Resolution 242 in 1967? Gautier contended Article 80 of the UN Charter effectively and specifically enshrines all previous obligations by the League of Nations. It states: "Nothing in this Chapter [Chapter XII] shall be construed in or of itself to alter in any manner the rights whatsoever of any states or any peoples or the terms of existing international instruments to which Members of the United Nations may respectively be parties."[17]

He concluded, "My work has led me to the conclusion that nothing happened since to take away the fundamental legal rights given to the Jewish people or Arab people in San Remo."[18]

Another scholar, Cynthia Wallace, agreed: "The rights thereby granted to the Jewish people . . . were aimed at the establishment of a Jewish national home throughout Palestine. These rights have never been rescinded."[19]

THE FIGHT FOR JERUSALEM

But what about Jerusalem itself? Gautier concluded:

> In fact rights have been granted to the Jewish people in respect to Jerusalem; that they're entitled to have sovereignty here. Then it's no longer appropriate to call them trespassers. It's no longer appropriate to say that they're wrongfully there, that they're thieves, that they've taken somebody else's land. If they are there as a right, then they should be treated properly as others who have been able to enjoy the rights that were granted to them in the same conferences and the same circumstances that I've referred to. So the fact that they are entitled to be in Jerusalem and all of Jerusalem under international law is very, very relevant in the political process.[20]

Yet this history of San Remo seems to have been lost in the political debate. Why?

Sandel believes that "there are people; there are powers who do not want this to be commonly known. Because if the agenda is to divide up the land and if the agenda is to internationalize Jerusalem, this goes completely contrary to what was pledged here ninety years ago. And we feel that we have a historical duty to just bring the facts on the table.

Because we are here dealing with historical facts and this should be known and this should be taken into consideration in the public debate."

He says when people hear this information, "It's like people are waking up from a slumber. They say, wow, that's very interesting." Some call it revolutionary. "This is revolutionary. It just means that something that has somehow been hidden for so many years is coming into the light. . . . I hope that the legal arguments which were made ninety years ago and which by now are deeply forgotten in the public debate even among Christians and supporters of a modern Israeli state would come into the light again and "people can see that there's a very clear, legal argument which can be made and which will really support Israel's biblical borders."[21]

Sandell, Gautier, and others believe these legal facts are significant because the legitimacy of the Jewish state is under assault. It's accused of being a usurper, a Western colonist entity, who simply by virtue of the horror of the Holocaust and the pity of the world gave them a stake in the Middle East. But the San Remo Resolution marks the time in international law, with the weight of more than fifty nations, that the Jewish people gaind a right to reconstitute their homeland in Palestine.

Yet the fight over Jerusalem will go on. The political process continues, and undoubtedly the fate of Jerusalem will remain on the world's political docket. The Palestinian Authority keeps insisting on the establishment of a Palestinian state with Jerusalem as its capital while its president, Mahmoud Abbas, questions the Jewish nature of Jerusalem.

Sandell believes beyond the political debate there are profound spiritual implications at stake for the nations of the world. The Bible says the Lord Himself will judge the nations "for dividing up His Land." That's why the message of San Remo is so important, why the nations need to know that the League of Nations recognized and granted Israel's historic claim to its former homeland. It's important because the legitimacy of Israel is an open question in the eyes of a significant part of the world.

The Bible speaks of a day when the nations of the world will gather around Jerusalem and that the city itself will become "a burdensome stone." The battle over Jerusalem will be the last, final, and great battle of history. In the meantime, the nations of the world are "in the valley of decision" over Jerusalem. How they decide may well determine the fate and future of their own nations.

10 PALESTINE: FACT AND FICTION

The victory march will continue until the Palestinian flag flies in Jerusalem and in all of Palestine.[1]
—PALESTINIAN LEADER YASSER ARAFAT

DATELINE: RAMALLAH

WHAT DID YOU THINK OF YASSER ARAFAT?

Arch-terrorist? Palestinian leader? Nobel Prize winner? Regardless of your opinion, Arafat played a major role in the Middle East for decades. From the time he first splashed on the cover of *Time* in December 1968, he dominated headlines and captured the attention of the world until his death in Paris on November 11, 2004. In fact, the day after he died—November 12—the world's media, including *Time*, showed up for his funeral in Ramallah. In the history of the Middle East, that day marked an important turning point. Why? It signaled the end of one era in the Israeli-Palestinian conflict and the beginning of another throughout the region and perhaps the world.

On that autumn day, we got a bird's-eye view of Arafat's funeral. For those who got to see it firsthand, the sight stamped an indelible memory. I went to the funeral to broadcast a live satellite transmission for the *700 Club*. Early that Friday afternoon, a colleague and I grabbed a taxi in Jerusalem and began the thirty-minute drive to Ramallah. The bright, warm, nearly cloudless day gave no hint of the spectacle about to unfold. We crossed the Israeli Army checkpoint separating Israel and the Palestinian-controlled city. Israeli guards insisted we sign waivers. If anything happened to us, they wouldn't be responsible.

As we drove through Ramallah, the neighborhoods crackled with an eerie silence. Streets normally filled with people stood silent and deserted. I had never seen Ramallah like this. Our destination? Arafat's compound called the Mukata. It once served as his headquarters; now it would serve as his cemetery. By this time of the day, nearly everyone in Ramallah had already flocked to the Mukata. As we drove closer, cars flooded the area. Finally, they clogged the roads so much we abandoned our taxi and continued on foot.

As we neared, the noise swelled. It was the kind of sound you hear when you're late for a football, baseball, or soccer game. As you get closer to the stadium, the roar of the crowd grows.

We finally reached the site of our satellite live shot, a three-story building just across the street from Arafat's compound. We climbed the stairs and walked out onto the roof. The view stunned me. Spread out before us stood thousands of people. They filled nearly every spot in sight to watch Arafat's return. They sat on rooftops, on walls, and in trees. One man perched himself on top of a light pole. They came to see history, mark the end of an era, and say good-bye to the only leader most Palestinian Arabs had ever known.

The world's media circled the compound. Every major media outlet —BBC, Fox, CNN, and dozens more—staked out rooftops and balconies ensuring the world would witness this landmark event. Earlier in the day, Egypt gave Arafat a state funeral in Cairo as his body made the trek from Paris to the West Bank. Now, Egyptian helicopters flew his body and entourage back to Ramallah.

Everybody anticipated Arafat's arrival. When the throng first caught sight of the Egyptian helicopters, they swelled with emotion. Whistles, shouts, shootings, and cheers rang out. The helicopters made a long, slow descent and flew just one hundred feet over our rooftop location. Landing in the compound, they stirred up a cloud of dust and the crowd into an even greater frenzy. When the dust settled and the helicopter blades stopped, Palestinian security forces tried in vain to maintain order and keep the crowd back. Instead, they swarmed the helicopters. Saeb Erekat, a longtime confidante of Arafat and the Palestinian's chief negotiator, opened the helicopter door. He tried to persuade the crowd to get back. They ignored him. Their size overwhelmed the outmanned (and apparently outgunned) security force that fired automatic weapons into the air to no avail. Pandemonium.

The sound of gunfire filled the air. Masked gunmen walked up and down the street toting automatic weapons. Inside the compound others shot in the air. Even uniformed police fired either to control the crowd or to celebrate. We didn't know which. Other gunmen—unseen from our view—fired incessantly. One sounded like the staccato burr of a heavy machine gun. The sounds reverberated above the melee. Running through my mind was the simple knowledge that "whatever goes up must come down." Every so often I put my hand on my head in a feeble attempt to stop one of those bullets. Later we heard falling bullets injured several people.

The frenzy reached its peak when Arafat's coffin disgorged from the helicopter. The crowd took over. They wrenched control of the coffin. Now it rode on a sea of humanity that took on a life of its own. Thousands wanted to touch the coffin, the flag, or the body. The crowd stirred up plumes of dust. The afternoon sun glistening through that dust painted a golden, surreal, and riveting scene. The coffin made its frenzied way around the compound and finally arrived at Arafat's grave. Given the mood of the crowd, officials seemed to bury him as fast as they could.

They buried a man one commentator called "a terrorist with a good public relations campaign." Another called him the "most dangerous man to the state of Israel." Yet, paradoxically, he received the red carpet treatment in Europe and was feted throughout the world. The Western media often lionized the man; watching some of their coverage, one might have thought Mother Teresa was being laid to rest instead of the father of modern terrorism. In fact, when Arafat left his compound a few weeks earlier, a BBC reporter wept.[2]

How do you explain the disparity? In part, the explanation lay in the fact that Arafat could simultaneously call for "the peace of the brave" in English and then call for "a million *shahids* [martyrs] to march to Jerusalem" in Arabic. Arafat, one Israeli politician told us, had a rare genius for this sophisticated, deceptive evil as he strove to implement his phased plan for the destruction of Israel. George Tenet, the former CIA director who spent time negotiating with Arafat, wrote in his memoir that "almost always, that last impenetrable barrier to peace had the same name: Arafat."[3]

When Arafat's body finally sunk beneath the earth, the crowd's emotional fervor subsided. They began to thin out. The gunfire died down. Many began to head home to break the fast of the Muslim holiday of Ramadan and leave behind the body and legacy of the man who profoundly influenced their lives. Saying good-bye to Arafat's body took a few frenzied hours, but saying good-bye to his legacy would take longer. Yet it seemed clear the throng and the world witnessed the end of an era and the beginning of another.

THE "ROAD MAP" OR THE ROAD TO JIHAD

Yasser Arafat's funeral marked one of the most incredible spectacles I'd ever witnessed. But life and history marched on.

Mahmoud Abbas carried Arafat's immediate legacy for Palestinians. Abbas—also known as Abu Mazen—functioned as Arafat's right-hand man for decades. At the insistence of the United States, he had served as prime minister since 2003. When new elections were held after Arafat's demise, he ran for president and won.

On January 15, 2005, Abbas took the oath of office as the new president of the Palestinian Authority. The Quartet—a combination of the United States, the European Union, the United Nations, and Russia—charged him with implementing the Palestinian requirements of what became known as the "Road Map" peace plan, officially known as "A Performance-Based Roadmap to a Permanent Two-State Solution to the Israeli-Palestinian Conflict." The US State Department had released that document nearly two years before on April 30, 2003.

What did this mean for Abbas? His first charge meant he had to "declare an unequivocal end to violence and terrorism and undertake visible efforts on the ground to arrest, disrupt, and restrain individuals and groups conducting and planning violent attacks on Israelis anywhere."[4] Simply put, they wanted Abbas to disarm and dismantle all Palestinian terror groups. Clear enough, but for the next year, Abbas not only refused to disarm those terror groups, he tried to incorporate them into his government.

Following is an example of what he did to undermine the "peace process."

It's Friday. The call of the muezzin draws thousands of Palestinian Muslims for prayer. A human stream cascades down the steps of the Damascus Gate. They pass stalls filled with the pungent smell of spices, fruits, and vegetables. They file through the gritty cobblestone streets—streets that echo with the memories of the Muslim heroes Saladin and Suleiman the Magnificent. You ascend with this human wave up to the place known to Muslims as the Harem al-Sharif or "Noble Sanctuary." Jews know it as the Temple Mount, the site of the first and second temples. Now it's the most contested piece of land on earth. The crowds come to pray. They come to listen. What kind of sermon do they hear? Who is persuading the hearts and minds of these Muslim worshippers?

Sheik Ibrahim Mudeiris, an employee of the Palestinian Authority (PA), preached this message broadcast on PA television:

We have ruled the world before, and by Allah, the day will come when we will rule the entire world again. The day will come when we will rule America. The day will come when we will rule Britain and the entire world—except for the Jews. The Jews will not enjoy a life of tranquility under our rule, because they are treacherous by nature, as they have been throughout history. The day will come when everything will be relieved of the Jews—even the stones and trees which were harmed by them. Listen to the Prophet Muhammad, who tells you about the evil end that awaits Jews. The stones and trees will want the Muslims to finish off every Jew.[5]

Mudeiris echoes the same ideology other Islamic sheiks do from Damascus to Cairo. This sermon is an example of an often ignored and seldom reported dynamic fueling the Israeli-Palestinian conflict, messages that proclaim Muslims will kill the Jews and rule the world. The stumbling stone to today's Middle East "peace process."

DECEPTION

Sheik Mudeiris works for the Palestinian Authority, the entity the United States and many nations say is a peace partner with Israel. But are they a real "partner for peace"? Itamar Marcus of the Palestinian Media Watch believes the partnership is a deception. He documented the official media of the Palestinian Authority in a three-hundred-page book called *Deception: Betraying the Peace Process.*

Marcus often seems like a voice crying in the wilderness, and his reports reveal a side of the conflict seldom reported. In their own words, statements, public announcements, and propaganda, the PA tells its people what they believe about the conflict. Marcus says the PA gives two messages: one in English meant to reach the media and negotiators and an Arabic message to their own people. "Often there is no resemblance between those two messages and that's what this book documents. This is the internal Palestinian world. This is what they don't want everybody to know. This is what they don't want everybody to hear."[6]

Sheik Mudeiris is one example. The PA's official mufti, Muhammad Hussein, is another. He quoted from the same Islamic Hadith as Mudeiris during an official PA rally. Here's the transcript of his introduction and speech:

> Our war with the descendants of the apes and pigs [i.e. Jews] is a war of religion and faith. Long live Fatah! (I invite you,) our honorable Sheikh. (PA Mufti Muhammad Hussein comes to the podium and says:) "47 years ago, the (Fatah) revolution started. Which revolution? The modern revolution of the Palestinian people's history. In fact, Palestine in its entirety is a revolution, since (Caliph) Umar came (to conquer Jerusalem, 637 CE), and continuing today, and until the End of Days. The reliable Hadith (tradition attributed to Muhammad), (found) in the two reliable collections, Bukhari and Muslim says: 'The Hour (of Resurrection) will not come until you fight the Jews. The Jew will hide behind stones or trees. Then the trees will call: 'Oh Muslim, servant of Allah, there is a Jew behind me, come and kill him. Except the Gharqad tree (which will keep silent)." Therefore it is no wonder that you see Gharqad (trees) surrounding the (Israeli) settlements and colonies.[7]

When news of his speech went public, Hussein protested his comments were taken out of context. But Marcus said Hussein was "basically saying that one of the conditions for the redemption for humanity is the killing of Jews by Muslims . . . this is not an isolated message." In *Deception*, Marcus notes several ways the PA media undermines the "peace process."[8]

One of the PA's messages is that the whole of Israel, not just the West Bank, is Palestine. For example, a PA-produced documentary shows that Acco, the Sea of Galilee, Haifa, and Jaffa are Palestinian lands, all currently part of modern-day Israel. This message buttresses the Islamic belief that land once under the control of Islam can never be relinquished to the "infidel." This belief puts Muslims under a religious obligation to win back that land. The fact that Jews hold sway in Palestine makes the affront that much more injurious. With this kind of indoctrination, Marcus despairs of a true peace between Israelis and Palestinians. When the PA raises a whole new generation of Palestinian children with the idea Jews stole their land, that all of Israel is theirs, and they have a religious obligation to take back the land, peace will be virtually impossible to achieve.

Marcus says, "It's part of the great deception. To the world they say it's a territorial war. To their own people they say it's a religious war for Allah. If it's a territorial war, you can compromise on territory. But if it's a religious war, you're prohibited from compromising."[9] And if there are no consequences or change within the PA, Marcus believes peace will remain elusive. "If that doesn't happen, there is no peace process, even if they're meeting in Jordan or meeting any place else, it's not a real peace process. As our book title says, it's just a deception process."[10]

The land that persists contentious between Israel and the Palestinian Authority remains Jerusalem. The rhetorical battle lines are intensifying over the fate of the capital of a future Palestinian state or Israel's "undivided and eternal capital." Yasser Arafat once proclaimed, "The victory march will continue until the Palestinian flag flies in Jerusalem and all of Palestine."[11] His protégé, Mahmoud Abbas, reaffirmed his mentor's dream: "There will be no peace, security or stability unless the [Israel] occupation, its settlements and settlers will be evicted from our holy city and the eternal capital of our state."[12]

Abbas also accused Israel of "Judaizing" Jerusalem: "[Israel's] purpose is to achieve its black goals: Destroying the Al-Aqsa Mosque, building the 'alleged Temple,' taking over the Muslim and Christian holy sites, and destroying its [Jerusalem's] institutions in order to empty it, uproot its residents, and continue its occupation and Judaization." Abbas's statement also said that all of Israel's archeological digs and tunnels "will not change the reality of the city . . . and will not create a [Jewish] right based on fantasy and legends."[13]

Despite a mother lode of archeological discoveries documenting the Jewish history of Jerusalem, Abbas continues to dismiss the evidence. The PMW reported Abbas and other PA leaders referred to the "alleged" Jewish temple nearly one hundred times in 2011 and 2012. The temple denials set up the ultimate showdown. Two sides are advancing toward a seemingly inevitable confrontation. That's when Jerusalem and the Temple Mount itself will be the most volatile issue of all.

That confrontation seemed to draw closer when on November 29, 2012, the U.N. General Assembly voted overwhelmingly—138 in favor to 9 against (Canada, Czech Republic, Israel, Marshall Islands, Micronesia [Federated States of], Nauru, Panama, Palau, United States), with 41 abstentions—to grant Palestine non-Member Observer State status. The vote fell symbolically sixty-five years to the day after the U.N. recognized Israel. Abbas called on the General Assembly to "issue a birth certificate of the reality of the State of Palestine."[14]

He also said, "We will accept no less than the independence of the State of Palestine, with East Jerusalem as its capital."[15]

DATELINE: THE GAZA BORDER, NOVEMBER 15, 2012

By 7:00 a.m. we arrived. About a dozen still photographers and one camera crew already scanned Gaza City for the latest rocket launch. We didn't have to wait long for another. Soon a plume of smoke streaked across the sky. Soon there were more—sometimes two or three at a time—rockets on their way to southern Israeli towns like Ashkelon, Ashdod, or Beersheva. It was another war just like Operation Cast Lead in 2008–2009. This war called Operation Pillar of Defense was Israel's latest attempt to stop the incessant rocket fire that put more than a million Israelis under the shadow of death. The numbers told a numbing story. Since 2005, Israelis endured more than eight thousand rockets fired by Hamas and other terror groups. Some openly wondered what other nation on earth would endure such a reign of terror? But it wasn't supposed to be this way. Israel withdrew entirely from the Gaza Strip in

2005 and evicted nearly ten thousand Jews with the promise of peace. The promise proved elusive.

We watched this unfolding battle feeling as if we were sitting in the front row of a shooting gallery. Gaza City lay just more than a mile over several rolling hills. The rockets streaked past and then up above and we could see other skinny streaks in the sky followed by little puffs of smoke and then the sound of booms. Israeli sirens wailed in the background. The skinny streaks and puffs of smoke were Israel's Iron Dome at work. The ingenious antimissile system could trail Hamas-fired rockets and knock them out of the sky. Few had ever seen such a technological marvel in action. It worked magnificently.

The war officially began on November 14 when Israel targeted Ahmed Jabari, the Hamas mastermind behind its rocket campaign. But in reality, the war represented only the outward manifestation of Hamas's longstanding commitment to kill Jews and destroy Israel. For example, in article seven of its charter, it says: "The Hamas has been looking forward to implement Allah's promise whatever time it might take. The prophet, prayer and peace be upon him, said: 'The time will not come until Muslims will fight the Jews (and kill them); until the Jews hide behind rocks and trees, which will cry: O Muslim! there is a Jew hiding behind me, come on and kill him!'"[16]

While the Iron Dome proved an amazing response to Hamas's rocket barrage, some rockets did get through. We saw the tragic result later that morning when three Israelis were killed in the town of Kyriat Milachi. They died when they didn't leave their apartment after the air raid siren. Yet throughout the course of the eight-day war the Iron Dome shot down more than 80 percent of the rockets fired from the Gaza Strip.

Within the first few minutes of the war, they succeeded in eliminating most of Hamas's long-range rockets. For the next eight days they hit fifteen hundred targets—Hamas infrastructure, smuggling tunnels, and ammunition caches. They flew hundreds of sorties over Gaza and dropped thousands of laser-guided bombs but with relatively few casualties. Tragically, some innocent Gazans died, but Israel made enormous efforts to minimize civilian casualties. They dropped thousands of leaflets pleading with Gazans to get out of harm's way. They sent thousands of text messages conveying the same warning and even called people directly by phone.

At the end of the war and with the truce just hours away, we talked with Don Gordon, an IDF spokesman when war breaks out and a Hollywood screenwriter in his other life. He said Operation Pillar of Defense incurred "the least loss of civilian life in any conflict in modern history . . . there is no country on the face of the earth that does more to minimize civilian casualties than Israel does to the degree that we endanger (our) own soldiers."[17]

He summed up the battle in simple terms: "Convince Hamas to stop trying to kill us. That's all they have to do. The old saying is, and it's true unfortunately, if Hamas would lay down their weapons, there'd be peace. If we were to lay down our weapons, we'd be dead."[18]

The war ended just hours after our interview with Gordon. Regardless of the outcome, Hamas declared victory. The climax came when Khaled Meshal, the political leader of Hamas, came to the Gaza Strip a few weeks later after an absence of more than forty years. A massive crowd of nearly half a million Gazans came to hear him speak. He rallied the crowd with his vision of Palestine:

First of all, Palestine—from the [Jordan] River to the [Mediterranean] Sea, from its north to its south—is our land, our right, and our homeland. There will be no relinquishing or forsaking even an inch or small part of it . . . since Palestine belongs to us, and is the land of Arabism and Islam, we must never recognize the legitimacy of the Israeli occupation of it. The occupation is illegitimate, and therefore, Israel is illegitimate, and will remain so throughout the passage of time. Palestine belongs to us, not to the Zionists.[19]

He saw no difference between Hamas-controlled Gaza and the West Bank:

> The West Bank is inseparable from Gaza, Gaza is inseparable from the West Bank, and they are both inseparable from Haifa, Jaffa, Beersheba . . . and Safed . . . the liberation of Palestine—all of Palestine—is a duty, a right, a goal, and a purpose. It is the responsibility of the Palestinian people, as well as of the Arab and Islamic nation . . . Politics are born from the womb of resistance. The true statesman is born from the womb of the rifle and the missile.[20]

He laid claim to Jerusalem:

> Jerusalem is our soul, our history, our collective memory, our past, our present, and our future. It is our eternal capital, to which we hold fast and which we will liberate, inch by inch, neighborhood by neighborhood, stone by stone, every place sacred to Islam . . . Israel has no right to Jerusalem.[21]

Some would see the war as the latest front lines in the battle over Jerusalem.

11 ALIYA: THE RETURN TO THE LAND

Hear the word of the LORD, O nations; proclaim it in
distant coastlands: "He who scattered Israel will gather
them and will watch over his flock like a shepherd."
—JEREMIAH 31:10 NIV

DATELINE: ODESSA, UKRAINE

WE ARRIVED IN THE UKRAINIAN PORT OF ODESSA, A CITY ONCE
ruled by the Czars and then by the Soviet Empire. But now it served
as a gateway for Jews from the former Soviet Union. We visited the
famous Potemkin Steps near the docks, where a workers uprising in 1905
supported by sailors of the battleship Potemkin made history and fore-
shadowed the Soviet Revolution twelve years later. But back in town, *olim*
(Hebrew for immigrants) from throughout the far-flung former Soviet
Union forged another history. We came to chronicle one more chapter
in the story of *aliya*. *Aliya* literally means "coming up or ascending," but
it's the term used to describe the return of Jews from around the world.

About sixty Jews gathered at the base of the Ebenezer Emergency

Fund, an organization formed to assist immigrating Jews. Gustav Scheller founded Ebenezer during the 1991 Gulf War. He used his expertise as a former travel agent to bring Jews back from the former Soviet Union. Ships provided the main mode of transportation, the same way these sixty Russian Jews and our CBN News crew would return to Israel. We started videotaping this group loading their belongings and boarding two buses.

While their trip appeared on the surface quite ordinary, underneath lay a modern-day odyssey and biblical miracle. Ebenezer provided the buses and the passage for a waiting ship. But why would non-Jews help Jews back to Israel? *Ebenezer*—which means "God has helped us"—sees itself as part of the fulfillment of the scripture in Isaiah 49:22 (NIV) that says, "This is what the Sovereign LORD says: 'See, I will beckon to the Gentiles, I will lift up my banner to the peoples; they will bring your sons in their arms and carry your daughters on their shoulders.'"

We followed the buses down to the dock and watched Ebenezer volunteers load the baggage onboard. We asked Vadym Rabochyy, the director of Odessa's Ebenezer base, about their goal. He explained, "We're just helping Jewish people come back home to Israel by all means: with our hands, with our legs, with our bodies, with our smiles."[1] A few hours later, along with a shout and salute from the Ebenezer volunteers, the ship pushed away from the dock. Within minutes it set sail through Odessa's harbor. Within a few hours, it plowed through the dark waters of the Black Sea. Each turn of the propeller pushed these sixty *olim* farther away from a familiar way of life and closer to—for many—the fulfillment of a dream.

For example, both a woman named Ludimer and her nine-year-old daughter held on to their own dream of a better life in Israel. She planned to join her husband, who had gone to Israel several months earlier to get a job. With a stiff but refreshing sea breeze buffeting the ship, she told us, "I don't know why, I can't explain, but I feel such a peace in my heart. . . . I heard back in Ukraine so many black testimonies, even threats sometimes from the people but despite all these words I have a peace in my heart. I have a confidence that everything will be fine. . . . I have a peace because I think that maybe really God gives it to me."[2]

On the ship's stern, we met with Richard Gottier, then the international chairman of Ebenezer, about *aliya*. While the ship's wake swept out to the horizon, he told us, "Jeremiah made the comment that the day will come when you will actually forget the God who opened the Red Sea and brought you out of Egypt, so great will be the return of My people from the land of the north and all the countries where I send them. And this *aliya* is one of the great miracles of all time."[3]

Since 1991, Ebenezer Emergency Fund has made more than 160 sailings from Odessa to Haifa. They brought tens of thousands of immigrants from the former Soviet Union to the land of Israel. Including air transportation, Ebenezer helped more than one hundred thousand immigrants to the promised land.

The voyage set sail through one of the most storied parts of the world. Our ship called the *Jasmine* was like some vessel out of the *Arabian Nights* churned out of the Black Sea. We entered Turkey's Bosporus Straights and its capital, Istanbul. The channel—clogged with shipping and boats of all kinds—straddles two continents, Europe and Asia. Istanbul's skyline reflects the fourteen-hundred-year-old struggle between East and West, Islam and Christianity. At one time, Istanbul, then Constantinople, sat as the capitol of the Holy Roman Empire. Dozens of minarets show Islam dominates this region now. The skyline mirrors today's revival of this ancient conflict. In one sense, our voyage seems to represent a challenge to Islam's supremacy and radical Islam's attempt to kill the Jews, destroy Israel, and thwart God's plan set forth in the Scriptures.

From Istanbul we passed through the Dardanelles, where the famous World War I battle of Gallapoli took place. Tens of thousands of soldiers, from Turkey, Britain, Australia, and New Zealand, lost their lives in one of the most brutal conflicts in the "war to end all wars." That war would eventually see the defeat of the Ottoman Empire and set the stage for establishing the state of Israel. After the Dardanelles, we sailed into the Aegean Sea and plowed through waters where Paul the apostle once sailed. From here his missionary journeys to take the gospel of Jesus Christ transformed the world.

We sailed near the island of Patmos where John penned the book of Revelation. Nearby, on Turkey's mainland stood the seven churches of Revelation: Pergamum, Smyrna, Sardis, Ephesus, Philadelphia, Thyatira, and Laodicea. They hearken back to the infancy of the Christian church and herald its future prophetic fulfillment.

Yet many of the *olim* were thinking not of history but of their own stories. The voyage gave them time to reflect on family and friends left behind and the future beyond the horizon. Our sailing in May 2004 took place during the dark days of the second Palestinian intifada. They knew the difficulties and dangers ahead. The intifada and strained economic times in Israel posed significant challenges. Those challenges cut the number of immigrants coming to Israel. But for now, they were resting, talking, or even dancing and singing along with the volunteers. They resounded with the scripture that says Jews will return to Zion with singing and dancing.

Throughout the voyage, the Christian volunteers tried to help the families make the transition to Israel. This again fulfilled that scripture from Isaiah: "Behold, I will lift My hand in an oath to the nations, and set up My standard for the peoples; they shall bring your sons in their arms, and your daughters shall be carried on their shoulders" (49:22).

One Russian couple felt overwhelmed by the help given to them by Christians. They told us: "The only thing I can say, it's like a fairy tale. It's amazing. You know, it's impossible to explain to our friends who stayed back in the Ukraine that all the assistance and all the help that we received here is free of charge and just out of love. They won't be able to believe it."[4]

Shirley, a native of South Africa, made more than one hundred sailings with Ebenezer and worked with hundreds of volunteers. She said these volunteers find it overwhelming to witness prophetic history with their own eyes: "They're overwhelmed by their experience of assisting God's people going home and seeing prophecy fulfilled right in front of their eyes. It's one thing to read about it, and it's another thing to actually experience carrying the olim in their hands; seeing the blind and the lame and others go, and it's really just an awesome experience to see God's Word being fulfilled right in front of your eyes."[5]

Another volunteer, Thoels, added, "It's really a touching experience to be a part of fulfilling God's prophecy. Carrying a girl on the shoulder or having a boy in the bosom. It's really something. . . . It is being fulfilled every day I can tell you in the former Soviet Union today. . . . You can see it on the ship here, you can see it on the [Ebenezer] bases, all over."[6]

We passed islands dotting the Aegean Sea that seem to fulfill the scripture from Isaiah 11:11 (NIV): "In that day the Lord will reach out his hand a second time to reclaim the remnant that is left of his people from Assyria, from lower Egypt, from Upper Egypt, from Cush, from Elam, from Babylonia, from Hamath and from the islands of the sea."

We passed Crete and Cyprus, then after three days the immigrants on this three-thousand-year voyage in the making saw the shores of the land God promised to Abraham. It was thrilling to see them watch the *Jasmine* navigate those last few minutes into the port of Haifa. A couple of years later this harbor would be closed by Hezbollah rockets, but for now their dreams of a new life were becoming a reality.

Despite the recent fall in numbers in the latter part of the decade, some believe Israel might be on the verge of a much greater *aliya*. Peter Malpass of Ebenezer explained, "I believe that we're probably on the threshold of the greatest ingathering of the Jewish people. It seems possible and we have many words from intercessors that there will be a huge exodus from the nations of the world into the land of Israel and it seems to be entirely in line with biblical prophecy."[7]

The story of *aliya* continues.

———

Two years later in 2006, CBN News documented another chapter in *aliya*, this time just after the Second Lebanon War. Forty-eight hours after the Katyushas stopped landing in northern Israel, 120 miles to the south, three planes touched down in Tel Aviv's Ben Gurion airport. The planes carried eight hundred Jews from England, Canada, and the United States. They came to live in the country that had just suffered through the longest war in its modern-day history. The fires surrounding Kiryat Shmona still smoldered, Israelis still mourned their dead, and others cared for their wounded, but these eight hundred decided to come to a land scarred by war with the threat of another to come.

You might ask, why come at all?

The Hebrew prophets would say, look to the Scriptures.

They would explain what happened on the tarmac of the Ben Gurion airport was no ordinary event but an extraordinary example of the Bible coming to life in our time. Throughout the Old Testament, Hebrew prophets foretold of a human exodus to come unparalleled in human history. Brock Thoene, coauthor of dozens of books on Israel's history, told us, "In the whole history of the world, no people, no nation has ever gone out of existence anything like two thousand years and then been reborn. So it's correct to say it's a miracle. But that is a dramatic understatement. Because the rebirth of Israel is a whole series of miracles."[8]

Here's what the prophet Jeremiah declared, "'However, the days are coming,' declares the LORD, 'when men will no longer say, "As surely as the LORD lives, who brought the Israelites up out of Egypt," but they will say, "As surely as the LORD lives, who brought the Israelites up out of the land of the north and out of all the countries where he had banished them." For I will restore them to the land I gave their forefathers'" (Jeremiah 16:14–15 NIV).

Isaiah wrote, "He will raise a banner for the nations and gather the exiles of Israel; he will assemble the scattered people of Judah from the four quarters of the earth" (Isaiah 11:12 NIV).

Ezekiel proclaimed, "For this is what the Sovereign LORD says: I myself will search for my sheep and look after them. As a shepherd looks after his scattered flock when he is with them, so will I look after my sheep. I will rescue them from all the places where they were scattered on a day of clouds and darkness. I will bring them out from the nations and gather them from the countries, and I will bring them into their own land" (Ezekiel 34:11–13 NIV).

This ancient prophetic dream continues, and Jews from the four corners of the world still return to the land of their forefathers, and new waves splash on the shores of Israel to repopulate the Jewish state and write new chapters in the history of *aliya*.

OUT OF THE EAST

We witnessed another chapter at Ben Gurion in 2009. A small but significant group of seven Chinese men set foot on Israeli soil for the first time. They flew from Beijing and come from the Jewish community in Kaifeng, China. Their community began more than one thousand years ago when historians believe Jews from Persia or Iraq settled in China. Their arrival marked the end of a nearly four-year bureaucratic struggle to get to Israel but also marked the fulfillment of a biblical promise several thousand years old.

Michael Freund, the founder of Shavei Israel, an organization committed to bringing Jews back to Israel, helped arrange their immigration. He said their arrival was prophetic: "The prophet Zechariah in chapter 8 tells us that God promises that He will save His people from the east, from the countries of the east and from the countries of the west. And here before our eyes, a group of Chinese Jews from the Far East are returning to the land. If that's not a miracle, I don't know what is."[9]

Freund says their ancestors once dreamed of going back to Israel. Now these men are fulfilling that dream, a dream shared by the few female Chinese Jews who immigrated four years before the men. One of these women told us, "I still remember my grandma always read her Bible like Isaiah 60 chapter says Hashem [God] will like the eagle bring His people back. And always this word and scripture came into my mind and I think it's true."[10]

After they arrived, these Chinese men went first to Jerusalem's Western Wall. They came to pray and begin their new life in Israel. Freund and others say this group represents a historic first, the initial group of Chinese men to move to Israel in history. He estimates two thousand Jews now live in China, and he hopes more will move to Israel.

Freund is also involved in bringing several thousand Jews called the Bnei Menashe. They represent one of Israel's "lost tribes." He calls the return of these Jews from China, India, and other settings on God's compass a sign of the times: "God is gathering His people in. And this is an event not only of theological significance but of tremendous historical significance as well. . . . We are witnessing the ingathering of the exiles from the four corners of the world. It's taking place before our very eyes."[11]

———

Immigration means a lot to every country. For example, the United States itself is primarily a nation of immigrants. But no other nation on earth can boast that its current history was foretold thousands of years before. No other country can say that after two thousand years, its sons and daughters have come home. No other state can claim a historic and biblical mandate to resettle land chosen and promised by God.

For the first time in two thousand years, there are more Jews living in Israel than in any other place on earth. This remarkable milestone calls to mind that one of the greatest miracles in modern times has been the rebirth of the nation of Israel and the return of the Jews to the land. Isaiah, Jeremiah, Ezekiel, and prophets throughout the Old Testament prophesied there would come a day when God Himself would call back Jews from the four corners of the earth to the land of Israel. It's one reason why many see Zechariah 8:4–5 being fulfilled in our day.

It says, "This is what the Lord Almighty says: 'Once again men and women of ripe old age will sit in the streets of Jerusalem, each with cane in hand because of his age. The city streets will be filled with boys and girls playing there'" (NIV). Now, after nearly two thousand years, that divine call is drawing Jews from the nations of the earth to the city of Jerusalem and throughout Israel. They're part of the story of *aliya*, the regathering of Jewish people to the land of Israel. It's a modern-day exodus many believe is both a miracle and a message to the world that God is faithful to His Word and He will gather His people to His land.

12 THE MOUNTAINS OF ISRAEL

But you, O mountains of Israel, you shall shoot forth your
branches and yield your fruit to My people Israel, for they
are about to come.
—EZEKIEL 36:8

And I will make them one nation in the land, on the
mountains of Israel.
—EZEKIEL 37:22

DATELINE: ARIEL, SAMARIA

WHAT WOULD YOU DO IF YOU CAME FACE-TO-FACE WITH A SUICIDE
bomber?

Menachem Gilboa answered that question.

It's October 27, 2002: a sunny autumn Sunday afternoon. Dozens of
Israeli soldiers gather at the corner gas station at the entrance to Ariel,
known as the capital of Samaria. They're waiting for buses to take them
back to their army bases after the Sabbath. Nearby, Menachem Gilboa
sits with his wife, Tova, and his friend Tuvia Gelbard. They're enjoying a

cup of coffee at a small café. They run the Eshel Hashomron Hotel next door. They came to Samaria years before to settle the land of the Bible and provide a haven for pilgrims and tourists.

Suddenly, Menachem notices a young man. Tall and blond, he looks Scandinavian. But he's walking with a small towel over his hand. *That's strange*, Menachem thinks. He goes up and greets him. He's not being polite. He wants to hear the young man's accent. Is he Arab? He comes close . . . about six feet away. He gets up in his face and pushes him. Then Menachem sees the bomb. It's hidden under the young man's coat. Thoughts race through Menachem's mind. What should he do? Menachem carries a weapon. He can shoot the bomber, but what if he hits the bomb? He'll die and so will many others around him. In an instant he decides.

He jumps the bomber and throws him on the ground. They begin a frantic life-and-death struggle. His life, and the lives of those around him, hangs in the balance. The towel comes off. It hid the cables between the bomb and its switch. The suicide bomber strains to put his fingers together, to hit the switch and detonate the bomb. Menachem strains just as hard to keep the bomber's fingers apart. Inches separate him from life and several pounds of dynamite. Menachem shouts, "Shoot him! It's a suicide bomber."

His cries fill the gas station. Some come running. "Shoot him!" he cries again. But the suicide bomber is shouting too. He screams that Menachem is the bomber in an attempt to confuse the situation. Someone comes close. It's a friend of Menachem's. He's got a gun, but he's afraid. What if he misses? How can he get a clear shot while they're wrestling? Now it's a scene. Everyone within earshot hears and sees what's going on. A shot rings out. The suicide bomber's frame slumps. Life oozes from his body. He's dead.

Exhausted but relieved, Menachem struggles to his feet and begins to walk away. It's over. Or is it? Another shot rings out. A flash, an explosion, and suddenly Menachem's body is thrown to the ground. He's in agony. His clothes are blown off, his body singed. He wonders, *What happened?*

Only later does he find out. After his life-and-death struggle—a heroic action that potentially saved dozens of lives—tragedy struck. One soldier in the crowd thought the bomber was still alive. From about seventy-five feet away, he shot at the bomber but hit the bomb. Three IDF soldiers died in the explosion. It wounded seventeen, including Menachem. Miraculously he survived but pieces of metal tore into Menachem's body. He faced weeks in the hospital, months of rehabilitation, and a lifetime of limited mobility. But he's alive and more determined than ever to stay in the land he calls home, the land of the Bible: Judea and Samaria.

JUDEA AND SAMARIA OR THE WEST BANK

Thousands of years ago the Jewish prophet Ezekiel declared there would come a day when the Jews would return to the land of Israel. When they did return, he said, they would resettle the mountains of Israel. This prophetic declaration is at the heart of one of the biggest conflicts in the world today. Why? Because what the prophet Ezekiel calls "the mountains of Israel" much of the world today calls the West Bank. For decades, one of the most familiar terms in the Israeli-Palestinian conflict has been the West Bank. It refers to land Israel captured from Jordan during the 1967 Six Day War.

From 1948 to 1967, Jordan controlled this area and gave it the name since it lies on the west bank of the Jordan River. But for thousands of years, the Bible has called this land Judea and Samaria. It's a land with the richest biblical history in the world. It's the land God promised to Abraham and his descendants—the promised land of the Bible—and the biblical heartland of Israel. It's the land of Bethel, where Jacob dreamed; Hebron, where King David first set up his capital; Bethany, the home of Mary, Martha, and Lazarus; Bethlehem, the birthplace of Jesus; and Jerusalem, where the first and second temples once stood.

Now the future the world is planning for the West Bank is very different from what the Bible lays out for "the mountains of Israel." What's the difference? While the Bible says the Jewish people will one day re-settle this land, the world insists this is the place for a future Palestinian state. So the promise of the Lord and the plans of the world are clashing in one of the biggest conflicts on the world stage today. These competing interests regularly crash into the headlines around the world.

More than three hundred thousand (and counting) Jews now live in the West Bank. To many, they represent an "obstacle to peace." To others, they are biblical pioneers following in the footsteps of the patriarchs and the words of the prophets. Throughout the years, we've often traveled to this land of contention and land of promise to meet the people called "settlers." Many of them, like Menachem, consider living in the land of the Bible a privilege, even in the face of death.

ELON MOREH

One of my first experiences in this area took place in early 2001. Bible teacher Billye Brim invited us to accompany her and her small group to a place called Elon Moreh. The intifada roared like a furnace by then. Frequent drive-by shootings marred the roads of Judea and Samaria, so we drove by armored bus to one of its many hilltops. Except this hilltop was different. Its summit marked the place where God first promised the land of Israel to Abraham, hence the promised land.

Genesis 12:6–7 says, "Abram passed through the land to the place of Shechem, as far as the terebinth tree of Moreh. And the Canaanites were then in the land. Then the Lord appeared to Abram and said, 'To your descendants I will give this land.' And there he built an altar to the Lord, who had appeared to him."

The first promise of the promised land.

On top of the mountain you get a spectacular view of the biblical heartland of Israel, the ancient city of Shechem, below, now called Nablus. It's a taste of the vista Abraham must have seen when God promised the land to him and to his descendants. While the view from the Himalayas, the Rockies, or the Alps might be more stunning, this vista is unlike any other on earth. This land, after all, is the one place on earth God promised to a particular people. Here God gave one of His elemental promises.

On a clear day, you can see the Mediterranean Sea to the west. The mountains of Samaria and Judea stretch out to all points of the compass. Toward the horizons, most of the major events of the Bible took place. Jewish history began on these hills and valleys. This is the Jewish heartland, its biblical patrimony.

Joseph is buried below in Shechem. To the south sits Hebron, where Abraham bought the cave of Malchpah and where David established his capital for seven years before it was Jerusalem. Farther south, Micah prophesized of Bethlehem, "Though you are little among the thousands of Judah, yet out of you shall come forth to Me the One to be Ruler of Israel, whose goings forth are from of old, from everlasting" (Micah 5:2).

For four thousand years, the history of this land and the destiny of the Jewish people have been entwined. It was a profound experience to be there.

With the valleys spread out below us, we asked Brim about her understanding of the "mountains of Israel." She told us, "Ninety-two percent of the Bible place names are in the mountains of Israel in what the Bible calls Judea and Samaria and the world calls the West Bank."[1]

Brim—who often brings Christian groups to Judea and Samaria—noted that in modern times Jews have been returning to the land for more than 120 years. She believes the Bible is clear about where they should live: "When God called them to come home, He particularly told them in Ezekiel 36 and in Jeremiah 30 and 31 that they were to return to the mountains of Israel and to build cities there."[2]

Brim quoted from Ezekiel: "But you, O mountains of Israel, you shall shoot forth your branches and yield your fruit to My people Israel, for they are about to come. For indeed I am for you, and I will turn to you, and you shall be tilled and sown. I will multiply men upon you, all the house of Israel, all of it; and the cities shall be inhabited and the ruins rebuilt" (36:8–10).

Brim said, "So the mountains of Israel, that's where He told them to go. And I believe that behind it all . . . the enemy of God is trying to stop it from coming to pass. And what the world calls, for instance, settlements, is what God calls cities, and says particularly to come back and inhabit and build, in the mountains."[3]

When we talked to Brim in 2001, the nations of the world—much like today—were trying to divide this promised land. She believed because of their plans, they were also in the process of being judged by how they dealt with the nation of Israel. Joel 3:2 (NIV) says, "I will gather all nations and bring them down to the Valley of Jehoshaphat. There I will enter into judgment against them concerning my inheritance, my people Israel, for they scattered my people among the nations and divided up my land."

It's a clash of ancient covenants and modern diplomacy. But as a rabbi once told me, God is the "Silent Partner" at the negotiating table. He has a stake in these negotiations too. Leviticus 25:23 (NIV) says, "The land must not be sold permanently, because the land is mine and you are but aliens and my tenants."

In the heart of Judea—or the West Bank—lies Jerusalem. The 1967 borders run right through modern Jerusalem, the potential dividing line between a future Palestinian state and the Jewish state. On the Palestinian side would remain the Temple Mount. Will Israel hold on to the most sacred site in all of Judaism? It's an ancient question.

About a forty-five-minute drive from Jerusalem is the town of Shiloh where that question was asked before. Shiloh marks the site of some of the most dramatic events in the Old Testament. It's where the tabernacle stood for 369 years. It's where Hannah prayed for a son. It's where that son, Samuel, ministered before the Lord. It's also where Joshua divided up the promised land to the twelve tribes of Israel. At that time, Joshua asked ancient Israel a question: "How long will you neglect to go and possess the land which the LORD God of your fathers has given you?" (Joshua 18:3).

That question resonates now for modern Israel.

13 PERSIA, PURIM, AND PRAYER

"Go, gather together all the Jews who are in Susa, and fast for me. Do not eat or drink for three days, night or day. I and my maids will fast as you do. When this is done, I will go to the king, even though it is against the law. And if I perish, I perish."
—ESTHER 4:16 NIV

DATELINE: SUSA, PERSIA

Mordecai recorded these events, and he sent letters to all the Jews throughout the provinces of King Xerxes, near and far, to have them celebrate annually the fourteenth and fifteenth days of the month of Adar as the time when the Jews got relief from their enemies, and as the month when their sorrow was turned into joy and their mourning into a day of celebration. He wrote them to observe the days as days of feasting and joy and giving presents of food to one another and gifts to the poor. (Esther 9:20–22 NIV)

THE CELEBRATION OF PURIM—BORN IN THE HEAT OF PERSIAN treachery more than twenty-three hundred years ago—continues to this day. Just as in ancient Persia, Jewish family and friends still send gifts to one another marking the deliverance of the Jews from Haman. They read the book of Esther in synagogues around the world. It's also celebrated by wearing costumes. For example, if someone from the United States showed up in Jerusalem during Purim, they might think it was Halloween in the middle of the fall rather than Israel on the cusp of springtime.

You'll likely see a mother with kids in tow dressed up like Spider-Man, Superman, or some other superhero. You might see a young girl dressed up as a young and beautiful queen. Or your waitress might come and take your order wearing rabbit ears. It's a lighthearted holiday, but underneath the merriment is a sobering story of intrigue with life and death consequences for the Jewish people and a lesson for today.

Purim is named for the *pur* or "lot" that Haman cast to destroy the Jewish people. It's where we get the term *lottery* and the expression "my lot in life." The book of Esther, sandwiched between Job and Nehemiah in the Old Testament, revolves around four main characters: the wicked Haman, the beautiful Queen Esther, her uncle Mordecai, and King Ahasuerus (or Xerxes in some translations). It's a story dripping with intrigue, worthy of any Hollywood script. In fact, Hollywood did do a movie called *One Night with the King*. The book of Esther carries the distinction as being the only book in the Bible that doesn't contain the name of God. But make no mistake: His hand is seen clearly throughout this powerful story of deliverance.

Esther 3:8–9 contains the main theme of the story. Haman, the Grand Vizier of the Persian Empire, tells the Persian king Ahasuerus, "There is a certain people dispersed and scattered among the peoples in all the provinces of your kingdom whose customs are different from those of all other people and who do not obey the king's laws; it is not in the king's best interest to tolerate them. If it pleases the king, let a decree be issued to destroy them" (NIV).

The "certain people" Haman wants to destroy are the Jews.

If this story sounds familiar, it is. For years the world has been watching a modern-day drama that echoes the book of Esther. It's the growing confrontation between modern-day Iran—roughly the same territory as ancient Persia—and the Jewish state of Israel.

Iran's leaders—the spiritual heirs of Haman—have thundered their genocidal threats against the Jewish people for years. Iran's president Mahmoud Ahmadinejad declared, "The existence of the Zionist regime is an insult to all humanity."[1] While their Supreme Leader Ali Khamenei bellowed, "The superfluous, mendacious and false Zionist [regime] will be eradicated from the geographical landscape."[2]

Different time. Different leaders. Same story: destroy the Jews.

SPIRITUAL BATTLEFIELD

The parallels between Haman of the book of Esther and Ahmadinejad and Khamenei today are striking. It's another potential genocide coming out of Persia and placing the Jewish people in jeopardy. It's also reminiscent of the twentieth-century world power that attempted to destroy the Jews. The mass rallies in Tehran calling for Israel's destruction model those chilling 1930s mass rallies in Nuremberg where Adolf Hitler called for the elimination of all Jews in Europe.

Some explain this striking parallel by using another book in the Bible, the book of Daniel. The book recounts the time when the biblical hero Daniel fasted and prayed for twenty-one days. The angel Gabriel responded to his prayer and fasting but the "Prince of Persia" opposed and delayed Gabriel. Some believe this same spiritual being—the Prince of Persia—is still operating today through Iran's ruling regime. Given this understanding, the confrontation between Iran and Israel takes on a spiritual dimension with profound consequences.

It also explains why in the book of Esther, when Mordecai tells the queen about Haman's wicked plot to destroy her people, she chooses a spiritual strategy. She tells Mordecai to ask the people to join her in a three-day fast before she tries to save her people. After the fast, she courageously approaches the king without being summoned—to do so could mean death even for the queen. She deftly exposes the plot to the king. Haman is uncovered and executed and, instead of being destroyed, the Jewish people are vindicated:

> On the thirteenth day of the twelfth month, the month of Adar, the edict commanded by the king was to be carried out. On this day the enemies of the Jews had hoped to overpower them, but now the tables were turned and the Jews got the upper hand over those who hated them. The Jews assembled in their cities in all the provinces of King Xerxes to attack those seeking their destruction. No one could stand against them, because the people of all the other nationalities were afraid of them. (Esther 9:1–2 NIV)

The Jews of Persia escaped annihilation then, but how will the Jews fare today when faced with another genocidal threat? Some are calling on their people to employ the same spiritual means Esther did twenty-three hundred years ago to combat this modern-day genocidal threat. One of them is Michael Freund, a devout Jew, a columnist for the *Jerusalem Post*, and the former communications director for Prime Minister Benjamin Netanyahu. He is, as we mentioned before, the founder of Shavei Israel. Freund wrote an op-ed piece titled "A Call to Psalms." In it, he exhorted both Christians and Jews to pray the psalms as a response to his recognition of the spiritual nature of today's spiritual battle. We spoke with Freund about why he issued such a call. Here are some excerpts from that interview:

> I think it's clear that Israel and the West are facing an immense battle, against a foe that is driven, not by economic dissatisfaction, not by poverty or lack of development, those are all factors. But the bottom line is that they are driven by a kind of deep-rooted religious fundamentalism, a kind of fanaticism that is unprecedented in modern history. And if our foes are resorting to their form of holy war, I think it's incumbent upon us not to abandon the sacred weapons that we

have in our arsenal, chief and foremost among them, the power of prayer. . . .

I think that such an event ("A Call to Psalms"), the echoes of such an event, would resound, from Washington to Moscow to Tokyo, but more importantly they would resound in the heavens above too. . . .

You know, I studied international relations as an undergraduate at Princeton University. And one of the things that the professors always stress is that the international arena is comprised of actors. There are actors on the world stage that are states, or leaders, or other entities. But what they don't tell you is that there is also a Director. This Director who is overseeing the actors, who is pulling the strings. Now each of us has the ability on a daily basis to have a direct conversation with the Director. To talk to Him about what we would like to see in the script that is world history. We dare not forego such an opportunity. We dare not ignore our ability as individuals, as communities, to have an input, to have a say, in how the future develops. No one out there should ever feel powerless about what's going on. Because at the end of the day we each have, through the power of prayer . . . the ability to influence events.[3]

CHANGING HISTORY THROUGH PRAYER

But have you ever considered a geopolitical standoff like this on a global scale and felt overwhelmed with the size and scope of the situation? It's the feeling you don't have a role to play or, if you do, your role is too small to matter. That events on the world stage will just play out while your life is removed from what's happening in today's headlines. But could you play a redemptive role in world history through prayer? Can intercession play a role in world politics? Do Christians have any influence on world events? In essence, do our prayers affect history?

CBN News anchor Wendy Griffith and coauthor Craig von Busek of CBN.com believe the answer to those questions is yes. In their book *Praying the News*, they cited examples from the fall of Communism to individual stories during 9/11 of effective intercession. They wrote, "When people pray in sincerity and unity according to the will of God revealed in the Bible, things change; headlines change. The ancient words of the apostle James are just as true today as they were when he wrote them under the inspiration of the Holy Spirit in the first century AD 'The effective prayer of a righteous man can accomplish much' [James 5:16 NASB]."[4]

They also cite the late Bible teacher Derek Prince. Prince wrote *Shaping History through Prayer and Fasting*, where he made the biblical case that Christians can change world events through these simple yet powerful spiritual tools.

Prince saw that firsthand as a British officer in World War II. It was during the critical North African campaign. Field Marshal Edwin Rommel, the "Desert Fox" of the German army, threatened to conquer all of North Africa. His seemingly invincible troops had pushed the British army back to the Egyptian border, and his battle-tested army stood at the door to the Middle East. Another British defeat would have opened up Egypt, the strategic Suez Canal, and what lay beyond, what the Jews then called Palestine. Their fate and the fate of the as yet unborn Jewish state hung in the balance.

Yet the British command suffered from a lack of leadership and appeared headed for defeat. In light of these desperate circumstances and just prior to the next pivotal battle, Prince prayed a simple prayer: "Lord, give us leaders such that it will be for Your glory to give us victory through them."[5]

Just a short while later, British prime minister Winston Churchill appointed General B. L. Montgomery, the son of an evangelical Anglican bishop, to be the commander of British troops. Montgomery rallied the British troops and led them to victory over Rommel's German corps at El Alamein. Here's how Prince described this profound answer to prayer:

> Without a doubt, the Battle of El Alamein was the turning point of the war in North Africa. Two or three days after the battle, I found myself

in the desert a few miles behind the advancing Allied forces. A small portable radio beside me on the tailboard of a military truck was relaying a news commentator's description of the scene at Montgomery's headquarters as he had witnessed it on the eve of the battle. He recalled how Montgomery publicly called his officers and men to prayer, saying, "Let us ask the Lord, mighty in battle, to give us the victory." As these words came through that portable radio, God spoke very clearly to my spirit, "That is the answer to your prayer."[6]

Today, we face similar dire circumstances. Iran is just one front of a worldwide spiritual battle at the end of the age. We're in a war. The threats are real. The stakes are high, and as usual, God is looking for intercessors: Ezekiel 22:30 reads, "I looked for a man among them who would build up the wall and stand before me in the gap on behalf of the land" (NIV).

Paul said many of these enemies are hostile forces from an unseen realm: "For we do not wrestle against flesh and blood, but against principalities, against powers, against the rulers of the darkness of this age, against spiritual hosts of wickedness in the heavenly places."

He goes on to exhort, "Therefore take up the whole armor of God, that you may be able to withstand in the evil day, and having done all, to stand" (Ephesians 6:12–13).

For Christians, prayer, fasting, taking up the whole armor of God, and standing in the gap are the spiritual weapons Paul wrote about in 2 Corinthians: "For though we live in the world, we do not wage war as the world does. The weapons we fight with are not the weapons of the world. On the contrary, they have divine power to demolish strongholds. We demolish arguments and every pretension that sets itself up against the knowledge of God" (10:3–5 NIV).

Israel can take heart in the example in the book of Esther. It still echoes down through the centuries, and Haman's fate serves as a warning to everyone who would thunder declarations against the Jewish people. Too often, their declarations boomerang. Haman died on the gallows he built for Mordecai, and the Jewish people designated for destruction were vindicated. Hitler's "thousand-year Reich" ended in ruins after twelve years, and out of the ashes of the "final solution" the Jewish state of Israel was born. Iran's Ahmadinejad should read the book of Esther and consider what his own fate might be if he continues to thunder against God's chosen people.

Home groups, prayer groups, and 24/7 houses of prayer both small and large all over the earth are part of God's great army of prayer. During Esther's time, God vindicated the Jewish people. He used a brave queen, a wise uncle, and a praying and fasting people. It's likely He will use the same kind of praying and fasting people for "such a time as this."

AN END-TIME OBSTACLE TO PRAYER

While many might recognize the scope of the spiritual battle raging today, my sense is that some minimize the value of prayer in these last days. Perhaps some feel a fatalistic idea that in the last days, everything that occurs is already set in stone and can't be changed through prayer. It's certain that biblical events prescribed by the Lord will take place, but in these last days, could the church and its power of prevailing prayer have a unique and profound part to play at the end of the age?

Joel Richardson addressed this issue in his book *Antichrist: Islam's Awaited Messiah*:

> I believe that while the Bible indeed gives us a general prophetic frame-work of what will happen in the last-days; *many of the specific details have yet to be determined.* God did not reveal every final detail for a reason. He rarely does. If He did, then we would be justified in simply waiting for the Antichrist to come and get us. We would be entirely justified in digging holes in the ground as secret hideouts to store our survival food. But instead, God desires us to actually wrestle with Him in prayer, not only for our own souls and our families, but also for the very nations that we live in and call home.[7]

Once again, perhaps it will be said that "history belongs to the intercessors.

> He goes on: "Never underestimate the ability of prevailing prayer to effect reality and the final end of any matter. Remember, the story is not over, until it has come to pass. I believe that it will be specifically the lack of, or the presence of an abundance of prevailing prayer that will literally determine the final chapter in the story of *many* nations."[8]

14 A WORLDWIDE CRESCENDO OF PRAYER

*My prayer for this Congress is that the movement
of prayer, this movement of mission will be joined
together to see the Great Commission accomplished in
the coming decades.*[1]

—PAUL ESHLEMEN, GLOBAL MEDIA OUTREACH

DATELINE: JAKARTA, INDONESIA

IN MAY 2012, EIGHTY THOUSAND CHRISTIANS FILLED INDONESIA'S national stadium in the heart of Jakarta. With our press passes, we stepped onto the field. I turned and saw a throng assembling for the first World Prayer Assembly in more than twenty years. It felt like watching another chapter of spiritual history. This chapter marked the growing crescendo of prayer in the church around the world. While tens of thousands gathered in the sweltering equatorial heat, an estimated two million joined the prayer meeting through the Internet or satellite throughout Indonesia's archipelago. Millions more would join through God TV's global broadcast. The stadium meeting capped a five-day meeting of Christian leaders from more than eighty nations around the world.

They knew their history.

More than twenty years ago, the last World Prayer Assembly in Seoul sparked an unprecedented evangelistic movement out of the Korean peninsula. Organizers in Jakarta like John Robb hoped for even greater results. He told CBN News, "We feel that the epicenter of world revival is going to be Asia and especially Indonesia. We see the World Prayer Assembly as kind of a stepping-stone toward the fulfillment of Habakkuk 2:14: 'For the earth will be filled with the knowledge of the glory of the LORD as the waters cover the sea.'"[2]

That the event took place in the majority Muslim country of Indonesia made the gathering all the more significant. Indonesian leaders said a massive prayer movement is already connecting hundreds of their cities and millions of believers there. As CBN News's George Thomas reported, "This historic gathering at the national stadium is just part of a week-long prayer event as tens of thousands of Indonesians have come together along with some 84 country representatives. Christians asking the Lord, 'Lord would you change the course of history, would you change the destiny of nations today through the power of prayer.'"[3]

The World Prayer Assembly is just one example of this growing prayer movement. On the other side of the world is another. Not far off Route 71 in Kansas City—part of America's heartland—the fires of intercessory prayer have not gone out for more than ten years. What started as an ember has grown into a raging fire stoked by hundreds of intercessors. Old and young, male and female, they are dedicated to keep the fires burning, to keep praise rising and to fill the "bowls of prayer" on God's altar. It's called International House of Prayer (IHOP), a ministry begun by Mike Bickle.

IHOP is emblematic of a new movement in the earth today—24/7 prayer, worship, and intercession. It's calling a new generation of Simeons and Annas to wait—and pray—for the coming of the Lord. They report: "There are now thousands of 24/7 prayer watches across the nations by a sovereign work of the Holy Spirit, and 215 nations regularly connect with the Global Prayer Room in Kansas City via webstream, including closed Muslim nations and North Korea."[4]

They're inspired by the biblical model of David's tabernacle and the historical example of Count Zinzendorf. Zinzendorf's Moravian prayer meeting lasted more than a century and birthed a worldwide evangelistic effort. "For more than one hundred years, beginning on August 26, 1727, there was a Moravian brother or sister somewhere engaged in prayer, twenty-four hours a day, seven days a week. Among the brethren this meeting was known as the "Hourly Intercession."[5] Their biblical model came out of Leviticus 6:13, which says, "The fire must be kept burning on the altar continuously; it must not go out" (NIV).

Bickle joined other Christian leaders like Lou Engle for a landmark prayer assembly in Jerusalem in the spring of 2008. The Call Jerusalem was a solemn assembly of twelve hours of prayer and fasting. They partnered with the annual Global Day of Prayer. At the time it might have been history's largest prayer meeting. It brought together an estimated one to two hundred million believers worldwide to pray on Pentecost Sunday, May 11, 2008.

God TV provided many of the satellite links between venues from South Africa to New Zealand. The event deeply moved Bickle. He said, "The most amazing thing is the fact that the thousands here in unity and in concert with the Global Day of Prayer up in venues all over the earth. So for the first time in history, I mean literally one or two hundred million people crying out for the breakthrough of God for the city of Jerusalem and the center of it, the base of it is here in Jerusalem. I mean, that's remarkable, to me, it's a sign of the times itself."[6]

Massive prayer meetings like the Global Day of Prayer are just one sign of a growing emphasis on prayer throughout the church. Anecdotal evidence from the "ends of the earth" supports this contention. A friend who travels through the South Sea Islands reports Christians cut off from the world's media are nonetheless spontaneously praying for Israel. Especially as Jerusalem is more and more threatened, believers seem to intuitively know how important it is to pray for the peace of Jerusalem in these days.

For years we've reported on the annual Day of Prayer for the Peace of Jerusalem, which occurs on the first Sunday in October every year. One year, organizers held it on the Haas Promenade overlooking Israel's capital. They prayed for this ancient bastion and came to fulfill God's command in Psalm 122:6, "Pray for the peace of Jerusalem." They represented a growing phenomenon on today's prophetic land-scape: Jerusalem is becoming the focus of prayer by believers all over the world.

Organizers and participants believe, as it says in their prayer guide: "Psalm 122:6 is a biblical mandate—a timeless prayer assignment from God—that has never been rescinded anywhere in scripture." Robert Stearns, the founder of Eagles Wings Ministry, and Pastor Jack Hayford of Church on the Way serve as cochairmen of this prayer meeting. While several hundred believers gathered to pray over Israel's ancient capital, God TV cameras provided a window for millions more to join in prayer.

Since its inception in 2004, it's become one of the largest prayer meetings in the world. It has grown exponentially and now includes more than 150,000 churches in more than 150 nations. It's one more sign that a crescendo of prayer for Jerusalem is rising in the hearts and minds of believers worldwide. Hayford, like many other leaders, sees prayer as crucial to fulfilling Jerusalem's prophetic destiny: "Prayer really is the key. Nothing can solve the gridlock of problem, even the things beyond Jerusalem that affect its peace, the rise of global anti-Semitism. . . . I don't know of anything that is going to tip the scales in the interest ulti-mately of global revival of what God does in this city."[7]

Stearns described Jerusalem's unique role: "This is the city for our present and our future. We see biblical prophecy being fulfilled here and we will see the day when Messiah will come and His government will issue forth out of this city."[8]

One prayer leader in the city told us, "I'd encourage everyone, even if it's just putting a little thing on your refrigerator saying 'pray for the peace of Jerusalem,' every day to just bring that up before the Lord. I think there's a power in a mass of people worldwide focusing on one thing that God has said very clearly we are to pray for."[9]

Another way to pray for Jerusalem is to pray God's Word. Penny Valentine, in a small, simple but significant book *Praying for the Peace of Jerusalem*, provides a prayer guide for informed and biblical prayer for the city. She believes the Bible is the best guide. "That way we will not pray with our own understanding, but in cooperation with the Lord, to help fulfill His perfect will."[10]

Valentine uses scriptures from both the Old and New Testaments as a guide to informed prayer. The goal is to pray for God's will. "In fact, true peace will not come to Jerusalem until it is again fully the House of the Lord, built together for His people both Jew and Gentile, and ruled over by the Prince of Peace. That is what we are praying for when we pray for the peace of Jerusalem—the fulfilling of God's plan."[11]

But people are not just praying for Jerusalem from the ends of the earth. Prayer is increasing in the city itself. Tabernacle of Praise stands as one of those prayer ministries. Founded in 1999 by Rick and Patti Ridings and called *Succat Hallel* in Hebrew, this house of prayer now prays twenty-four hours a day, seven days a week.

Ridings told us: "If this [worldwide prayer] is happening all over the world, how much more important that it happen in Jerusalem. So we feel that the Scriptures that talk about the Gentiles coming from the nations to worship at the throne of Jerusalem, that we're starting to see the fulfillment here in Jerusalem as more and more from the nations' people are coming to pour out their lives in worship and in prayer to the Lord here."[12]

But Succat Hallel is just one facet of the 24/7 prayer movement within Jerusalem. Another 24/7 ministry is called the Pavilion Prayer Tower. It occupies the top floor of one of Jerusalem's tallest office buildings. Pastor Wayne Hilsden of King of Kings Congregation began the ministry. Hilsden says within the last few years they have had what he calls "a remarkable burden of intercessory prayer" come upon them. It's part of this unprecedented movement of prayer in the city, concentrated prayer that might not have been heard since the book of Acts and the Upper Room.

> We've never seen that before where hundreds of people now, committing themselves to prayer watches during the day and now even in the night hours as well. I just believe that that's a signal that God is about to do something great . . . and when God is about to do something great, He prepares His intercessors to pray into His purposes, He wants co-laborers in the work He's about to do and the key laborers in the bringing about of His eternal purposes are those who pray. So it's remarkable and it's happening in our day.
>
> One ministry that pioneered praying within and for the city is the Jerusalem House of Prayer for All Nations. Tom Hess began this ministry in 1987 to establish a twenty-four-hour prayer watch to pray for the peace of Jerusalem and for the nations of the world. He and his wife, Kate, bring Christians from around the world for an annual convocation and mobilize intercessors globally.[13]

They and millions more around the world are fulfilling the biblical exhortation in Isaiah 62:6–7: "I have posted watchmen on your walls, O Jerusalem; they will never be silent day or night. You who call on the Lord, give yourselves no rest, and give him no rest till he establishes Jerusalem and makes her the praise of the earth" (NIV).

Isaiah also penned one of the strongest declarations to pray for Jerusalem. Isaiah 62:1 says, "For Zion's sake I will not hold My peace, and for Jerusalem's sake I will not rest. Until her righteousness goes forth as brightness, and her salvation as a lamp that burns."

15 | DREAMS, VISIONS, AND PERSECUTION

*Look among the nations and watch—be utterly
astounded! For I will work a work in your days which
you would not believe, though it were told you.*
—HABAKKUK 1:5

It was the best of times; it was the worst of times.
—*A TALE OF TWO CITIES* BY CHARLES DICKENS

DATELINE: CHRIST CHURCH, JERUSALEM

WE RENDEZVOUSED WITH ALI IN THE SHADOW OF JERUSALEM'S
Christ Church, the oldest Protestant church in the Middle East. The
church sits just inside the walls of the Old City near the Jaffa Gate. We
arranged to talk with Ali about the changes in the Middle East but also
about his own life story. We had heard about Ali and wanted to hear his
unusual saga. Christ Church hosted Ali and many others like him who
came from throughout the Fertile Crescent to attend a unique conference called "At the Crossroads." Ali, like many of those who came, calls
himself a "Muslim Background Believer" or "MBB." They represent the

growing number of Muslims throughout the Islamic world who believe that Jesus Christ is the Son of God. Through his translator, Ali told us his story.

He grew up in Turkey and lived a tumultuous life. As an adult, he fell under the grip of alcohol. He beat his wife, groused at his neighbors, and led an unhappy, aimless existence. As a nominal Muslim, he decided to make the Islamic pilgrimage to Mecca called the Hajj. He thought by becoming a devout Muslim, he'd straighten his life out. He traveled to Saudi Arabia with several friends. The night before he planned to walk around the black stone known as the Kaaba, part of his Islamic requirements, he fell asleep and had a dream.

In the dream, Jesus appeared to Ali.

Ali told me, "First Jesus touched my forehead with His finger. And after touching me, He said, 'You belong to Me.' And then He touched me above my heart. '. . . follow Me, you belong to Me,' He said. Then I woke up. . . . So I decided, okay, I'm not going to finish the Hajj, the pilgrimage. Whatever it takes, I'm going to follow that Voice."[1]

Ali told his friends what happened. They dismissed the dream, but he insisted it was real. To their chagrin, he followed the instructions in the dream and left Mecca. He made a profession of faith to his wife and members of his village and despite bumps along his new road of faith, he now serves as a pastor in one of Turkey's churches. His transformation dramatically affected his family.

His mother told him, "You are not the same child that I bore and raised. Because after I raised you and brought you up, you started drinking alcohol and did all kind of bad things. But now God has changed you. God has disciplined you and you've become an incredible person."[2]

Ali personifies many former Muslims who have come to faith in Jesus through a dream. A DVD called *More than Dreams* that's been distributed throughout the Muslim world dramatized Ali's story and four other similar testimonies. A new book called *Dreams and Visions: Is Jesus Awakening the Muslim World?* chronicles many more. I've known its author, Tom Doyle, for several years. I've come to admire the work he, his wife, and others do through e3 Ministries throughout the Middle East. Before the book's publication, he sent me the manuscript and asked for an endorsement. As I read through the book, I found myself spellbound and brought to tears or sometimes laughter by the amazing testimonies and inspiring stories. One story in particular gripped me: the story of Dina or, as the book says, "One Tough Burka."

Dina served in Iran's Female Secret Police (FSP). She and her cohorts stalked other women who violated even the most minor infraction of Sharia Law. Yet secretly she watched a Christian satellite program called *Iran Alive!* hosted by Hormoz Shariat, called by some the "Billy Graham of Iran." As a regular caller, she challenged, bellowed, shouted, and ridiculed Shariat over the phone for his Christian beliefs. She thought they were pathetic and reviled him with cries like, "You Christians are going to hell." One night, however, one call took an unexpected turn. Dina confided to Hormoz that she and her mother—who suffered from terminal cancer—planned to kill themselves during his program.

Stunned for a moment, Hormoz composed himself and asked Dina to give Jesus one week. If nothing happened in a week, she could go ahead and kill herself. She accepted his "foolish challenge" and pledged to call back one week later and commit suicide on his program "if you are brave enough to take my next call."[3] Hormoz promised to take the call, but he asked Dina for one more thing. He asked her to pray to accept Jesus as her Savior. Reluctantly she prayed.

One week later, Hormoz got the call. Tom tells the rest of the story:

Hormoz finished another call. His eyes widened as the name of the next caller came up on the screen. He glanced at Donnell, who monitored the incoming calls just off camera. Eyes matching his, she nodded and mouthed, "Yes, it's Dina."

"Welcome back, Dina. How are you?"

"Hormoz, last week I repeated the words you told me to say, but I didn't take them seriously." The TV host nodded into the camera as

Dina continued. "But God did. Tonight my mother is with me again. She's *standing* here beside me!"

This time, it was Hormoz who struggled to hold back tears. "And?"

"I didn't want Jesus to be the answer. All week long, I thought of everything in my life that was negative. I was trying to feel depressed. But each time I tried to concentrate on my problems, I was flooded with peace. I would stop by the mirror, amazed at the smile on my face. As for my mother, she's well, Hormoz. She's well! And so am I! Jesus is everything you promised. Thank you, my friend."[4]

Time after time when I read this account, it brings tears to my eyes. I wrote this endorsement: "*Dreams and Visions* is a record of part of the ongoing Book of Acts in the earth today! And as thrilling as a movie script. Meet the precious saints in the Muslim world who literally risk it all to serve Jesus, who is graciously appearing in dreams and visions."[5]

As Doyle says, Jesus is on the move in the Muslim world!

Doyle and his wife, JoAnn, want believers around the world to join this spiritual revolution through prayer. Tom said, "Not everybody is going to go to the Middle East, but they can pray. And no government, no leader can block intercession around the world. That's one thing that can get into any country so we need to pray as believers that God would continue to push the gospel out to the ends of the earth."[6] Doyle came to our Jerusalem studio and told us, "I think God is a fair God that He's righteous and just and people are seeking and they don't know where to go. Maybe they don't have a Bible, maybe there's no missionary in the village. He'll get the message to them somehow."[7]

I've met several former Muslims like Ali whose lives have been transformed by this "Glorious Intruder." These MBB testimonies rise like a clarion call for the church to pray for the Muslim world that's been historically and unusually resistant to the gospel. The veil that shrouded the Muslim world for centuries is being shredded. While the Arab world is experiencing unprecedented political upheaval, this phenomenon—often unseen and unreported—is a modern-day spiritual earthquake shaking the foundations of Islam. You can't understand today's Middle East completely without knowing about this supernatural phenomenon.

AT THE CROSSROADS

One organizer of the At the Crossroads conference told me they wanted to let people know that, along with the changes through the Arab Spring seen on the news, the kingdom of God is also on the move. "We should be encouraged by that," he said.[8] Under the surface of the Fertile Crescent, spiritual tectonic plates are moving from Mecca to Tehran to Morocco and the world of Islam is being shaken, even in countries "closed" to the gospel.

Iran is one of those countries. I interviewed on the phone an evangelist to Iran whom I'll call C. He said in Iran dreams and visions are the primary ways Muslims come to faith in Jesus. The dreams are often similar. Jesus usually comes dressed in white. He brings hope. His instructions are often specific. For example, "In the next two or three days you will meet someone who will tell you more about Me."

C estimates about eight out of ten believers in Iran come to Jesus through a dream or vision. He feels this phenomenon is unique in church history. He knows it's a very special time for Iran and hopes it lasts. He says the apostle Paul with his passion for evangelism would love to have seen Iran's revival. More Muslims have come to faith there in the past fifteen years than in the previous three hundred.[9]

According to the book *Iran: Desperate for God* by the Voice of the Martyrs (VOM), "the fastest growing movement in the entire Muslim world today are Muslims converting to Christianity."

According to native Iranian pastors, the evangelical church in Iran before the Islamic Revolution of 1979 numbered a mere few hundred believers. Today, the evangelical following is estimated at over one million strong. In 2006, even Iranian president Mahmoud Ahmadinejad decried the rate of Muslim conversions to Christianity in his country. VOM estimates Iran's underground churches are currently experiencing an annual growth rate of 20 percent, the highest rate worldwide, followed by Afghanistan at 16 percent.[10] C adds that Iranians are so spiritually hungry and dissatisfied with Islam it takes about five minutes to lead someone to faith in Jesus, fifteen minutes if it's a "tough case."

But dreams and visions are just one way Muslims are embracing Jesus. While in Persian Iran dreams and visions are the main way God is revealing Himself, in the Arab world another missionary—I'll call him T—says satellite television is a modern-day evangelistic wonder. He came to the conference and constantly travels in and out of Arab countries. One evening we sat in the Christ Church courtyard and enjoyed the sweet evening Jerusalem breeze. He described the view he sees as he traverses these spiritual fault lines penetrating the world of Islam.

He identified satellite television as the number one way the gospel is reaching Muslims in Arab countries. He says, "The Arabs love their TV and their TV is their window to the world."[11] There are now no less than eight Christian satellite TV networks beaming the gospel into the Muslim world. In addition, a Bible film community called the *God's Stories* Series (godsstories.com) is producing films in Arabic that have been downloaded millions of times throughout the Middle East. They've finished stories from Adam and Eve to David and plan to soon release the story of Jesus.

One factor driving Muslims to Jesus is the profound dissatisfaction many Muslims feel about Islam. One Kurdish pastor and a former Muslim paraphrased a Kurdish proverb that says, "If we cannot taste the bitterness [of Islam], we cannot know the sweetness [of Jesus]."[12] "C," our missionary friend, said most Iranians are fed up with Islam, and most gave up on it decades ago. He estimates Iran's population is only 5 percent radical Muslim. "If people could speak freely, they'd tell you they hate the regime. Few go to the Friday mosque, and while the Western media may portray it one way, it's not the reality."[13]

T exclaimed, "We are living in exciting times! They never heard these things before. [We] are standing on the prayers of others sown years before."[14] He's right. Muslim evangelism has been one of the least fruitful endeavors in church history. Men like Samuel Zwemer, the father of Muslim evangelism, and Roy Whitman, one of the first evangelical preachers in Jordan, labored for decades with precious little visible spiritual fruit. They could only dream of such fruit as is found in these days.

Throughout its nearly fourteen-hundred-year history, Islam has been like an impenetrable fortress resisting attempts to scale its spiritual walls. But that history is being rewritten. The organizers of the conference wanted to show Israel and the world that the "fields are indeed white unto harvest," as Jesus said. They also want Western Christians to see those "white fields," be gripped by His love for Muslims, and help share God's Good News to this needy field of humanity. Already there's a new emerging church where Muslims in significant numbers are shifting their allegiance from the Muslim prophet to Jesus.

T cited those numbers, for example, in Algeria, which has the fastest-growing church in North Africa. He also noted the MBBs are "starting to rise up; becoming less afraid and more willing to speak out." This new boldness is breaking "the shell of fear." He says this is the future of the Middle East and added, "I'm willing to die for this. I was willing to die for Allah. Now I'm willing to die for this."[15]

Some see these stories, testimonies, and claims as just a harbinger of things to come in the Muslim world. Some expect that millions more Muslims will embrace Jesus Christ.

MUSLIMS LOVING ISRAEL, JEWS, AND JERUSALEM

When MBBs come to faith in Jesus, one unique characteristic—some would say an amazing one—is that they often fall in love with Israel and the Jews. Many want to come to Israel and connect with the land. One organizer said, "They want to see where Jesus walked, where He ministered, where He was crucified, where He was buried, where He rose again, and where He's coming back. Many of them came to Jerusalem at great personal risk." They journeyed from countries where it's illegal to come, but for many it was the trip of a lifetime.

Some who came from Middle Eastern countries met Jews who fled that same homeland. In the streets and in the markets they told them, "We came from where your parents and grandparents came from. We're from there, and we want you to know you're not alone. And regardless of what our politicians are saying, we love you and, indeed, we pray for the peace of Jerusalem." The change of heart is significant since most of these MBBs grew up in the epicenter of anti-Semitism and were raised to hate Israel and the Jews.

Dr. Jurgen Bühler of the ICEJ (International Christian Embassy Jerusalem) shared this testimony of his meeting with an Algerian pastor:

> A look at Algeria is also encouraging. . . . The revival started among the Berber tribes but is spreading now to other sectors and new fellowships are cropping up all over the country. But what is equally exciting is that these new Christian believers share a passionate love for Israel. The pastor asked me: "Our brothers back home love what you are doing for Israel. Can we open a branch of the International Christian Embassy for Algeria?"[16]

JEWS BELIEVING IN JESUS

These MBBs parallel a phenomenon happening among Jews. For example, when the following story hit the headlines of Israel's newspaper several years ago, it revealed a side of Israel not seen since the book of Acts.

When fifteen-year-old Ami Ortiz saw the package, he thought it was like any other holiday gift. It was Purim, and many people sent friends and family presents celebrating the time when God delivered the Jewish people from the wicked plot of Haman. He thought the package was beautiful. He didn't know this "gift" would change his life forever. He had come home early this holiday while his parents had chosen to spend the day in Jerusalem. Their housekeeper, Marina, took the package from outside the door and put it on the kitchen table. She left Ami with the package while she took out the rubbish to the container down the street. Ami called his mother to see if he could open it. "Yes," she said.

Marina described what happened next. "I heard this loud boom! It was this big, huge explosion. The air was shaking and I thought, *Oh my God, what's happening here?*"[17]

Three stories down and half a block away, she could feel the rush of the wind from the explosion. She raced back upstairs to see what had happened. She found Ami on the floor, bloodied and near death. The explosion destroyed the apartment. She heard Ami say, "Jesus, Jesus," and then roll over. The bomb had punctured Ami's lungs, blown off two toes, sprayed his body with shrapnel, and left him nearly blind. Ami was alive but barely. An ambulance came and took Ami to Tel Aviv's best pediatric hospital. David and Leah Ortiz, Ami's parents, rushed to the hospital. The doctors gave them the bad news: Ami probably would not survive the night.

But miraculously, Ami did survive that first night—and the second. But Ami's ability to survive, much less walk, run, or play his favorite sport basketball, was in doubt. His parents endured the pain of watching their son suffer. His mother, Leah, told us, "To see the violence that was done to his body. How this bomb just mangled his body. It's very, very hard. And it's just a lot of pain, a lot of emotional pain to go through this with your child."[18]

Yet through the days, weeks, and months Ami made what even the medical staff called a miraculous recovery. For example, Ami wasn't able to see at first. Now his vision is 20/20. His father, David, gave the credit to the Lord, "God is the God of the impossible. He is able to turn darkness into light in an instant."[19]

The story of the bombing and his miraculous recovery went throughout Israel and literally around the world. Thousands of letters, well wishes, and prayers flooded the Ortiz home. The family said prayer is what sustained them through their dark night of the soul. But why would someone send a bomb to the Ortizes? Why would they have to go through this dark time?

Eighteen months later, the answer came. Police finally arrested the man responsible for the bombing. "Jack" Teitel told investigators he wanted to wipe out Messianic Jews from the land of Israel. The Ortizes are Messianic Jews, Jews who believe that Jesus—*Yeshua* in Hebrew—is the Jewish Messiah. But Teitel's attempt to eliminate Messianic Jews backfired. Instead, their story and their faith spread throughout Israel and around the world.

Channels 1 and 2—Israel's national broadcast stations—profiled Ami and highlighted this new phenomenon within Israeli society, the growth of the Messianic Movement. David said, "It's been a year of God just bringing up in media who's Yeshua and could the Jewish people really accept the Lord and still remain Jewish. So the gospel has been preached." Leah added, "I believe that's what the Lord meant to do through an extremely painful, painful situation is that [Ami's] face—people love him in Israel and they love him all over the world and it's through that that the gospel is being preached."[20]

Ami's story portrayed the Messianic Movement, which is often maligned and misunderstood, in a sympathetic way, particularly when soft-spoken Ami chose to forgive the man who tried to kill him. Even after losing body parts and admitting that was hard to deal with, amazingly, Ami carried no bitterness toward Teitel. Ami told us, "I don't feel hate. I don't see a reason for it. I could say they're blind by their hate. They think it's the right thing. You can't blame a blind person for running over you, so I don't see. It's just not there. It wasn't there from the beginning. I don't even know how to explain it but it's just not there. No hate at all."

I asked, "Have you forgiven them?"

"Yeah, I have."[21]

David and Leah echoed Ami's feelings:

Forgiveness has to be. It has to be. I'm convinced that Yeshua died for these people too. And even though they did what they did, God's love is great enough to forgive them. . . . Forgiveness was a necessity for us. And it is true that if we can't forgive others then, I mean the Lord has done so much for us and so much to forgive us; then if we don't forgive others, He won't forgive us. It doesn't matter what the situation is. It has to be. It's a command of the Lord. Because of the great price that He went through, that He paid in order to forgive us.[22]

On April 9, 2013, an Israeli court sentenced an unrepentant Teitel to two life sentences plus thirty years for his attempted murder of Ami, the murders of two Arabs, and other violent acts. The court said Teitel's so-called "holy work had become dust under his feet and that his actions contradicted the values of the Jewish state."[23] Once again the Ortiz's said, "We all forgave him."[24]

This extension of forgiveness by Ami and his parents struck a chord in many of the reporters who covered this case. So, in a most dramatic way, the phenomenon of Jews believing in Jesus spread throughout Israel and the Jewish world. The question was raised: Can a Jew believe in Jesus and still be a Jew? The presumption for centuries had been if a Jew believes in Jesus, he or she no longer remains a Jew but becomes a Christian.

Yet Knut Hoyland, the international director of the Caspari Center in Jerusalem, an organization that tracks the Messianic Movement in Israel, told us, "Well, if we go back to the New Testament, the first believers were all Jewish, and if you go through history there have been Jewish believers in Jesus throughout history. Jesus was Jewish. So in many ways, it's a natural way. Jesus came as the Messiah for the Jews and we as Gentiles have had the privilege of sharing the gospel, but we have received it from the Jewish people. We owe them much, and it's perfectly natural to be Jewish and believe in Jesus, but not everyone in the Jewish community or the Israeli society will see it that way."

Hoyland told us the Messianic Movement has likely doubled in the last ten years. Now perhaps as many as ten thousand or more Messianic Jews worship and practice their faith within Israel. Their congregations have spread throughout the country. Asher Intrader leads one called Revive Israel Ministries and oversees Ahavat Yeshua congregation in Jerusalem and Tiferet Yeshua congregation in Tel Aviv. He believes the growth of the Messianic Movement within Israel holds prophetic significance:

> One of the verses that is very important to us is in Matthew 23. Yeshua said, "You will not see me again until you say 'Blessed is He who comes in the name of the Lord." We understand in that chapter, He was talking to the same people that had Him crucified and rejected Him. So we see that Yeshua was addressing our people, the Jewish people here in Israel. There will be a turning to Him and an invitation both for Him to come back. This phrase also has a legal and covenantal meaning in Hebraic thought and grammar. It means to choose or make someone King. It's more than just a welcoming invitation. It is an expression of authority. It's a coronation statement. It's a welcoming and saying, "Blessed is He who comes in the name of the Lord." King Messiah is the whole concept. So we believe our people are becoming ready to do that. Now, the 10–15,000 of us that are already here; we are praying and declaring this statement continuously. So we have already begun the process. However, as more and more people get saved, we will be building a critical mass. The kernel is in place, but we have not reached the total critical mass yet. But our people have returned to the land, and all of us here in the Land believe in that prayer and all are doing it.[25]

Intrader sees a revival coming to Israel centered in Jerusalem:

> We believe that the world is coming toward a revival that's of a similar pattern that we see in Acts chapter 2, but the size of it will be worldwide. It will be like Acts 2 in a worldwide scope. We are on the way to a worldwide revival that will be rooted in Jerusalem. . . . The first revival in the book of Acts that launched the gospel going around the world started in Jerusalem. The last revival that will lead to Him coming back must be centered in Jerusalem as well. Yeshua arose into heaven from Jerusalem and will return there.[26]

SIGNS, WONDERS, AND MIRACLES

Another phenomenon happening in the Middle East is the reports of miracles. Canon Andrew White also spoke at the conference. Few people have experienced danger or escaped death like White. He pastors the Anglican Church St. George's, where his flock has been decimated by terror attacks throughout the long and bloody Iraqi conflict. Terrorists killed, murdered, kidnapped, or assassinated nearly three hundred of his flock. In his book *The Vicar of Baghdad*, he shares his experiences and some of the miraculous happenings in the onetime hometown of King Nebuchadnezzar.

We met with White at his hotel and with the Mount of Olives in the background sat down for an interview. White is a large man with a larger heart. His cerebral palsy seems to exaggerate his thick British accent. According to White, the age of miracles is not over and he shared this story to prove it. They staff a medical clinic at the church, and a man named Achmed came to see White to transfer his daughter from a Baghdad hospital to their clinic:

[Achmed] came up and said, "I really need you to treat my daughter. She is so ill. She's at Medical City, the big university hospital. And the doctors said, 'There's nothing we can do, she's in our hospital already.'" So he sent him to me. And I saw him and I prayed for him. And I said, "Go see your daughter now." And he was a Muslim. I said, "All the time you're going just say the name of Jesus. In Aramaic it's, 'Yesua, Yesua, Yesua, Yesua.'

And so he went there, he got to the hospital and just got into the ward and one of the doctors came up to him and said, "Achmed, I'm so sorry, your daughter has just died." He cried and screamed with anguish. And he walked into the room and saw her lying covered in her bed. And he pulled the blanket back, went to her, and said, "Yesua, Yesua, Yesua." And he cuddled her and put his arms around her. And she sat up and said, "Daddy, can I have some food now? I'm hungry."

So when he came and told me what happened, I said, "Don't worry, it's happened before." It just didn't happen with Jairus's daughter, it also happened recently. The bishop of Rochester, the former bishop who's actually a Pakistani, Michael Yusef Ali, said to me, "In Pakistan there was a man whose daughter died and he went up to her and cuddled his daughter and she sat up and she said, 'Dad, can I have some food?'" So there's resurrections and there's hungry people all over the world![27]

The daughter of Jairus, whom White referred to, was the story Mark told about Jesus in Mark 5:35–43. The similarities are striking.

PERSECUTION

One Christian worker at the conference said, "So we see the harvest that we've all proclaimed and prayed and fasted for is upon us, but it comes in an environment of persecution as well as blessing."[28] This persecution is experienced not only by MBBs but by Christians throughout the Middle East and particularly on the fault line between Islam and Christianity.

Ayaan Hirsi Ali, a Muslim woman, spoke out about the pervasive and ongoing persecution by Muslims against Christians in the Middle East and beyond. She cites attacks on Christians from Sudan to Egypt, Nigeria, and Pakistan; from West Africa and the Middle East to South Asia and Oceania. She calls it "Christophobia" and compared it to "Islamophobia." She says:

> The scale and severity of Islamophobia pales in comparison with the bloody Christophobia currently coursing through Muslim-majority nations from one end of the globe to the other. The conspiracy of silence surrounding this violent expression of religious intolerance has to stop. Nothing less than the fate of Christianity—and ultimately of all religious minorities—in the Islamic world is at stake.[29]

As Nina Shea, the director of the Hudson Institute's Center for Religious Freedom, pointed out in an interview with *Newsweek*: "Christian minorities in many majority-Muslim nations have lost the protection of their societies."[30]

Whether MBBs or Christians, the Middle East is spawning stories of great faith in the midst of severe persecution. Consider the story of Fatima Al-Mutairi. She was born into a well-known Bedouin tribe in a religiously zealous town and named after Fatima, the fourth daughter of Muhammad. According to Tom Doyle's account, her family expected no less than absolute devotion to Islam.[31]

Yet on the Internet Fatima began to hear stories about Muslims coming to faith in Jesus through dreams. After chatting with others online about who this Jesus was and devouring the New Testament, she embraced the One others said was "a powerful, gentle Person who overwhelmed him or her, not with unendurable shame as the Muslim leaders did, but with a pure love that reached deep inside."[32]

She became well-known on the Internet under her pen name "Rania" for her poetry about Jesus. Until the day her brother found her poems and Christian communications. Doyle tells the rest of the story:

> When Fatima returned home, her brother announced to the family that she had devoted herself to the infidel faith, a faith for which she would now die. To confirm the stunning revelation, the raging cleric asked Fatima, "Are you a Jesus follower?"
>
> Her answer was simple: "Yes. Yes I am."
>
> He took her cell phone, so she could not call for help—not that anyone in Buraydah would have come to her rescue—and locked Fatima in her bedroom. For the four hours she awaited her execution, the computer that had brought Christ to her brought Rania's last words to the world. To her online church and beyond, she sent out one last poem on the Internet: [It reads in part . . .]

May the Lord Jesus guide you, O Muslims, and enlighten your hearts that you might love others. We do not worship the cross, and we are not insane. We worship the Lord Jesus, the light of the world. . . .

And the Messiah says: "Blessed are the persecuted." And we for the sake of Christ all things bear. What is it to you that we are infidels?

Enough—your swords do not concern me, nor evil, nor disgrace. Your threats do not trouble me, and we are not afraid.

And by God, I am unto death a Christian—Verily I cry for what passed by, of a sad life. I was far from the Lord Jesus for many years.

Oh History record and bear witness, Oh witnesses! We are Christians—in the path of Christ we tread.

Take from me this word, and note it well. You see Jesus is my Lord, and He is the Best of Protectors. . . .

As to my last words, I pray to the Lord of the worlds.

Jesus is the Messiah, the Light of clear Guidance. That He changes nations, and sets the scales of justice aright.

And that He spread Love among you Oh Muslims.

Minutes after she clicked Send for the last time, Fatima's brother entered the room. He beat her cruelly, breaking bones and rupturing skin. Finally, he cut out her tongue and dragged her outside where he burned her alive.[33]

Fatima's story seems right out of the book of Hebrews: "Others were tortured, not accepting deliverance, that they might obtain a better resurrection" (11:35). This is the era of the Middle East today. A time of great blessing and a time of great persecution.

The best of times; the worst of times.

16 BACK TO JERUSALEM

This gospel of the kingdom will be preached in all the world as a witness to all the nations, and then the end will come.

—MATTHEW 24:14

DATELINE: HONG KONG

WE WAITED IN LINE, BOUGHT OUR TICKETS, AND STEPPED aboard one of the most exotic modes of transportation in the world, Hong Kong's *Star Ferry*. About every ten minutes—day and night—the ferry runs between Hong Kong Island and the Kowloon Peninsula across the famed Victoria Harbour. For $2.50 it was a bargain. It felt like stepping back into a Humphrey Bogart or Charlie Chan movie.

Seeing the striking Hong Kong skyline, listening to the churning waters, and sitting with the locals on their daily commute was an awesome experience. My friends who had been to Hong Kong before said I had to try it. I wasn't disappointed. But our main goal in Hong Kong wasn't to ride the ferry but to find out more about one of the most significant spiritual trends in the world, the Back to Jerusalem movement.

While Hong Kong straddles the fault line between East and West, China and the world economically, it also opens a window into China's spiritual past and its future. We came to interview Dennis Balcombe, one of the first Western evangelists to enter China when it reopened its doors in the 1970s. His autobiography, *One Journey, One Nation*, chronicles how God dramatically led him to the People's Republic of China. We met Balcombe in his crowded and cluttered Revival China Ministries International offices and tapped into his extensive knowledge of China's church.

First, Balcombe explained that for decades he's witnessed the gospel in China preached with biblical "signs and wonders." That means sick people healed, deaf people hearing, blind eyes opened, and even some people raised from the dead. The growth of the home church in twentieth-century China remains one of the most remarkable in church annals. During the Communist takeover in the 1940s, the government expelled all the foreign missionaries. It seemed a mortal blow to the church. For years little news emerged of what was happening spiritually within this Asian giant. The church appeared dead or dormant.

But what took place away from the eyes of the world was nothing short of miraculous. From an estimated 700,000 Christians in the 1940s, the church grew to an estimated 100 million Christians or more by the twenty-first century. The Communists expunged the missionaries from the land, but they couldn't uproot the gospel seed these missionaries had planted in China's rich soil.

Now one dream has captivated many of those Christians, the dream of completing Jesus's Great Commission and taking the gospel all the way "back to Jerusalem." Balcombe told us, "They believe that when they get back to Jerusalem the gospel will have gone around the world one time and Jesus will come back."[1]

The Chinese church sees itself at a pivotal juncture in the spread of the gospel around the world. It's almost as though they see themselves as the runners on the last lap of Christian evangelism. If you look into the record of the book of Acts nearly two thousand years ago, the apostle

Paul says he tried to take the gospel into Asia. But Luke, the author of Acts, wrote that the Holy Spirit had another idea:

> Paul and his companions traveled throughout the region of Phrygia and Galatia, having been kept by the Holy Spirit from preaching the word in the province of Asia. When they came to the border of Mysia, they tried to enter Bithynia, but the Spirit of Jesus would not allow them to. So they passed by Mysia and went down to Troas. During the night Paul had a vision of a man of Macedonia standing and begging him, "Come over to Macedonia and help us." After Paul had seen the vision, we got ready at once to leave for Macedonia, concluding that God had called us to preach the gospel to them. (Acts 16:6–10 NIV)

This "Macedonian call" took the gospel west instead of east. It's hard to overestimate the impact this call had on the world. It spawned Western civilization from Europe to North and South America. Now two thousand years later, its westward advance has splashed upon the shores of Asia. The Chinese church hopes to complete the circumnavigation of the gospel and reach the finish line in Jerusalem.

Balcombe explains, "They feel this way: we received the gospel from the West so we are going to take it back to where it began. . . . So they talk and pray about it all the time . . . it's going around the world and when the gospel comes back to Jerusalem, they believe that is when Jesus will come back."[2]

They're not talking about a conference in Jerusalem but a bold, unprecedented vision to evangelize the world from China to Jerusalem. This quest is one of the most ambitious plans to complete the Great Commission in the world today. If Matthew 24:14 will be fulfilled, the gospel has to reach the ends of the earth, including that part of the world between China and Jerusalem. Yet, historically, this region has been one of the most resistant areas to the good news of Jesus. It includes the Muslim, Buddhist, and Hindu worlds.

Missionaries often refer to this region as part of the "10-40 Window."

The 10-40 Window signifies that part of the world 10 to 40 degrees latitude north of the equator and stretching from Japan to Morocco. The Chinese church plans to retrace the ancient trade routes through the 10-40 Window. These routes once connected East and West, like the northern Silk Road, the central mountain Silk Road, and the coastal Silk Road. Centuries before, traders along these routes—like Marco Polo—brought spices back from the East to the West. Now, instead of spices, these modern-day spiritual adventurers hope to bring the scent and savor of the gospel from east to west.

It's a daunting task, and some wonder if this Mount Everest of evangelism can be scaled. But the leaders of the Back to Jerusalem movement say yes. They believe the church in China has been both called and prepared by the Lord to complete this task in part because it's been forged in the furnace of persecution. They estimate it might require thousands of missionaries to complete the task.

Whatever the figure, the requirements for these missionaries might surprise many Westerners. Their number one qualification is a willingness to "give their utmost for His highest." Simply put, some are willing to die and be buried outside of China. Many in the Chinese church believe only this level of commitment can penetrate these seemingly impenetrable areas with the gospel.

Many of them want to specifically reach Muslims. Balcombe says, "So they would say, look at these one billion Muslims who don't believe in Jesus. Who's going to reach them? They would say that is our job and we aren't afraid of dying or persecution. We are afraid of disobeying God's Great Commission to take the gospel to the whole world. So this is basically why we think [the] Chinese are more suitable than any other nation."[3]

Behind this evangelistic thrust stands China's economic growth. China's growing economic strength and political relations are opening up opportunities for Christians to leave the confines of China and spread the gospel. They're sending workers throughout the region to work on economic projects. Some of them are working as "tentmakers," as the apostle Paul once did. This unique set of circumstances—the Chinese church's "Macedonian call," its preparation through long years of persecution, and China's economic and political expansion—is blowing to fill the sails of this gospel vessel.

Peter Tsukahira, author of *God's Tsunami: Understanding Israel and End-Time Prophecy,* wrote that this movement has global implications:

> We live in a time when it is possible to envision the events leading up to the completion of Jesus' Great Commission. One day in the not too distant future, the Chinese government policy against believers in China will be changed. The massive underground network of house churches will surface, and the unbelieving world, along with many Christians all over the world, will be stunned by their sheer numbers and the strength of their faith. God has invested so much over the years in the Chinese church. Many martyrs, both Western and Chinese, have shed their blood on Chinese soil, and now tens of millions pursue lives of faith in defiance of official (and unofficial) government persecution. Today, China, in spite of its great size, is also one of the world's fastest growing economies. One day it may be the world's largest. God's Hand is behind this, and His purposes are being fulfilled in China. This nation will lead the Christian world in taking action to complete God's work of bringing in the "fullness of the Gentiles."[4]

THE HEAVENLY MAN

We met with one of the leaders of the Chinese church infused with this "Back to Jerusalem" dream. Ironically, we traveled not east but west to the pastoral hills of western England and the quaint village of Hereford. The River Wye runs through it. The English composer Edward Edgar once wrote some of his famous symphonies in Hereford. But we came not to hear an Edgar symphony like "Pomp and Circumstance" but a modern-day composition some say is being orchestrated by the Spirit of God. In an oak-lined room of the Green Dragon Hotel in the center of town, we sat down with Brother Yun, one of the pioneers of this modern Back to Jerusalem movement. Also known as "The Heavenly Man," he came to England as part of his effort to spread the word to the church in the West about the Back to Jerusalem movement.

I had read the book about Yun's life called *The Heavenly Man*. Like many others I came away deeply moved by this man's sacrificial life for God. Who wouldn't? We settled down with Brother Yun and his interpreter, Brother Ren. Surrounded by lights, cables, and three cameras, I sat riveted by his tales of faith, miracles, and courage in the face of torture and persecution. We talked about both his remarkable testimony and this growing phenomenon of the Chinese Back to Jerusalem movement.

Yun's life story parallels the powerful history of China's home church movement. Signs and wonders brought thousands to faith in Jesus through his evangelism, but it also aroused the attention of the police. As a result, Yun spent time in jail, lots of time. When he wasn't in jail, he lived on the move. When persecution broke out in one place, he would move to the next. During those days under the Cultural Revolution, the government sent thousands of pastors, evangelists, and workers to labor camps. They even tried to expunge Bibles from the land. If they found a person with a Bible, he was immediately sent to prison.

Yet the furnace of persecution forged a fire in this "Heavenly Man." He prayed before he was tortured. He thanked God for the morsels he received in prison. Through it all, he possessed an infectious joy we experienced firsthand during our interview. He spontaneously broke out in song not once but twice during our talk. I've never had that happen before or since.

Yun says that many of the gospel pioneers behind the Back to Jerusalem movement formed the backbone of the Chinese revival for the past several decades and bring a unique résumé to this mission. They've operated in signs and wonders, carried a passion for lost souls in their bones, and helped evangelize the vast outreaches of China. Many have been tortured, imprisoned, and persecuted for their faith.

Yun expressed a childlike but tenacious faith in evangelizing this part of the world:

Every day, my faith is increased and I truly believe today and in the very soon future, Jesus is going to open the door for gospel in Buddhist nations, in the whole India, in the entire Muslim world. We believe that India and the Buddhist world will be filled not with idol temples, but it will be filled with the glory of Jesus Christ. And the same blood of Jesus that is now cleansing the entire continent of Africa today is powerful enough to cleanse the entire Arabic continent and the Muslim world. . . . I am not opposing any other religion, I am just proclaiming that Jesus Christ is the Lord and King of the whole universe and everything belongs to Him. . . . From my own experience, I have understood, Jesus is the eternal way, the eternal truth and the eternal life. And there is no other name given to us than we could be saved by.[5]

Yun also feels that this world-changing evangelism will go on despite changes in the world: "Even though the Bible tells us very clearly that the end-times will be filled with wars and disasters and one nation and people group [rising up] against another. But at the same time when this start to happen, this is also going to be an uprising of the unity and salvation when Jesus is going to bring salvation to multitudes of nations."[6]

Evangelism can be hard work even for the most zealous of disciples, so to meet this need they've established centers to provide training for hundreds and thousands of eager missionaries on their mission all the way back to Jerusalem. The training consists of four main areas: Bible study, languages, cross-cultural training, and practical teachings. On the biblical front, two of the primary requirements are "a passionate understanding of the central message of the cross of Jesus Christ and also (a belief in need to fulfill) the Great Commission."

There are other parts of the church—besides the Chinese—who see themselves as participating in the Back to Jerusalem effort. For example, in April 2005, we traveled all the way to the southern tip of Africa and met a missionary couple with an amazing story to tell.

OUT OF AFRICA

Hundreds of black Africans lined up one behind the other at the edge of the crystal blue waters of the Indian Ocean. They waited patiently. Christian worship music squawked out of a portable sound system. Many swayed with the music. The sound of "Hosanna" filled the air. Multicolored robes like the one in *Joseph and the Amazing Technicolor Dreamcoat* splashed color on this panoramic scene. Sea and sky met somewhere on the horizon and painted a reassuring blue background. The crowd waited until one by one they stepped into the churning surf.

They inched toward two people in the waves. The two—a black African pastor and a white woman missionary—reached out and grabbed the hands of those stepping into the water. They held their hands up high, prayed for them, and baptized them into the cold, refreshing waters of the Indian Ocean. Dozens danced and celebrated all around the two as they rode the swells. Some lay on the shoreline, overcome—they said— by the power of the Spirit of God. The white woman with the blonde hair dotted the scene like an exclamation point in the sea of black faces. She joined the celebration and jumped up and down with arms raised as though the home team had just scored the winning touchdown. For her, this was winning . . . winning souls.

The two stayed for hours until everyone was baptized. Pemba—a town on Mozambique's northern shoreline—marked the site of this baptism. Most of these new Christians had practiced a blend of Islam and syncretism, a kind of spiritual amalgam. For decades—perhaps centuries—this area remained untouched by the Christian gospel. Some veteran missionaries even called it unreachable. So the sight of hundreds of Africans being baptized signaled the dawn of a new day for the good news in this region and turned a new page in the spiritual history of these people.

The scene stirred up visions of the apostle Peter's command on the day of pentecost two thousand years earlier: "Repent and be baptized, every one of you, in the name of Jesus Christ for the forgiveness of your sins. And you will receive the gift of the Holy Spirit" (Acts 2:38 NIV). On that day the church burst into history and the gospel began its march around the world when three thousand souls were saved. That march has continued from that day to the day we witnessed the baptisms in Pemba, on one of the prettiest beaches in the world when the tide rolled in and their sins were washed away.

Magellan, the sixteenth-century Portuguese explorer, plied the waters near Mozambique as he circumnavigated the globe hundreds of years earlier. This scene marked another circumnavigation, the story of the gospel of Jesus Christ going around the world and back to the place where it all began, back to Jerusalem.

After the baptisms, the white woman with the blonde hair came up out of the water. Heidi Baker greeted us: "Welcome to my country." Known as Mama Baker to many, she had several children clinging to her. She kissed them, hugged them, and held their hands. Although it seemed obvious she spoke the local language, love seemed the language that mattered most.

We came to do a report on what we heard was one of the most remarkable revivals in the earth today. Yet Mozambique seemed an unlikely place for a revival that stands poised to sweep up the east coast of Africa all the way back to Jerusalem. For nearly a generation, disasters and destruction scarred this nation on the southeastern coast of Africa. A brutal civil war devastated the country for twenty years, and in the year 2000 some of the worst floods in its history battered the nation. Even today, coming to Mozambique struck me like coming to another planet.

It's beyond third-world poor. Rubbish lines the streets. Abandoned cars dot some of the "nicer" parts of the capital, Maputo. Some houses were no more than a few pieces of tin hung together. We saw a number of people living near the city's dump called the Boccaria. They survive off the refuse of others. The dump reminded me of a scene out of Dante's *Inferno*. Smoke rose from the mountains of rubbish as people picked through this surreal panorama for their daily bread.

Yet in the midst of this hellish environment and desperate poverty, heaven kissed this piece of God's earth. A nascent spiritual renewal brought hope to the hopeless, showed signs of altering the character of a country, and promised to change the face of Africa and even the Middle East. After spending time with the people involved in this revival, I am convinced that in one of the poorest nations on earth live some of the richest people I know.

Several days after the baptisms, we interviewed both Heidi Baker and her husband, Rolland. Heidi bubbled with childlike enthusiasm when she talked about what's happening in Mozambique. "We're in revival," she beamed. "It's amazing. It's a time of glory; we've waited our whole lives for this."[7]

Heidi and Rolland Baker possess an unquenchable faith in the power of the Holy Spirit to transform lives. They began reaching out to Mozambique's poor and needy in 1995 when they established Iris Ministries. Nearly fifteen years later, they're in the middle of what some believe is an unprecedented revival. Rolland explained, "We come into villages here and they find out Jesus is real and they're just screaming at us. They're just demanding—'We want Jesus now. We want a church now. We want a pastor now. Not tomorrow.'"[8]

While they're now seeing multitudes come to Jesus, their vision spans far beyond Mozambique's horizon. They desire to take the gospel of Jesus Christ up through Africa and all the way back to Jerusalem. Rolland Baker says the vision came supernaturally: Here's his explanation:

Person after person after person has had vivid, intense visions of flames of revival starting from South Africa and southern Mozambique and just spreading up north further, further, further into the Moslem areas and into really difficult places and tense places and war-torn areas and famine-torn areas. And just going and going and going until Africa is in fact saturated with the gospel and the gospel just keeps going through Saudi Arabia and keeps going through the Near East all the way back to Jerusalem. And God finishes what He wants to do. God knows how to glorify His Son and He knows how to bring His Son back to this world. He's just able and we don't want to miss out. We want to be right in the path of that progress.[9]

Heidi Baker had one of those visions:

I was praying and worshipping God and I saw a vision of fire. Fresh fire from God and it was Holy Spirit fire and it was just burning, blazing fire. And it went from Southern Africa and it went all the way up into Northern Africa, Sudan, Egypt, until Jerusalem. And the Lord said this movement, this revival that we're seeing that is fruitfulness flowing out of intimate love. That this revival we were called to reach all the African nations until Jerusalem. That Jerusalem was our goal. That Jerusalem was the heart of God and we would reach Jerusalem. So it's something we say all the time in Arco-Iris, until Jerusalem, Ate Jerusalem. So we've planted now into Sudan. We've hit every African country until Sudan and we're about to get into Egypt until we're in Jerusalem.[10]

TO THE ENDS OF THE EARTH

Oddly enough—for all its significance—this "last lap of world missions" is one of the least known facts of the twenty-first century. On February 15, 2005, CBN founder Pat Robertson addressed the National Press Club in Washington DC and called the advance of the Christian gospel "the most underreported story in the world."[11] He noted,

For the past century, the world has been experiencing the most profound revival of the Christian religion in all of history. This has taken place in the midst of two world wars and the rise of Communism, but here are the startling facts. At present, Christianity is by far the world's largest religion encompassing one-third of the world's population. Christianity has been and still is growing at a much faster rate than the population of the world. . . . In 1900, there were 10 million

Christians in Africa representing 10 percent of the population. Today there are 360 million Christians in Africa, representing just under half of the total population of that continent. According to Penn State University distinguished Professor Philip Jenkins, author of a land-mark book *The Next Christendom: the Coming of Global Christianity*, the greatest move of the last century was not Communism or capitalism. Jenkins says, "Do the math and the winner is spirit filled Christianity known as Pentecostalism." The growth of Christianity has taken place in the Southern Hemisphere and Asia outside of the radar of most western media. The new Christianity represents a return to the Bible, to a faith in a supernatural Jesus who saves from sin, heals diseases, and overcomes the power of evil. While the American media is fixated on priestly sex abuse and homosexual marriages, the real story is on simple faith and supernatural power exploding around the world. . . .

My organization [CBN] broadcasts . . . in two hundred countries and many, many languages. And since 1990, our in-depth statistical surveys show that an incredible 369 [now 600] million people world-wide have professed faith in Jesus Christ through our broadcasts. Of note are the 14 million handwritten letters that have been received in our office in Kiev in the Ukraine from all over the former Soviet Union now called the Commonwealth of Independent States. They have been huge responses in Nigeria, Indonesia, the Philippines, Central and South America. . . . Our staff is discovering something else that is not being reported in the Western press that throughout the Muslim world there is a profound spiritual hunger and willingness for the people to know more about Jesus Christ and the New Testament.[12]

Since Robertson delivered his address, another significant development took place with important implications for the future of world missions. On January 29, 2008, mission leaders held an historic and unprecedented meeting called Call2All in Orlando, Florida. Six hundred Christian leaders gathered for the meeting that brought together CEOs of the primary mission organizations and leaders of the international prayer ministries. This combination of mission and prayer organizations represented a historic breakthrough in the progress of the Great Commission. This partnership represents a first in the history of the Christian gospel.

Two major mission organizations in the world—Campus Crusade for Christ begun by Bill Bright in 1951 and Youth with a Mission started by Loren Cunningham in 1960—hosted the meeting. These two organizations represent 12 percent of the mission work force in the earth with almost fifty thousand full-time staff and five hundred thousand part-time staff. This marriage of prayer and missions could well represent an exponential surge for the gospel.

You might wonder what this all has to do with Jerusalem. Well, this gospel, this "power of God unto salvation," this gospel with signs and wonders, is a movement sweeping the nations of the earth and is blowing by the wind of the Holy Spirit back to the place where it all began, back to Jerusalem. While we mentioned China and Mozambique, other churches around the world indicate they, too, feel that the Holy Spirit Himself is urging them to take the gospel back to Jerusalem.

Few might note or record the departure of thirty-six Chinese missionaries toward Jerusalem or a meeting in the bush of Mozambique where a village comes to Jesus, but it's all part of an end-time harvest of souls that many believe will help close the end of this age. While "wars and rumors of wars" might get the headlines, this often unseen and unreported phenomenon is an elemental part of the times in which we live. In this story of salvation's history, the Holy Spirit is orchestrating a crescendo of evangelism that will sweep the gospel of Jesus Christ back to the place where it all began.

17 INTO THE FURNACE

Says the LORD, whose fire is in Zion, and whose
furnace is in Jerusalem.
—ISAIAH 31:9

We're not in Kansas anymore.
—DOROTHY FROM *THE WIZARD OF OZ*

DATELINE: CONTINENTAL FLIGHT OVER THE ATLANTIC

WOULD YOU BRING YOUR FAMILY TO A WAR ZONE?

That's the question I had to answer in the fall of 1998. I was flying on my way to Israel, my third trip to the promised land. As the Continental flight roared above the Atlantic, I pondered the future of my wife and three children. Should we leave the safety and security of the United States for the Middle East cauldron?

Just two weeks before my trip, Michael Patrick, then executive producer of CBN News, sent out an e-mail that changed my life. He asked for a volunteer to open the CBN News Bureau in Jerusalem. If you've ever read a letter, e-mail, or note that all of a sudden rocked your world, you know how I felt. I literally pushed myself away from the computer screen. My heart raced. The implications rushed through my mind. How could we make the cultural leap from suburban America to the Middle East? Would my wife want to go? What about my children? What impact would this have on their lives? We led a fairly comfortable secure life in a quiet town. Did we want to exchange that life for a life in the most contentious place on earth?

Would we move to a war zone?

My 1998 trip included several story assignments, but my most pressing task was to find the answer to this question. I knew I had to pray. My prayers, though, took a turn I had never experienced before. When I prayed, I felt that I was to offer up my children back to God. I had never felt such an urge. The question that burned in my heart was: Would I surrender them to God in the way that Abraham offered up his son Isaac? No, I wasn't going to literally lay them on an altar but offer them back symbolically and emotionally to God in prayer. I didn't consider myself to be what some people call a "prayer warrior." It proved to be one of the hardest times in my life.

During that time, I remember listening to a song I had sung many, many times before: "I Surrender All." I thought how many times I glibly sang that song without realizing what it really meant. Now, I felt that I was being asked to "surrender all." I loved my children. They were the joy of our lives. I hope this doesn't sound too hard-hearted, but was I willing to allow someone else—even God—decide their fate? Yet, with His help, I persevered. I continued to pray and experienced what many old-time Pentecostals used to call "breaking through." After a particularly meaningful time of prayer, I realized that I really had given my children—the most precious things in the world to me—back to the One who gave them to me in the first place.

I wasn't prepared, however, for what happened next. I felt God's fierce love for them, a fierceness that surprised me. It brought new meaning to the scripture that says God is a Warrior. I know it sounds a bit silly to compare my love with His, but I suddenly knew His love was far greater than mine and that He would take care of them, even in a war zone. I didn't know then how important this realization would mean in the days to come.

My first introduction to Israel had come in 1996. CBN News sent my colleague John Waage and me to produce several news stories. Like Christian pilgrims to the Holy Land for the past two thousand years, that experience dropped a plumb line in my life. Life before and after would be measured by that experience—a spiritual and emotional line of demarcation. I felt the truth of what the tour guides say: "Israel may be three hundred miles long, thirty miles wide, but it's three thousand years deep." The depth of three millennia of Bible history is sown throughout Israel's rocks, fields, hills, and countryside. My one regret? That my wife and children did not share my experience at that time. I did not know then that one day we would all share the experience of living in the Land of the Bible.

My second visit to Israel came the next year, 1997. On that trip, I listened to the late Bible teacher Derek Prince speak at a conference. I sat riveted while he shared his experiences as a young man, fresh out of the British army in 1948 and poised to start a new life in the Middle East. I remember vividly when he told one particular story. He spoke with an elderly woman about his desire to live in Jerusalem. She wisely told him, "But, Derek, you don't choose Jerusalem. Jerusalem chooses you." Have you ever felt words pierce your heart? Well, when he said that sentence, it pierced my heart like an arrow. I'm not sure what Prince said after that. I simply sat stunned with the realization that maybe Jerusalem had somehow "chosen me." I hid those words in my heart.

When I returned from my third trip in 1998, I volunteered to start the CBN News bureau in Jerusalem. While my family and I fully expected to go the next year, in 1999, budget decisions constrained us and we postponed our trip until the following year. In May 2000, CBN president Michael Little gave us the go-ahead. We made our plans and scheduled our arrival in the middle of August 2000, to coincide with the upcoming school year. We didn't know then what turmoil, danger, and conflict lay before us.

Three thousand years ago, the Hebrew prophet Isaiah cried out that Jerusalem is a furnace: "Says the LORD, whose fire is in Zion and whose furnace is in Jerusalem" (Isaiah 31:9). When we arrived in that summer of 2000, we immediately began to feel the heat.

When CBN News sent me over from the United States to establish a news bureau in Jerusalem, the timing proved uncanny. Five weeks after we arrived, the second Palestinian intifada led by Yasser Arafat erupted. The Arabic word *intifada* means "struggle," and suddenly we found ourselves in the middle of one of the most violent periods of struggle in the history of the Palestinian-Israeli conflict.

Its turmoil covered the land like a fog. Our isolated and somewhat insulated life in the United States ended. As one family member put it— just like Dorothy in the *Wizard of Oz* once said—"We're not in Kansas anymore." Not only did we find ourselves in a different land with new languages and an unfamiliar culture, but regular terror attacks, suicide bombings, and shootings punctuated daily life. We found ourselves talking around the dinner table not just about what the kids had done at school that day but often about where the latest bombing took place or if we knew someone who was close to the explosion—wounded, or even killed.

In those pre-9/11 days, the war on terror took on a whole new and personal meaning.

Would you keep your family in a war zone?

THE FIRST BOMBING

The first Jerusalem bombing—early afternoon, November 2, 2000— touched our entire family. I had joined dozens of other correspondents in the Isrotel Hotel's press room on Jaffa Street, one of Jerusalem's main thoroughfares. Just a few blocks away, the Anglican International School prepared to let out their students—including my children—for the day.

The press gaggle waited expectantly for a joint announcement by then Israeli prime minister Ehud Barak and Palestinian chairman Yasser Arafat. The press and public expected a joint cease-fire declaration by the two leaders that would douse the fires of the nascent intifada. By then, the intifada—just a few weeks old—had become the worst civil disturbance within Israel in more than fifty years and a story splashed across the world.

The Barak-Arafat announcement—scheduled for 2:00 p.m.— lingered in limbo for almost an hour. But instead of an announcement, sirens suddenly filled the air. One after another, ambulances sped past the pressroom. The news traveled fast. A car bomb had exploded just a few blocks from us, not far down Jaffa Street near Mahane Yehuda, Jerusalem's biggest open-air market.

Twenty or more reporters—including myself—raced out of the briefing room. As we ran down Jaffa Street, now filled with ambulances, crowds streamed toward the blast site. Shomron Street marked ground zero. A car loaded with more than twenty pounds of explosives had transformed the quiet, narrow, cobblestoned street into a death zone. The scene—one repeated dozens of times over the next few years—was utter chaos.

Hundreds of policemen, firemen, reporters, and onlookers swarmed the entrance to Shomron Street. Firefighters doused the flames of the car wreckage. The bomb squad scoured the area for more bombs. Volunteers from ZAKA—a religious disaster relief organization—searched for body parts. They took the grisly job of collecting human remains to be buried according to Jewish law. It seemed in the midst of this evil, their work took on a sacred air. TV journalists staked out spots for their live reports. Police—including a half dozen on horseback—strained to keep the crowd from the site of the terror attack.

Nearly one hundred Orthodox Jews gathered and shouted, "Death to the Arabs!" Desperate family members came to see if a loved one might have been hurt or killed in the bombing. Instinctively, everyone wanted to let their family and friends know they were okay. Many people got frustrated when they discovered the flood of calls from the same location at the same time simply overwhelmed Israel's cell phone network. Their phones proved useless.

Two blocks away, the students from the Anglican International School had dismissed for the day just in time to hear the explosion. Immediately school officials closed the front gate. Two of my children remained inside, but inexplicably no one knew the whereabouts of our youngest child, Grace. Halfway across the city, my wife anxiously waited for news. She heard about the bombing but wasn't prepared for the word that two of our children were safe but one was missing. Where could she be? Was she near the bombing? And why doesn't anyone know where she is?

Back on Shomron Street, the impact of the bombing became deadly clear. The blast killed two people, wounded nine, and shook a neighborhood that once again had become a terrorist target. In July 1997, an explosion in the same area had killed sixteen people, and another attack in November 1998 had wounded twenty-one. It was obvious the bomb makers wanted to make this crowded market their target.

On the home front—after desperate phone calls and nearly an hour after the bombing—my wife finally solved the mystery of our missing third child. Just before the bombing, the swimming coach took the younger students off school grounds and headed for practice. Oblivious to all the commotion, they swam peaceably at a pool on the outskirts of Jerusalem.

November 2, 2000, marked the first of many bombings in Jerusalem and our family's first close call. Later that evening, weary from the ordeal, but relieved we were all safe, we gathered around the family dinner table. We talked through the day and how we would handle similar situations in the future. We thanked God that despite the danger, He had protected us. It proved a sobering introduction to life in Jerusalem for years to come. Certainly not what we had expected when we landed at Ben Gurion airport two and a half months earlier.

It became like living in the valley of the shadow of death.

Early on during the intifada, one Palestinian activist cried, "The battle over Jerusalem has begun." So it had. We found ourselves in the midst of that battle, not knowing then how deep or desperate it would become. We lived with the constant threat of terror attacks. Like many other Jerusalemites, we got used to random checkpoints on the roads and ubiquitous security checks at the supermarket, restaurant, or movie theatre.

Even in the best of times, Jerusalem contains an emotionally and spiritually charged atmosphere. It can wear you down or out. Now, with this conflict playing out day by day, we went from one adrenaline surge to another. Often you woke up in the morning to face the next terror attack. The experience was numbing.

When we first arrived in Israel, we didn't know then we would have a front-row seat to witness the pain, suffering, and horror of one of the most traumatic epochs in this centuries-old Arab-Israeli conflict. Some of the more vivid memories: hearing machine-gun fire from nearby Gilo during our home group meeting, or listening to the roar of Apache attack helicopters while I prayed at bedtime with Grace. Others include getting a phone call from our daughter Kathleen to pick her up after a bus blew up two blocks from school. She heard the explosion, silence, metal falling, and then people screaming. Or my son Philip and me at a checkpoint watching an Israeli tank turret swivel around, then staring down its barrel and realizing it's time to "get out of Dodge."

During those early days, a friend and more than twenty-year veteran of Jerusalem said, "I got thrown into the deep end of the pool." Things began to explode—literally and figuratively—around us. We knew we were coming into a war zone, but we didn't know we'd find ourselves on the front lines. The experience made us appreciate life, knowing that wherever you are, eternity is not far away. It highlighted the brevity—and fragility—of life.

Daily life became a gruesome reality. The deadly and devastating impact of a suicide bomber shattered real people and real lives. It's rare for a reporter to arrive at the scene of an attack without being kept at a distance by the police. Emergency services typically arrive on the scene moments after an attack and control access to the bomb site. But on February 22, 2004, a bus blew up near the home of veteran journalist Stan Goodenough. Our home was just three blocks away and we heard the explosion. Goodenough made it quickly to the scene and captured in words the devastation of the suicide attack on Bus 14:

> For a while I was alone, the only nonofficial person able to take in the detail of it all. . . . The yawning rear doorway revealed more orange, yellow and red flesh, lumps of bodies in the aisle between the seats. Near the front door, a portable pink cassette player lay on its side. Forensic personnel in white coveralls, dark red cloth booties covering their shoes and pink-stained disposable gloves shielding their hands, picked their way through the mix of metal and human debris. . . . I watched now as police passed objects through the back window of the bus. A shredded army shirt—it's frightening how a bomb blast can rip off people's clothes—some bullets, books, bags, and at least five children's backpacks, pink and blue and red. As one officer gingerly (tenderly?) searched through the school bags, I wondered about the mothers and fathers who had packed their kids' lunches just a little while before, and who must have been frantically trying to get news of their loved little ones after hearing that horrible sound.[1]

Those suicide attacks came with grisly regularity. In the midst of this terror, Psalm 91:1 became a favorite scripture: "He who dwells in the secret place of the Most High shall abide under the shadow of the Almighty." God's shadow did envelop us. I learned to love His shadow. We had to put our trust in the Lord and our lives into His hands. Even more difficult as parents, we had to put our children into His hands. One of the hardest things had to be letting your son or daughter go to meet their friends knowing it might be the last time you'd see them again. We took what precautions we could and tried to let them have as normal a social life as possible during those hellish days. Parenting seminars didn't prepare us for this.

But through the violence and death that enveloped us, He watched over them and kept us all under His wings. Those wings became our refuge. We found out what it meant to live in the midst of terror. We learned the importance of knowing where God has called you. Peace and protection came from walking in the center of His will, even in the midst of suicide attacks. We discovered that when you're where He wants you to be, His calling is a strong anchor in the midst of any storm. The other anchor proved to be the knowledge we had surrendered our children to Him and His quiet assurance that He would watch over them even in a war zone, even in the valley of the shadow of death.

We learned lessons in that valley about ourselves and the times we all live in.

We learned it was time to "watch and pray" as Matthew said about the five wise virgins: "Watch therefore, for you know neither the day nor the hour in which the Son of Man is coming" (Matthew 25:13).

We learned that as much as our world shook, the book of Hebrews said a greater shaking is coming: "'Yet once more I shake not only the earth, but also heaven.' Now this, 'Yet once more' indicates the removal of those things that are being shaken, as of things that are made, that the things which cannot be shaken may remain" (Hebrews 12:26–27).

We learned it's time to look up: "Now when these things begin to happen, look up and lift up your heads, because your redemption draws near" (Luke 21:28).

We learned investing in eternity is the best investment: "Do not lay up for yourselves treasures on earth, where moth and rust destroy and where thieves break in and steal; but lay up for yourselves treasures in heaven, where neither moth not rust destroys and where thieves do not break in and steal. For where your treasure is, there your heart will be also" (Matthew 6:19–21).

We learned who to keep our eyes on: "Let us lay aside every weight, and the sin which so easily ensnares us, and let us run with endurance the race that is set before us, looking unto Jesus, the author and finisher of our faith" (Hebrews 12:1–2).

Our faith was tested when Jerusalem roared like a furnace during the intifada. Many did not survive; others came out scarred, wounded, and broken. We did live through the furnace. I can only explain our survival on the strength of Psalm 91 and His mercy: "He who dwells in the secret place of the Most High shall abide under the shadow of the Almighty" (v.1).

Our family's introduction to Jerusalem stamped a mark on our hearts. Yet each one of us may eventually rendezvous with Jerusalem, either the earthly or the heavenly one.

18 RENDEZVOUS IN JERUSALEM: A DATE WITH DESTINY

God is restoring the focus once again to Jerusalem. The place of beginnings is also the place of ending.[1]
—RUTH HEFLIN, *JERUSALEM, ZION, ISRAEL AND THE NATIONS*

The history of Jerusalem is the history of the world; it is more; it is the history of Heaven and earth.
—BENJAMIN DISRAELI, *TANCRED*

In this house and in Jerusalem, which I have chosen out of all the tribes of Israel, I will put My name forever.
—2 KINGS 21:7

DATELINE: JERUSALEM, CROSSROADS OF HISTORY AND PROPHECY

JERUSALEM'S GEOGRAPHY SEEMS TO PLACE IT AT THE HUB OF the world. It lies near the crossroads of the ancient trade route the Via Maris, the Way of the Sea. It also sits at the seam of Africa's Great Rift Valley that struts through Israel's backbone. During history's epochs, it's been the focal point of armies and generals from Alexander the Great to

Napoleon. Great nations like the Assyrians, Babylonians, Egyptians, and finally the Ottomans plundered its people and goods. Then for centuries, Jerusalem faded into obscurity. It languished as a backwater town in a decaying empire with barely a hint of its former glory.

Now it's blazed its way back onto the world's center stage. Politically, diplomatically, evangelistically, and even militarily Jerusalem lies at the epicenter of world attention. While all roads may have one day led to Rome, and Caesar once placed the Golden Column as an ancient lodestar, history's inexorable march ends in Jerusalem.

For better or worse, good or evil, the world is on its way to the city of David. The fate of this city, the diplomatic discussions over its future, and the political tempests it creates show the prophet Zechariah had it right; there will be a rendezvous of the nations coming to Jerusalem. He knew one day the nations of the world would focus on Jerusalem, and he prophesized the city would shoot back to the forefront of the world's agenda. Here's how he put it:

> This is the word of the LORD concerning Israel. The LORD, who stretches out the heavens, who lays the foundation of the earth, and who forms the spirit of man within him, declares: "I am going to make Jerusalem a cup that sends all the surrounding peoples reeling. Judah will be besieged as well as Jerusalem. On that day, when all the nations of the earth are gathered against her, I will make Jerusalem an immovable rock for all the nations. All who try to move it will injure themselves." (Zechariah 12:1–3 NIV)

In July 2001, Pat Robertson dedicated our CBN News Jerusalem bureau and alluded to this same prophecy: "This is the navel of the earth. This is the place where prophecy is going to be fulfilled. It's not Washington, it's not Bonn, it's not Paris, it's Jerusalem that's going to be the focus of the attention of the world and that's what's happening right now actually. The nations of the earth are once again beginning to look at Jerusalem."[2]

SIGNPOSTS ON HISTORY'S HIGHWAY

Dateline Jerusalem meant to set out various markers along today's history. They include the circumnavigation of the gospel back to Jerusalem. It began on Jerusalem's Mount Zion when three thousand souls were saved, and now the gospel is making its way back to the eternal finish line, the Mount of Olives. Jews—scattered all over the earth—have begun to make their trek back to their ancient homeland. The regathering of the Jewish people from the four corners of the world is something that's never happened before. A people once dispersed for two thousand years preserved their identity and at a specific moment in history migrated back to their homeland and settled where the prophets foretold they would.

The biggest spiritual revival among the Jews since the book of Acts is also unfolding. Muslims, too, are coming to faith in Jesus as never before in the fourteen-hundred-year history of Islam. Signs and wonders often accompany these heavenly visitations.

Christians around the globe seem drawn to make their way to Jerusalem. They're rediscovering their attachment to this city. They're also—as never before—making common cause with God's chosen people during their time of crisis and standing with them "for such a time as this." Believers also pray fervently for the peace of Jerusalem from the far-flung South Sea Islands to the center of the city itself.

Millions of Muslims covet this city too. "'Armies carrying black flags will come from Khurasan [Iran]. No power will be able to stop them and they will finally reach Eela [the Dome of the rock in Jerusalem] where they will erect their flags.'"[3] This quote is just one of many that denotes some Muslims see Jerusalem as their next, final, and ultimate destination. It foretells a brewing battle over the control of the city. The ultimate conflict appears to be over control of the Temple Mount, the pinnacle issue at the end of the age.

That's the view of Simon Montefiore, author of the seminal work *Jerusalem: The Biography.* We interviewed Montefiore, the great nephew of Moses Montefiore who established the first neighborhood outside

Jerusalem's Old City. We sat under the shadow of the iconic Montefiore windmill, restored by Christian Zionists. Montefiore remarked,

> I think it [Jerusalem] will be becoming more and more the center of the world. First of all there are more and more believers, Muslim, Jewish, but also Christian believers who look to Jerusalem, who look to the Temple Mount for Judgment Day, for the Apocalypse. And the number of believers in the three great Abrahamic religions is actually increasing even though we sort of think we're in an increasingly secular world out there. And that means that Jerusalem will become more and more significant. But also if you look at the tectonic plates that are moving. First of all, the history of Jerusalem is always decided by what happens in Cairo and Damascus, the great sort of cities in the Middle East, that's all up in the air. There's the Israeli-Palestine conflict. There's Iran versus America. There's Iran versus Israel. So there are vast divergences, vast conflicts, and all of them center on these fragile stones. After all, what is Jerusalem? Jerusalem is really the Temple Mount, one structure, tiny, tiny space in which all of us believe, all of us look for the future.[4]

I believe Montefiore. He also mentioned the Temple Mount is the place where God met man and man met God. This holy place will one day be the focal point of world attention and consternation.

THE CENTRALITY OF JERUSALEM

Jews, Muslims, and Christians revere Jerusalem but for different reasons.

For the Jews, it's hard to underestimate its significance. Jerusalem threads its way through the fabric of Jewish religion, culture, customs, and its rites of passage. When a Jewish couple marries, the groom recites Psalm 137:5–6: "If I forget thee, O Jerusalem, let my right hand forget her cunning. If I do not remember thee, let my tongue cleave to the roof of my mouth; if I prefer not Jerusalem above my chief joy" (KJV).

When Jews pray, they face Jerusalem. In Jerusalem, they face the Temple Mount. The "arks" where the Torah scroll is kept in Jewish synagogues throughout the world face Jerusalem. The Hebrew Scriptures mention Jerusalem 349 times. Throughout history, the Jews are the only people who made it their capital. Yet it's not just a political capital but a spiritual beacon.

During their most holy Jewish holidays, Jews acknowledge Jerusalem. After the Passover Seder finishes, the liturgy concludes with the words "Next year in Jerusalem." After their daylong Yom Kippur (Day of Atonement) fast, the prayer book ends with, "Next year in Jerusalem." For three millennia, it's been enthroned at the core of Jewish thought and faith.[5]

That's why June 7, 1967, remains such an important date in Jewish consciousness and such a pivotal day in world history. On that day during the Six Day War fought between Israel and a coalition of seven Arab armies, Israeli paratroopers led by Mordechai Gur captured Jerusalem's Old City. His cry "into his field radio—'The Temple Mount is in our hands'—entered the pantheon of national symbols of the State of Israel."[6] For the first time since the destruction of the second temple and the Roman destruction of Jerusalem in AD 70, Jews once again controlled the Temple Mount. "It unleashed an enormous sense of historical longing among the Jewish people worldwide."[7]

For Muslims, the capture in 1967 of the Temple Mount (Harem al-Sharif to them) stands as a *nakba*, Arabic for "catastrophe." The dream of Jerusalem's reconquest stirs the hearts of many Muslims worldwide. The rallying cry increasingly used to stir up Muslim fervor is "The Al-Aksa Mosque is in danger," the main mosque on the Temple Mount. This message accuses the Jews of physically undermining and destroying the mosque. While it's a fabrication, they disseminate this libelous story through film, cartoons, and sermons to the Muslim masses, who unfortunately seem too eager to believe the lie.

Sheikh Raed Salah, the head of the northern branch of the Israeli Islamic Movement, champions this message, and his message has a meaning.

In the long term this libel is also intended to help consolidate global Islam around Jerusalem as the capital of the envisaged global caliphate. In the world according to Salah . . . not only does Israel lack any historical or religious right to Jerusalem, and not only is the Temple a figment of the imagination. Jerusalem, in Salah's view, was a Muslim Wakf in its entirety, and must revert to exclusive Muslim rule and become capital of the caliphate. This global entity will amend the Muslim world's fragmentation into states and constitute part of the conquest of Christianity, Europe, and the West as a whole. Salah, whose doctrine is clear cut, speaks openly of "the global caliphate whose capital is Jerusalem, which will be 'the last stage in the history of the Muslim nation until the End of Days.'"[8]

Some of Salah's teachings found expression in the 2012 Global March on Jerusalem. During the march in venues from Jakarta to Jerusalem, millions of Muslims demonstrated against Israel's control of the city. They stated on their website, "The march will demand freedom for Jerusalem and its people and to put an end to the apartheid, ethnic cleansing and Judaisation policies affecting the people, land and sanctity of Jerusalem."[9]

Yet after three thousand years, it's unlikely the world will loosen the tenacious Jewish attachment and grip to Jerusalem. Now with the Muslim fierce, full-throated cry to take Jerusalem back, it appears the stage is being set for an apocalyptic showdown on this fault line between Judeo-Christian and Islamic civilizations.

Could this erupt into a diplomatic showdown of biblical proportions? For example, what will happen if the United Nations recognizes a Palestinian state and Israel refuses to divide Jerusalem or allow international troops—of whatever nationality—to enter? The diplomatic pressure might be enormous on Israel to divide its eternal capital between a Jewish and a Palestinian state. Could this set up the scenario the prophet Zechariah envisioned thousands of years ago? He wrote, "I [the Lord] will make Jerusalem a cup of drunkenness to all the surrounding peoples, when they lay siege against Judah and Jerusalem" (Zechariah 12:2) and "For I will gather all the nations to battle against Jerusalem" (Zechariah 14:2).

JERUSALEM: CENTER STAGE

Jerusalem therefore looks like God's center stage, and it appears He's drawing the nations to a rendezvous in Jerusalem and their date with destiny. Known as the "naval of the earth," "the rock of creation," "the womb of the kingdom of God," the destiny of the nations—and our own—seems to be linked to a city, a place, a King, and a coming kingdom. The prayer "Your kingdom come" prayed for two thousand years might be on the cusp of being answered.

The battle of the end-times will be the battle over this city, and the battle has already begun. Israel and Jerusalem will increase in importance in the eyes of both earth and heaven in the coming years. It's in the center of the world and in the center of what He's doing. Ultimately, it's a scene He is creating. After all, the Bible says God is going to do something: "It will be in the latter days that I will bring you against My land, so that the nations may know Me, when I am hallowed in you, O Gog, before their eyes" (Ezekiel 38:16). "Thus I will magnify Myself and sanctify Myself, and I will be known in the eyes of many nations. Then they shall know that I am the LORD" (Ezekiel 38:23). Like a casting director, He chooses the characters to be part of the story that's being played out today.

This story of the end of the age ripples through the world. What can one say about the unprecedented natural disasters striking the earth in the last several years? Here are some headlines: "Huge Quake and Tsunami Hit Japan," "Japan's Worst Disaster Since 1945," "Volcano Keeps World Grounded," "Two Million Displaced in Chile Quake," "Quake Devastates Haitian Capital."

Given this backdrop of geopolitical events, spiritual trends, and natural disasters, could we be living on the verge of prophetic events foretold thousands of years ago? Is something remarkable happening in our time? Remember the flotilla? After that incident, rabbis released a statement saying we've entered the Gog–Magog period of history prophesized by Ezekiel. Could we be living in the days Jesus talked about on the Mount of Olives? Here's what He said two thousand years ago:

> Watch out that no one deceives you. For many will come in my name, claiming, "I am the Christ," and will deceive many. You will hear of wars and rumors of wars, but see to it that you are not alarmed. Such things must happen, but the end is still to come. Nation will rise against nation, and kingdom against kingdom. There will be famines and earthquakes in various places. All these are the beginning of birth pains. (Matthew 24:4–8 NIV)

When history's trends merge with biblical prophecies, then something truly profound is unfolding in our time. Many agree. Forty-one percent of Americans think they will be alive when Jesus returns,[10] and He said He would return to Jerusalem. To me, coming to Jerusalem was like walking into a history book—like watching prophecy unfold and the Bible come alive. You can see the headlines of the newspaper and the pages of the Bible overlap. The world today certainly is convulsing, and the nations are rising up against nations.

THE DAYS OF NOAH

Jesus also mentioned when He returned it would be like "the days of Noah": "And as it was in the days of Noah, so it will be also in the days of the Son of Man: They ate, they drank, they married wives, they were given in marriage, until the day that Noah entered the ark, and the flood came and destroyed them all" (Luke 17:26–27).

It's an interesting phenomenon, but there are now two life-size replicas of Noah's ark in the world today. We visited them both. One of them sits in Hong Kong's harbor. It rises near a suspension bridge and next to one of the world's busiest waterways. It's a unique story of how a government, a developer, and Christian organizations worked together.

The government needed to use an island to build that suspension bridge and connect Hong Kong with its new airport. They wanted to develop the island for its residents and decided to include a theme park. An eight-year-old girl came up with the idea for the park—Noah's ark. When I saw it first, I was stunned by its size. It's huge! It's the same dimensions as Noah's ark: three hundred cubits long, fifty cubits wide, and thirty cubits high. They built it on land, so it doesn't float. It includes a conference center, a hotel, restaurants, and an exhibit hall. The builders wanted it to be family friendly and a sign of hope in troubled times.

The director at the time, Matthew Pine, said, "If we can find a vessel to pass through those storms, those floods in our lives that may even threaten our very lives, that we can pass through, have a new beginning, have a new hope, as it was in Noah's day."[11]

Half a world away and an hour's drive south of Amsterdam lies another ark, but this one floats. Johan Huibers, a Dutch carpenter, had a dream in 1992 that Holland was flooded. Despite objections from his wife, he built a small replica of Noah's ark. Six hundred thousand people visited that replica, but Huibers eventually built a life-size ark.

How do you build an ark? Huibers told us, "I didn't make plans, you know. I had no drawings. I had nothing. I had the will to build a boat, and I asked God every day; give me the ideas, how to do it and God gave me day by day, so it was very easy." He says he built the ark "to tell the people about the ark; who is God? That people [will] start to read the Bible again. The Bible is just put away somewhere in the house. Nobody cares about it, but I will open their mind that they will start to read again in the Bible. . . . When you read the Bible, God will be there and give you all the answers."[12]

Huibers believes the ark is a sign of the days we're living in, just as in the days of Noah. "They are terrible, like the same situation as in the time of Noah. Nobody cares about God, nobody cares about each other.

They kill each other for nothing. Unbelievable. . . . There are floods all over the world, earthquakes, and you can read it every day in the newspapers. Volcanos. I think we are very nearby the end of the days."[13]

THE VIEW FROM JERUSALEM

I love to run. My love of running began at St. Mary's Boys High in Lynn, Massachusetts. Our track team had a terrific coach named Joe Abelon. He took a team that had not won a track meet in its outdoor season in my freshman year, and in four years we became the third best Cross Country team in New England. We often ran the trails of a nature reserve called Lynn Woods. Now I have the opportunity to run the streets of Jerusalem.

One of the paths I've enjoyed the most is the Haas Promenade. This ribbon of sidewalk starts in Jerusalem's Abu Tor neighborhood and snakes up through a promenade studded with olive trees and small greenery. It's a great place to exercise. When you reach the top it offers a stunning view of Jerusalem. The vista spans the breadth of biblical history.

You can see the Mount Moriah that Abraham first saw more than four thousand years ago. The father of the faith strode toward that mount to sacrifice his son Isaac. There he forged a covenant with the Almighty that would forever alter the relationship between God and man. Here David set up his capital three thousand years ago. Here Solomon built the first temple, where he placed the ark of the covenant.

From this vantage point you can also see the settings for the greatest story ever told: the Mount of Olives where Jesus wept over the city and where He gave His Olivet discourse, setting out the conditions of the end of the age found in the writings of Luke and Matthew. The Garden of Gethsemane lies at the base of the mountain where He agonized over the cross. Farther west Golgotha sits where He was crucified, died, and rose again.

As I've run, sweated, and panted, I've often thought about the earth-shaking and history-ending events that will take place in this city one day. I've wondered, if people really knew what will unfold here one day and who is coming, would they be lined up standing-room only in anticipation of Jerusalem's prophetic promises?

It's a city pregnant with prophecy and yet still longing for its fulfillment. It's not only at the center of the promised land but a city of promise. This promise was not only for the Jewish people but for the whole world. As Isaiah prophesized:

"Rejoice with Jerusalem and be glad for her, all you who love her; rejoice greatly with her, all you who mourn over her. For you will nurse and be satisfied at her comforting breasts; you will drink deeply and delight in her overflowing abundance." For this is what the LORD says: "I will extend peace to her like a river, and the wealth of nations like a flooding stream; you will nurse and be carried on her arm and dandled on her knees." (Isaiah 66:10–12 NIV)

Yet the promise of Jerusalem's future now still seems more like an impression, not yet fully clear. It's similar to how Jerusalem often appears in the morning during some of its more beautiful moments, shrouded by an early morning mist. Like a watercolor painting or the apostle Paul's image of "through a glass, darkly" (1 Corinthians 13:12 KJV), it wraps Jerusalem in a prophetic destiny waiting to unfold.

While this city now is clouded in controversy and conflict, and its future portends great danger, the city's ultimate future is a glorious one. The world may scoff, but history and prophecy will intersect through this city one day. There is no other city in the world like Jerusalem. There's a sense in the word itself that Jerusalem reflects both an earthly city and a heavenly one. It's the city God calls His own.

In fact, from a bird's-eye view, the topography of Jerusalem spells the Hebrew letter *shin*, which is a letter connoting God. That's why when the Lord said in 2 Kings 21:7, "In this temple and in Jerusalem, which I have chosen out of all the tribes of Israel, I will put my Name forever" (NIV)

He meant it literally. It's unlike any other place on earth since one day this will be the city where the Lord of heaven establishes His kingdom on earth.

One day everyone will have a connection with Jerusalem. All our destinies will one day intersect through Jerusalem. It's why many Christians come to Jerusalem to celebrate the Feast of Tabernacles. This feast of the Lord instituted in Leviticus is a reminder of the time when the Israelites lived in booths after He delivered them out of Egypt. Zechariah says that feast will also be celebrated in the messianic age:

> And it shall come to pass that everyone who is left of all the nations which came against Jerusalem shall go up from year to year to worship the King, the LORD of Hosts, and to keep the Feast of Tabernacles. . . . In that day "HOLINESS TO THE LORD" shall be engraved on the bells of the horses. The pots in the LORD's house shall be like the bowls before the altar. Yes, every pot in Jerusalem and Judah shall be holiness to the LORD of hosts. (Zechariah 14:16, 20–21)

A LOVE STORY

Everybody loves a love story. It's the grand theme for the ages, and it will be one of the main melodies during earth's end-time symphony. From the beginning of Genesis to the end of Revelation, the Bible bursts with God's great love for His people and the world. It's God's love letter of His often unrequited love. It's first a love story of His passion for His chosen people. In Deuteronomy 14:2, He said, "The LORD your God . . . has chosen you to be a people for Himself, a special treasure above all the peoples who are on the face of the earth."

Eventually He used them to bring salvation to the world from one of their own. John 3:16 says, "For God so loved the world He gave His only begotten Son, that whoever believes in Him should not perish but have everlasting life."

For the Christian, the climax of the age ends with a love story.

Many Christians come to Jerusalem to deepen their love. We followed one Christian group from New Life Church in Virginia Beach, Virginia, during their visit. For most Christians it's a powerful and sometimes life-changing experience. One pilgrim told us, "When you read the Scriptures, you're kind of looking at it in black and white, but you come here, it really jumps off the page, it makes the Bible jump off the page and you're able to see really in color. You're like wow, this is real! This is really what our faith is built upon."[14]

They walk in the same places Jesus walked, like the Garden of Gethsemane. Another said through tears, "I don't ever have to be in the Garden of Gethsemane pleading before the Father because Jesus did it already."[15]

The other highlight for many is another garden, the garden tomb. Richard Meryon, its director, told us, "What we do have here in the garden is a perfect representation of the biblical accounts at the end of the four Gospels."[16] One of their tour guides says, "As you go through the whole story of what Jesus' life meant, what His death and resurrection meant, it's like you see the lights go on in people's eyes. They suddenly get it. And I've had Christians tell me I've been a Christian my whole life, thirty or forty years, but it's only now for the first time I really get it. I really get it was a real Man, God in my place. It was salvation paid at an incredible cost but absolutely permanently established."[17]

This relationship between Jesus and His church is another signpost along the way. It's a growing romance between a bride and her Bridegroom. Song of Solomon throughout describes this intimate relationship. I thought of that again on the Haas Promenade during a wedding ceremony. I looked to the Mount of Olives and realized that's where Jesus will come for His bride: "He has taken me to the banquet hall, and his banner over me is love. . . . The voice of my beloved! Behold, he comes leaping upon the mountains, skipping upon the hills. My beloved is like a gazelle or a young stag. Behold, he stands behind our wall; he is looking through the windows, gazing through the lattice. . . . My beloved is white and ruddy, chief among ten thousand. . . . I am my beloved's, and my beloved is mine. . . . Make haste, my beloved" (Song 2:4–5 NIV, 8–9; 5:10; 6:3; 8:14).

In Eastern tradition, the bridegroom would leave his betrothed and go to prepare a place for her in his father's house. He left but promised to return. This return is stirring the hearts of believers in Jesus around the world. It's a lovesick bride pining for the Bridegroom and a divine romance played against the backdrop of a world in chaos. It's an intimacy described by Isaiah:

> You shall no longer be termed Forsaken, nor shall your land any more be termed Desolate; but you shall be called Hephzibah [My Delight Is in Her], and your land Beulah [Married]; for the LORD delights in you, and your land shall be married. For as a young man marries a virgin, so shall your sons marry you; and as the bridegroom rejoices over the bride, so shall your God rejoice over you. I have set watchmen on your walls, O Jerusalem; they shall never hold their peace day or night. You who make mention of the LORD, do not keep silent, and give Him no rest till He establishes and till He makes Jerusalem a praise in the earth. (Isaiah 62:4–7)

The Christian knows it's not really the end, but a beginning. It's not the end of the world, just the end of the age and the start of a new age with the One they've been waiting for.

That's why their cry is: "Even so, come quickly, Lord Jesus."

ACKNOWLEDGMENTS

...E PUBLICATION OF *DATELINE JERUSALEM* IS A CELEBRATION
...he ones who made it possible.

...*Dateline Jerusalem* would not have been possible without my wife,
...anding beside me when we set out on the adventure of a lifetime.
...ust 2000, we arrived with our three children to a new land, a dif-
...ulture, and an unfamiliar language. Then five weeks later the
...tifada exploded into our lives—literally. Bus bombings, terror
...d suicide bombers suddenly became part of our daily rou-
...your steadfastness *Dateline Jerusalem* would not have been
...ndured, stood strong, and knew the One who called us
...s—and more importantly for our children.

...—Philip, Kathleen, and Grace—came along on our
jou... d for the adventure. They truly fulfill Proverbs 23:24:
"The... other) of godly children have cause for joy. What a
pleasu... wise children." You all fill our hearts with joy and
you we... perilous first days with courage and grace. You lived
Dateline... to ...w with Philip's new bride, Caitlyn, and Kathleen's
husband, ... e two more godly companions "on the journey."
You all ma... f the sweetest words in the English language.

One of t... eetest words is *brother*. Kevin, Brian, and Jeanne,
you're my heroes who have stood by me in those critical times of my life.
You're the best companions a brother could ask for along life's journey.
It's been a long way since Standish Road but we had the best parents—
Chris and Anne—four kids ever had. With His help we carry on their

legacy of goodness and godliness. They set the example for us and they'll be waiting for us at the end. What a reunion that will be!

Our earthly family reunions—now more than thirty years and counting—are where we renew all our family ties. *Dateline Jerusalem* is a fruit of that family unity.

My other family, CBN, is the fertile soil where *Dateline Jerusalem* could flourish.

CBN founder Pat Robertson allowed me to follow God's call to His promised land. Pat's involvement in Israel spans six decades since he first arrived in 1968. He made a vow to the Lord that he and all the organizations he founded would always stand with Israel. He's stayed true to that vow. *Dateline Jerusalem* is a product of that faithfulness. Now that vow and support are being fulfilled by his son, CBN CEO Gordon Robertson. Their support has been invaluable.

It was Michael Little, CBN's president, who told me in May 2000 to prepare to leave for Israel and establish a news bureau for CBN. I didn't know then how indispensable his support would be for CBN News Jerusalem, me, Liz, and our children. He's not only boss but also mentor, adviser, and friend. During that initial launch of the bureau into the unknown, it was Michael Patrick who helped oversee those first few years of the bureau.

Since then, Rob Allman built on that foundation. As news director for CBN News, I've benefited by his experience, news judgment, and godly leadership. It's been a privilege to serve under his leadership. He's helped us through some tough spots, none tougher than the crucible of the Arab Spring in Cairo's Tahrir Square.

It's been my highest professional privilege to work with a group of outstanding and godly journalists at CBN News. It's been a blessing to work alongside Drew Parkhill, John Waage, Gary Lane, Stan Jeter, Dale Hurd, Andrea Garrett, Lee Webb, George Thomas, Steve Little ("There's camels in the street!"), Ben Gill, Donna Russell, Charlene Israel, Mark Martin, Lorie Johnson, Drew Newman, Sarah Cron, Shoshannah Nunez, Caitlyn Burke, Chuck Calfant, Robin Mazyk, Paul Strand, Tracy

Winborn, Erick Stakelbeck, and David Brody. By the way, David and Erick, I won't forget the time when we sat down and prayed about the books the Lord put on our hearts.

It's been my privilege to lead the CBN News Bureau in Jerusalem. They are wonderful and faithful "watchmen and women on the walls of Jerusalem," telling His story "for such a time as this": Julie Stahl, Tzippe Barrow, Jonathan Goff, Yehuda Chamarro, Annika Kopp, Naomi Stahl, Lesly Bertell, and Nissim Lerner. Before our current team, Yoel Shoshani and I labored shoulder to shoulder for years. Before Yoel, Bill Hobson served faithfully and helped put CBN News on a solid foundation. For several key years, John Waage provided an insight that few Middle East analysts can provide. While he does it now from a distance, it's no less prescient or insightful. Thanks for reviewing *Dateline Jerusalem* and offering sage advice.

What a blessing to be a part of the fellow soldiers of the CBN staff who faithfully take the Good News of Jesus Christ to the ends of the earth. Jay Comiskey knew—and knows—the value of Jerusalem and how it intersects with the destiny of CBN. And to the CBN partners who help us all—whether in Jerusalem or the Philippines or other places around the globe—and undergird us in prayer and support to carry on the work. They are the often unsung heroes in this story.

Regent University helped me get started on a career in journalism. Professors like Bob Schihl and Harry Sova helped me to see what a holy calling it can be and set me on solid intellectual and biblical footing.

Discouragement threatened to abort *Dateline Jerusalem* before it was born. Chief encourager was my friend and prayer partner Stan Goodenough. He did not waver in his belief the book would be written one day. He along with others lifted me up in prayer and cast discouragement back to the shadows. Dov Geldman came alongside for a season and proved a threefold cord is not easily broken. Other invaluable encouragers were G. G. Conklin, who believed in the book when it was just a dream and Tom Doyle, who believed when I didn't.

For security reasons, many others cannot be identified. They labor in the dangerous harvest fields of the Middle East. They gladly bear that burden, and their understanding and insights contributed greatly to my understanding "of the times" as expressed through *Dateline Jerusalem*. They are the hidden heroes of the modern Middle East, those of whom the Bible says, "the world is not worthy."

Throughout our time here in Israel, we could not have survived without the prayers of faithful intercessors who have lifted our hands and hearts. They have stood in the gap for Liz, me, and our children. They have also steadfastly prayed for *Dateline Jerusalem*. Without their prayers I know *Dateline Jerusalem* would still be a dream.

The dream became a reality when Craig von Busek introduced me to his book agent David van Diest. David believed in the project—he simply "got it." His professional expertise, advice, and efforts got *Dateline Jerusalem* to the right publisher.

That publisher—Thomas Nelson—has been a joy and delight to work with. Bryan Norman, Kristen Parrish, Janene Maclvor, Chad Cannon, Kimberly Boyer, Emily Lineberger, and their wonderful team have help shepherd this neophyte through the publishing process. Their heart to honor the Lord and passion to get the word out on *Dateline Jerusalem* has been inspiring.

My biggest gratefulness goes to the God of Israel who gave me a love for His land and His people when I first set foot on His Holy Land in 1996, to His Son Jesus Christ—my Savior—who sustains me and gives me the privilege to live and work in the city He loves, and to the Holy Spirit, my Counselor who leads me with His still small voice. Without them I can do nothing. As the psalmist said, "Unless, the Lord builds the house we labor in vain."

To all, thank you. The best is yet to come!

NOTES

INTRODUCTION

1. "Milliarium Aureum," www.penelope.uchicago.edu/~grout /encyclopaedia_romana/romanforum/milliariumaureum.html.

CHAPTER 1: IN THE EYE OF THE STORM

1. "Open Letter to Hilton Worldwide," http://hiltoncairoappeal.tumblr.com.
2. Ibid.

CHAPTER 2: THE ARAB SPRING OR ISLAMIC WINTER

1. "Mubarak Intensifies Press Attacks with Assaults, Detentions," Committee to Protect Journalists, www.cpj.org, February 3, 2011.
2. "Apologists or Extremists," The Investigative Project, July 9, 2008.
3. Ibid.
4. MEMRI, translation of Sheik Yousuf Al-Qaradawi's Tahrir Square speech, February 18, 2011.
5. Ibid.
6. Palestinian Media Watch, "PMW Translation of 'Jihad Is the Way' by former leader of Muslim Brotherhood in Egypt," December 4, 2011.
7. Gideon Rachman, "In Cairo, with the Muslim Brotherhood," *Financial Times*, April 21, 2011.
8. Barry Rubin, "Brothers in Arms: The Muslim Brotherhood Takes Over the (Sunni) Arab World," www.pjmedia.com, November 20, 2011.
9. Con Coughlin, "The Arab Spring Was No Prelude to Democracy," *Telegraph*, May 31, 2012.
10. Joel Brinkley, "Islamists in Egypt, Libya, Tunisia not democratic," www .sfgate.com, April 15, 2012.
11. "The Muslim Brotherhood," Intelligence and Terrorism Information Center, June 19, 2011.
12. Zvi Mazel, CBN News interview, June 25, 2012.

13. "Mr. Erdogan's Turkey," Michael Rubin, *Wall Street Journal*, October 19, 2006.
14. Marina Nemat, CBN News interview, February 22, 2011.
15. Ibid.
16. Speech by Israeli prime minister Benjamin Netanyahu to a Joint Meeting of the U.S. Congress, www.pmo.gov.il, May 24, 2011.
17. Al-Sharq Al-Awsat, "Egypt, Fasten Your Seat Belts," MEMRI Translation, www.memri.org, June 26, 2012.
18. CBN News interview, April 9, 2012.
19. "Christians Begin to Flee Egypt," www.ChristianNewsToday.com, April 14, 2011.
20. Damien McElroy, "Radical Islamist Groups Gaining Stranglehold in Egypt," *Telegraph*, April 17, 2011.
21. Lela Gilbert, *Saturday People, Sunday People* Lela Gilbert, Encounter Books, 2012, 232.
22. Nina Shea, "Can Mideast Christians Survive?" National Review Online, June 27, 2012.
23. Ibid.
24. "Egyptian Revolutionaries take on Radical Islam," Daniel Steinvorth and Volkard Windfuhr, Spiegel Online, November 26, 2012.
25. Ibid.
26. "What Is a Constitution Anyway?" by Samuel Tadros, Center on Islam, Democracy and the Future of the Muslim World, January 7, 2013.
27. Ibid.
28. "Egypt's Morsi in 2010: Obama Insincere; We Must Nurse Our Children and Grandchildren on Hatred of Jews Those Who Support Them," Dispatch 5138, MEMRI, January 10, 2010.
29. "Egypt's Morsi 2010: No to Negotiations with the Blood-Sucking, Warmongering 'Descendants of Apes and Pigs'; Calls to Boycott U.S. Products," Clip 3702, MEMRI, January 16, 2013.
30. Ibid.
31. "Egyptian Muslim Brotherhood: The Attack on Israeli Embassy— A Legitimate Act of Protest," MEMRI Daily, September 12, 2011.
32. "Egyptian Cleric Safwat Higazi Launches Muslim Brotherhood Candidate Muhammad Mursi's Campaign," MEMRI, Special Dispatch No. 4739, May 18, 2012.
33. Ibid.
34. NBC Nightly News, interview of Richard Engel by Brian Williams, April 13, 2011.

CHAPTER 3: TURKEY: THE RISE OF THE CALIPHATE

1. Itamar Marcus, "Gaza Flotilla Participants Created War Atmosphere before Confronting Israel," Palestinian Media Watch bulletin, May 31, 2010.
2. CBN News interview, June 8, 2011.
3. Gursel Tekin, CBN News interview, June 8, 2011.
4. Egemen Bagis, CBN News interview, June 8, 2011.
5. Michael Rubin, "Mr. Erdogan's Turkey," *Wall Street Journal*, October 19, 2006.
6. Janet Levy, "Turkey and the Restoration of the Caliphate," *American Thinker*, March 10, 2011.
7. Ibid.
8. Daniel Pipes, CBN News interview, March 15, 2012.
9. Ibid.
10. Bari Weiss, "The Tyrannies Are Doomed," *Wall Street Journal*, April 2, 2011.
11. Boaz Ganor, CBN News interview, April 12, 2012.
12. Israeli Foreign Ministry press conference, May 31, 2010.
13. Ibid.
14. "Turkish Prime Minister Erdogan: Israel's Attack on the Mavi Marmara Constitutes a Casus Belli," MEMRI, Special Dispatch No. 4130, September 13, 2011.
15. Barry Rubin, "Turkish-Israeli Relations in the Shadow of the Arab Spring," www.gloria-center.org, April 27, 2012.
16. Simon Henderson, "Turkey's Threat to Israel's New Gas Riches," www.washingtoninstitute.org/policy, September 13, 2011.
17. Daniel Pipes, "Is Turkey Going Rogue?" www.danielpipes.org, September 27, 2011.
18. "Erdogan to Arab League: Israel to 'Pay a Price,'" Stephen Brown, FrontPageMag.com, September 14, 2011.
19. Ethan Bronner, "Threat by Turkish Premier Raises Tensions with Israel," *New York Times*, September 9, 2011.
20. Marcus, "Gaza Flotilla."
21. Ibid.
22. Ibid.
23. Ibid.
24. Steven G. Merley, *Turkey, the Global Muslim Brotherhood, and the Gaza Flotilla*, Jerusalem Center for Public Affairs, 2011, 10.
25. Ibid., 7.
26. Ibid., 8.

27. Ibid., 11.
28. Ibid.
29. Andrew McCarthy, "OIC and the Caliphate," National Review Online, February 26, 2011.
30. Levy, "Caliphate."
31. Ibid.
32 Ibid.
33. Ibid.
34. Ibid.
35. Ibid.
36. Daniel Pipes, "An Apology to Turkey," www.danielpipes.org, March 22, 2013.

CHAPTER 4: THE TWELFTH IMAM: IRAN'S AMBITION

1. Address by H. E. Dr. Mahmood Ahmadinejad, president of the Islamic Republic of Iran, www.un.org, September 17, 2005.
2. "1967: Israel Launches Attack on Egypt," BBC On This Day: 1950–2005.
3. Nazila Fathi, "Wipe Israel 'Off the Map' Iranian Says," New York Times, October 27, 2005.
4. Joel Rosenberg, "State of the Epicenter," www.epicenterconference.com, September 13, 2012.
5. Eli Lake, "Israel's Secret Iran Attack Plan: Electronic Warfare," Daily Beast, November 16, 2011.
6. "Cyberattacks on Iran: Stuxnet and Flame," New York Times, August 9, 2012.
7. Jim Finkle and Joseph Menn, "Some Flame code found in Stuxnet virus," Reuters, June 12, 2012.
8. Dan Rowinski, "The Flame Virus: Spyware on an Unprecedented Scale," www.readwriteweb.com, May 30, 2012.
9. CBN News interview with Pat Robertson and Israeli general Benny Gantz, August 9, 2006.
10. Ibid.
11. 700 Club, August 9, 2006.
12. "Netanyahu: It's 1938 and Iran Is Germany; Ahmadinejad Is Preparing Another Holocaust," Haaretz, November 14, 2006.
13. Ibid.
14. Report by the director general, International Atomic Energy Agency (IAEA), November 8, 2011.
15. Amos Yadlin, Strategic Assessment for 2013; Institute for National Strategic Studies, February 4, 2013.
16. "Netanyahu—'Gunter Grass Has Hurt Us Profoundly,'" WELT am SONNTAG, April 22, 2012.

17. "PM Netanyahu Addresses UN General Assembly; www.mfa.gov.il, September 27, 2012.

18. Ahmadinejad, UN Address.

19. Ibid.

20. George Thomas, "Inside Iran," CBN News, July 7, 2006.

21. Ron Cantrell, CBN News interview, March 2006.

22. "The World's Muslims: Unity and Diversity," Pew Forum on Religion and Public Life, August 9, 2012.

23. Ron Cantrell, CBN News interview, March 2006.

24. Erick Stakelbeck, "Iranian Video Says Mahdi Is 'Near,'" CBN News, March 28, 2011.

25. Ibid.

26. Lt. Col. (ret.) Michael Segall, "Iran Signals Its Readiness for a Final Confrontation," Jerusalem Center for Public Affairs, November 14, 2011.

27. Dore Gold, *The Rise of Nuclear Iran: How Tehran Defies the West* (Washington, DC: Regnery Publishing Inc., 2009), 217.

28. Joel Richardson, *The Islamic Antichrist: The Shocking Truth about the Real Nature of the Beast* (Los Angeles: WND Books, 2009), 27.

29. Ibid., 27.

30. Ibid., emphasis in the original.

CHAPTER 5: ISRAEL: PRESSED ON EVERY SIDE

1. Yoav Zitun, "IDF General: Likelihood of Regional War Growing," YNet, May 9, 2011.

2. "Hezbollah Spread Out over Southern Lebanon," CBN News, April 5, 2011.

3. "American Civil War: Major General John Buford," by Kennedy Hickman, About.com Military History.

4. "Syrian Rebel Founding 'Robin Hood Brigade' Vows to Conquer Israel, Iran and Europe," MEMRI, Dispatch 5078, October 21, 2012.

5. "The End of Syria?" Begin-Sadat Center for Strategic Studies, January 2013.

6. Zitun, "IDF General."

7. Ibid.

8. Ibid.

9. "Home Front Command holds major exercise in the Center," *Jerusalem Post*, November 3, 2011.

10. Julie Stahl, "Surrounded by Foes, Israel Preps for Bioterror," CBN News, December 7, 2011.

11. "World Opinion: Israel's Right to Exist on Trial," CBN News, March 28, 2010.
12. Ibid.
13. Ibid.
14. Ehud Barak, "Strategic Overview: Speech at the Herzliya Conference," February 2, 2012.
15. "Memorable Quotes for Fiddler on the Roof," http://www.imdb.com /title/tt0067093/quotes.

CHAPTER 6: THE HOUSE OF WAR AND THE HOUSE OF PEACE

1. "Know Thy Enemy: The Battle Against Islam," CBN News, April 8, 2008.
2. Moshe Sharon, CBN News Interview.
3. Ibid.
4. Ibid.
5. Ibid.
6. Ibid.
7. Bernard Lewis, CBN News Interview.
8. Moshe Sharon, CBN News Interview.
9. Ibid.
10. Michael Oren, *Power, Faith and Fantasy: America in the Middle East 1776 to the Present* (New York: W.W. Norton, 2007), 27.
11. Andrew C. McCarthy, *The Grand Jihad: How Islam and the Left Sabotage America* (New York: Encounter Books, 2010), 58, emphasis added.
12. Raymond Ibrahim, "Muslim Brotherhood Declares 'Mastership of the World' as Ultimate Goal," Jihad Watch, January 1, 2012, emphasis in the original.
13. Raphael Shore, CBN News interview, November 2007.
14. Moshe Sharon, CBN News interview.
15. Professor Bernard Lewis, CBN News interview, April 2008.
16. Ibid.
17. Ibid.

CHAPTER 7: THINKING THE UNTHINKABLE

1. Ayatollah Hashemi Rafsanjani, quoted in "Rafsanjani Says Muslims Should Use Nuclear Weapon Against Israel," Iran Press Service, December 14, 2001, http://www.iran-press-service.com/articles_2001/ dec_2001/rafsanjani _nuke_threats_141201.htm.
2. Anthony H. Cordesman, "Iran, Israel and Nuclear War: An Illustrative

Scenario Analysis," CSIS: Center for Strategic and International Studies, November 19, 2007.

3. Ibid.
4. Rafsanjani, "Muslims Should Use Nuclear Weapon."

CHAPTER 8: THE ISRAEL YOU NEVER KNEW

1. Martin Fletcher, CBN News interview, July 27, 2011.
2. Ibid.
3. Ibid.
4. Ibid.
5. Ibid.
6. Mosab Yousef Press Conference, Media Central, June 19, 2012.
7. Julie Stahl, "Israel's Save a Child's Heart Builds Bridges," CBN News, March 27, 2011.
8. Ibid.
9. Ibid.
10. Ibid.
11. "Israeli Irrigation Expert Wins World Food Prize," Associated Press, June 13, 2012.
12. Karin Kloosterman, "Pushing Back the Desert with Ancient Wisdom," www.israel21c.org, June 17, 2012.
13. Israel Kasnett, "A True Light among Nations," *Jerusalem Post*, January 6, 2012.
14. Abigail Klein Leichman, "Step Aside, Gutenberg, Israel Is About to Revolutionize Printing—Again," www.israel21c.org, May 7, 2012.
15. Dan Senor, *700 Club* interview with Pat Robertson, December 6, 2009.
16. Nicky Blackburn, "Made in Israel: The Top 64 Innovations Developed in Israel," www.israel21c.org, April 22, 2012.
17. Mark Twain, "Concerning the Jews," *Harper's*, 1899.
18. Mark Twain, *The Innocents Abroad* (1869), chapter 56.
19. Julie Stahl, "Israel's Land of Milk and Honey: Prophecy Fulfilled," CBN News, September 29, 2011.
20. Ibid.
21. Jon Felder, "Israeli Agriculture: Coping with Growth," Jewish Virtual Library.
22. Pauline Dublin Yearwood, "In the Desert: Why Israel Is a Model for Some of the World's Driest Countries," Chicago Jewish News, January 5, 2007.
23. Stahl, "Milk and Honey."
24. Ibid.

25. Twain, "Concerning the Jews."
26. "Memorable Quotes for Fiddler on the Roof," http://www.imdb.com /title/tt0067093/quotes.
27. Derek Prince, CBN News interview, June 1996.
28. "Why Israel?" Derek Prince Ministries International, P.O Box 19501, Charlotte, NC, 28219-9501, (704) 357–3556.
29. Ibid.
30. Ibid.
31. Ibid.

CHAPTER 9: SAN REMO: JERUSALEM'S FORGOTTEN HISTORY

1. Tomas Sandell, CBN News interview, San Remo, Italy, April 2010.
2. "PA Daily Accuses Israeli Government of Forging History, Stealing Land and Inciting Against Palestinians," Palestinian Media Watch, January 25, 2012. "Editor of PA Daily: Israel Steals Palestinian Land, Food, Graves and Culture," Palestinian Media Watch, March 15, 2012. Ruthie Blum, "PMW Documentation Reveals PA Violence Promotion and Demonization," Palestinian Media Watch, July 31, 2012.
3. Tomas Sandell, CBN News interview, San Remo, Italy, April 2010.
4. Ibid.
5. "The Balfour Declaration," November 2, 1917, www.mfa.gov.il.
6. Richard Gautier, CBN News interview, June 12, 2012.
7. "Israel Rights as a Nation State in International Diplomacy," www.jcpa .org, September 18, 2011.
8. Richard Gautier, CBN News interview, June 12, 2012.
9. "The Mandate for Palestine," July 24, 1922, www.avalon.law.yale.edu, emphasis added.
10. Richard Gautier, CBN News interview, June 12, 2012.
11. "The Mandate for Palestine," July 24, 1922 www.mfa.gov.il, emphasis added.
12. Eli Hertz Interview, CBN News, April 2010.
13. "The Mandate for Palestine," July 24, 1922. www.mfa.gov.il.
14. "Mandate for Palestine: The Legal Aspects of Jewish Rights," Eli E. Hertz, www.mythsandfacts.org, emphasis in the original.
15. Cynthia D. Wallace, Ph.d. "Foundations of the International Legal Rights of the Jewish People and the State of Israel," executive summary, September 2011.
16. "San Remo's Mandate: Israel's 'Magna Carta,'" CBN News, April 25, 2011, http://www.cbn.com/cbnnews/insideisrael/2010/July/San -Remo-Resolution-Revisited/.

17. Richard Gautier, CBN News interview, June 12, 2012.
18. Ibid.
19. Cynthia D. Wallace, Ph.D., "Foundations of the International Legal Rights of the Jewish People and the State of Israel," executive summary, September 2011.
20. Richard Gautier, CBN News interview, June 12, 2012.
21. Tomas Sandell, CBN News interview, San Remo, Italy, April 2010.

CHAPTER 10: PALESTINE: FACT AND FICTION

1. Yasser Arafat, "The Palestinians in Their Own Words," in a speech at the University of Beirut, December 7, 1980, www.iris.org.il.
2. "BBC Reporter Weeps over Arafat's Fate," www.honestreporting.com, October 31, 2004.
3. Hilary Leila Krieger, "Tenet Blames Arafat for Being 'Barrier to Peace,'" *Jerusalem Post*, May 2, 2007.
4. "A Performance-Based Roadmap to a Permanent Two-State Solution to the Israeli-Palestinian Conflict," Avalon, April 30, 2003, www.avalon. law.yale.edu.
5. "Palestinian Friday Sermon by Sheik Ibrahim Mudeiris: Muslims Will Rule America and Britain, Jews Are a Virus Resembling AIDS," MEMRI, May 13, 2005.
6. Itamar Marcus, CBN News interview, January 25, 2012.
7. "PA Mufti Calls for the Killing of Jews Quoting Islamic Hadith," Palestinian Media Watch, January 9, 2012.
8. Itamar Marcus, CBN News interview, January 25, 2012.
9. Ibid.
10. Ibid.
11. Arafat, "The Palestinians in Their Own Words."
12. "Abbas and PA Leaders Use the Term 'Alleged Temple,'" Palestinian Media Watch, August 23, 2012.
13. Ibid.
14. "Full Text of Mahmoud Abbas's Speech to the UN General Assembly," www.timesofisrael.com, November 29, 2012.
15. Ibid.
16. "The Hamas Charter," www.terrorism-info.org, May 2, 2006.
17. "Why Israel Went to War," CBN News interview with Dan Gordon, Jerusalem Dateline Blog, November 24, 2012.
18. Ibid.
19. "Transcript: Hamas Terror Chief Gaza Speech," www.algermeiner, December 10, 2012.

20. Ibid.
21. Ibid.

CHAPTER 11: ALIYA: THE RETURN TO THE LAND

1. Vakym Rabochyy, CBN News interview, May 2004.
2. Ludimer (Russian olim), CBN News interview, May 2004.
3. Richard Gottier, CBN News interview, May 2004.
4. Russian couple, CBN News interview, May 2004.
5. Shirley (Exodus volunteer), CBN News interview, May 2004.
6. Thoels (Exodus volunteer), CBN News interview, May 2004.
7. Peter Malpass, CBN News interview, May 2004.
8. "The Miracle Called Israel," CBN News interview, September 27, 2008.
9. "Lost Tribes of Jews from China, India Make 'Aliya,'" CBN News, November 16, 2009.
10. Ibid.
11. Ibid.

CHAPTER 12: THE MOUNTAINS OF ISRAEL

1. Billye Brim, CBN News interview, 2001.
2. Ibid.
3. Ibid.

CHAPTER 13: PERSIA, PURIM, AND PRAYER

1. "Iran: Israel's Existence 'Insult to All Humanity,'" Associated Press, August 17, 2012.
2. "This Year's Qods Day in Iran: Israel's Elimination Is Imminent—And More Possible than Ever Before," MEMRI, Special Dispatch No. 4893, August 17, 2012.
3. Michael Freund, CBN News interview, February 2004.
4. Wendy Griffith and Craig von Busek, *Praying the News: Your Prayers Are More Powerful than You Know* (Ventura, CA Regal, 2011), 14.
5. Derek Prince, *Shaping History Through Prayer and Fasting* (New Kensington, PA: Whitaker House, 1973), 80.
6. Ibid., 82.
7. Joel Richardson, (Antichrist: Islam;s Awaited Messiah (Enumclaw, WA: WinePress, 2006, 218.
8. Ibid., 219.

CHAPTER 14: A WORLDWIDE CRESCENDO OF PRAYER

1. George Thomas, "Muslim Indonesia Hosts Historic Christian Gathering," CBN News, May 18, 2012.
2. Ibid.
3. George Thomas, Christian World News, May 18, 2012.
4. "Partners," International House of Prayer, November 2012.
5. "The Roots of the 24/7 Prayer Movement," Intercessors Arise International.
6. Mike Bickle, CBN News interview, May 11, 2008.
7. Pastor Jack Hayford, CBN News interview, 2006.
8. Rev. Robert Stearns, CBN News interview, 2006.
9. Ibid.
10. Penny Valentine, *Praying for the Peace of Jerusalem* (Tahilla, 2004), 9.
11. Ibid., 14–15.
12. Rick Ridings, CBN News interview, 2007.
13. Pastor Wayne Hilsden, CBN News interview, 2007.

CHAPTER 15: DREAMS, VISIONS, AND PERSECUTION

1. "Dreams, Visions Moving Muslims to Christ," CBN News Story, July 3, 2012, and interview with "Ali," May 2012.
2. Ibid.
3. Tom Doyle with Greg Webster, *Dreams and Visions: Is Jesus Awakening the Muslim World?* (Nashville: Thomas Nelson, 2012), 76.
4. Ibid.
5. Ibid.
6. Tom Doyle, CBN News interview, November 2011.
7. Ibid.
8. "T," Conference Organizer, CBN News interview, May 2012.
9. "C," CBN News interview, June 2012.
10. Dr. Jurgen Buhler, "Revival Spring from Arab Winter," ICEJ executive director, www.int.icej.org.
11. "T," CBN News interview, May 2012.
12. Kurdish pastor, CBN News interview, May 2012.
13. "C," CBN News interview, June 2012.
14. "T," CBN News interview, May 2012.
15. Ibid.
16. Dr. Jurgen Bühler, "Revival Spring from Arab Winter," ICEJ executive director, www.int.icej.org.

17. "Ami's Miracle: Thriving after Holiday Bomb," CBN News story and CBN News interview with David and Leah Ortiz, May 4, 2009.
18. Ibid.
19. Ibid.
20. Ibid.
21. Ibid.
22. Ibid.
23. "Justice Served in Terror Attack on Jewish Family," CBN News Story, April 12, 2013, www. cbnnews.com.
24. Ibid.
25. "Israel's Messianic Jews: Some Call It a Miracle" and CBN News interview with Asher Intrader, July 13, 2008.
26. Ibid.
27. Rev. Canon Andrew White, "The Vicar of Baghdad," CBN News interview, May 2012.
28. "T," Conference Organizer, CBN News interview, May 2012.
29. "Ayaan Hirsi Ali: The Global War on Christians in the Muslim World," Ayaan Hirsi Ali, *Newsweek*/Daily Beast, February 6, 2012.
30. Ibid.
31. Doyle with Webster, *Dreams and Visions*.
32. Ibid, 58–59.
33. Ibid, 60–61.

CHAPTER 16: BACK TO JERUSALEM

1. Dennis Balcombe, CBN News interview, October 2010.
2. Ibid.
3. Ibid.
4. Peter Tsukahira, *God's Tsunami: Understanding Israel and End-Time Prophecy* (2003), 128, www.Gods-Tsunami.com.
5. Brother Yun, CBN News interview, May 2004.
6. Ibid.
7. Heidi and Rolland Baker, CBN News interview, June 2005.
8. Ibid.
9. Ibid.
10. Ibid.
11. Pat Robertson, "The Explosion of Global Christianity: The World's Most Important Unreported Story," address to the National Press Club, February 15, 2005.
12. Ibid.

CHAPTER 17: INTO THE FURNACE

1. Stan Goodenough, "A Twisted Corpse, a Severed Leg," Jerusalem Newswire, February 23, 2004.

CHAPTER 18: RENDEZVOUS IN JERUSALEM: A DATE WITH DESTINY

1. Ruth Heflin, *Jerusalem, Zion, Israel and the Nations* (Hagerstown, MD: McDougal Publishing, 1999).
2. CBN News Jerusalem Bureau dedication by Pat Robertson, July 2001.
3. Joel Richardson, *The Islamic Antichrist: The Shocking Truth about the Real Nature of the Beast* (Los Angeles WND Books, 2009), 45.
4. Simon Sebag Montefiore, CBN News interview, August 2012.
5. Eli E. Hertz, "Jerusalem's Jewish Link: Historic, Religious, Political," www.MythsandFacts.org, August 14, 2012.
6. Nadav Shragai, *The "Al-Aksa Is in Danger" Libel: The History of a Lie*, Jerusalem Center for Public Affairs, 3.
7. Dore Gold, CBN News interview, January 2007.
8. Nadav Shragai, *The "Al-Aksa Is in Danger" Libel: The History of a Lie*, Jerusalem Center for Public Affairs, 73.
9. "Global March on Jerusalem," www.gm2j.com.
10. Pew Research Center The Databank: "41%—Jesus Christ's Return to Earth," April 21–26, 2010.
11. "Life-Size Noah's Ark Opens in Hong Kong," CBN News, July 15, 2011.
12. "Life-Size Ark Replica Takes Shape in Holland," CBN News, August 28, 2011.
13. Ibid.
14. "Record Number of Tourists Visit Israel," CBN News, June 20, 2010.
15. Ibid.
16. "The Garden Tomb: Where Jesus Rose Again?" CBN News, April 8, 2012.
17. Steve Bridge, CBN News interview, March 2010.

INDEX

ABOUT THE AUTHOR

CHRIS MITCHELL'S FIRSTHAND EXPERIENCES AND REPORTING uniquely qualify him to expound on and explain the major trends and developments sweeping the Middle East and affecting the world. With an eye on the front page of the newspapers and the pages of the Bible, Mitchell provides the biblical perspective readers are so hungry for today.

Mitchell has served as the Bureau Chief for CBN News since August 2000, living and working in Jerusalem since that time and has worked for CBN since 1989. He holds an MA in communication from Regent University and a BA in history from the University of New Hampshire. He's married to his lovely wife Elizabeth and is the proud father of three children: Philip, Kathleen, and Grace.